"This Book of Starres"

Drawing of George Herbert by Robert White (1670)

"This Book of Starres"

LEARNING TO READ GEORGE HERBERT

James Boyd White

Ann Arbor
THE UNIVERSITY OF MICHIGAN PRESS

Copyright © by the University of Michigan 1994
All rights reserved
Published in the United States of America by
The University of Michigan Press
Manufactured in the United States of America
∞ Printed on acid-free paper

1997 1996 1995 1994   4 3 2 1

A CIP catalogue record for this book is available from the British Library.

Library of Congress Cataloging-in-Publication Data

White, James Boyd, 1938–
    "This book of starres" : learning to read George Herbert / James
Boyd White.
        p.   cm.
    Includes bibliographical references (p.) and index.
    ISBN 0-472-10505-1 (acid-free paper)
    1. Herbert, George, 1593–1633—Criticism and interpretation.
2. Reader-response criticism. I. Title.
PR3508.W48   1994
821'.3—dc20   93-46407
                                                            CIP

Grateful acknowledgment is made to the following publishers and libraries for permission to reprint
previously published materials: Bodleian Library for two pages of the Herbert Manuscript, MS Tanner
307, fols. 15v and 139v, reproduced by permission of the Bodleian Library, University of Oxford; Dr.
Williams's Library for two pages of the Herbert Manuscript, reproduced by permission of Dr.
Williams's Library, London; Henry Holt and Company, Inc., for "Range-Finding" by Robert Frost
from *The Poetry of Robert Frost,* edited by Edward Connery Lathem, © 1969 by Holt, Rinehart, and
Winston, Inc., reprinted by permission of Henry Holt and Company, Inc.; Houghton Library for the
sketch of George Herbert by Robert White, reproduced by permission of the Houghton Library,
Harvard University; New Directions Publishing Corporation for "The Red Wheel Barrow" by William
Carlos Williams from *Collected Poems 1909–1939,* vol. 1, © 1938 by New Directions Publishing
Corporation, reprinted by permission of New Directions Publishing Corporation; Oxford University
Press for quoted material from *The Works of George Herbert,* edited by F. E. Hutchinson, © Oxford
University Press 1941, 1953, reprinted by permission of Oxford University Press.

To the memory of my mother

Starres are poore books, & oftentimes do misse:
This book of starres lights to eternall blisse.

—George Herbert, "The Holy Scriptures" (II)

George Herbert

Born in 1593, in Wales, George Herbert was a younger child in an aristocratic family of seven sons and three daughters. His father died when he was three years old; his mother moved the family first to Oxford, then to London, where she became a well-known and much-admired figure in intellectual circles. (John Donne wrote a famous poem, and a funeral sermon, in her honor.) Herbert, not rich though some of his relatives were, was educated at Westminster School and Trinity College, Cambridge, where he became first a Fellow and then University Orator. In that capacity he came to the attention of the Court of King James. He seems to have had aspirations for high public office, with its attendant fame and power. He represented Montgomery in Parliament for two brief terms, at the end of which, in 1625, King James died and with him, apparently, any hopes for preferment. In 1626 Herbert was made prebend of the church at Leighton Bromswold, in Huntingdonshire, near the new religious community of Little Gidding. This church had become much dilapidated; he restored it beautifully, at his own expense and that of other members of his family. In 1630 he became rector of Bemerton, in Wiltshire, where his kinsman the Earl of Pembroke was his patron. He died in 1633, leaving behind a manuscript book of English poems, called *The Temple; or Sacred Poems and Private Ejaculations,* none of which had been published. On his deathbed he directed that they be given to his friend Nicholas Ferrar, the founder of Little Gidding, with instructions to publish them if he thought them valuable, otherwise to destroy them.

The Temple contains almost all his English poems, all of which are on religious subjects. He had written Latin verse for many years, but it was generally more topical, sometimes polemical, in character. Some years after *The Temple* his prose work, *A Priest to the Temple* (generally known by its subtitle, *The Country Parson*) was published, presenting in highly idealized terms the role of the country priest.

His first biography, published in 1670, was by Isaak Walton, who described Herbert as an Anglican saint. Herbert's English poetry has gone through various degrees of popularity; at present he is regarded by many as one of the most important poets of the seventeenth century, by some as one of the greatest masters of the short poem in English. He seems to have had great influence on later English and American poets, including Emerson, Dickinson, and Frost.

Contents

Preface

Although I had known some of George Herbert's poems well for decades, I began reading his poetry systematically only a few years ago, while on sabbatical leave in Cambridge. The few poems I already knew were wonderful, yet perplexing and often impenetrable; they haunted my mind. I knew I did not fully understand them, let alone the others I occasionally tried to read, and here was an opportunity not to be missed. I made it my major project to read *The Temple,* at first through slowly, then at the rate of one poem a day, taking elaborate notes and committing many of the poems to memory. As I did this, the particular poems not surprisingly came to take on greatly increased life and meaning, partly through simple familiarity and partly because I began to read them in light of each other. Difficult as they were, and are, they gradually grew more natural to me: I found their obscurities somewhat clarified, their silences less troubling, and came, more generally, to regard them not as a sequence of discrete artworks but as the sustained expression of one mind reaching out to others. I began to learn the language in which they were composed.

This book is the record, and to some degree the enactment, of this engagement with the poetry of George Herbert. It has been a difficult, though highly pleasurable, book to write, for it has not been obvious to me how to talk about such a sustained and detailed experience as the reading of these poems has been. This kind of experience does not result in the acquisition of knowledge in the usual sense, after all, nor in the addition of new items of aesthetic appreciation, but in a change in one's own imagination.

It is perhaps closest to the experience of travel, which cannot be reduced to photographs or views or anecdotes, but works a shift in one's sense of the world and one's place within it. And like travel, it is hard to report on. The first venture into a new culture, of a day or a week say, is relatively easy, for one's experiences are still few enough to observe and grasp from the outside, and one retains one's sense of the world left behind, and hence of a possible audience. But after months or years the particulars overwhelm the mind and shift their meaning. You are no longer observing, you are changing; and when you write a letter home, even in English, it is with a sense that you no longer speak the old language in the same way. You are now outside the world you left behind; when you do return to it you will feel like an outsider. As the strange becomes familiar, the familiar becomes strange. So too, in my experience, with reading of George Herbert: the result has been to shift the way I perceive and live in the world, a transformation of the self. This is in a sense no surprise—I had experienced much the same thing in living for years with the *Iliad* and the *Odyssey,* and to a lesser degree with other works as well—but it does present a central problem of thought and expression. How is one to think and talk about such an experience?

My own way of imagining it is to say that in working through these poems I began to learn the language in which they are composed. The account of reading Herbert presented in this book is largely shaped by this image: I try to show how Herbert creates a language in his poems, how this language can be learned, and something of what this learning can mean to the reader. In doing this I mean to make a more general suggestion as well, namely that it is helpful to think of the reading of any book of poetry, or prose too, as a kind of language-learning, and of writing as a kind of language-making.

By "language" I do not mean simply diction and grammar, but the ways in which a poet selects and transforms all the materials of meaning available to him or her. For poets do not simply use the words of their language as if each carried a certain determinate meaning, like freight in a freight car; they give active meaning to the particular words they use, in each poem and across their poems, and not to words only: to images, gestures, forms, voices, tones, attitudes towards the reader, allusions, in short to all the stuff out of which the poetry is made. In using his language the poet remakes it, and what he makes is in the end different from what anyone else makes: it is his version of a common inheritance.

Learning the work of a poet is not linear, one item at a time, first this, then that, but complex and simultaneous, just like learning a language in fact. You cannot really get part of it till you get the whole. In learning Greek, for example, the optative has meaning only against the indicative and subjunctive, the perfective against the aorist and continuative, and the same is true in learning the vocabulary, gestures, and tones of voice of a particular poet as well: each item is part of a larger system of difference and analogy, from which it derives its meaning. This at least has been my own experience. For years I would take a small volume of Herbert's poems with me on vacation, turning to them with an eagerness based on the three or four I knew well, yet finding the rest of the poems intractably opaque. Not understanding the issues they addressed or the way they did so, not able to hear their voices with confidence, I was not able to make sense of them. Only after working through a great many poems did I begin to feel that I knew how to go to work on one that was not already familiar. It is this experience of gradual acculturation that I wish to capture here and make available to the reader. This means that the shape of this book is not linear either, but closer to a spiral, as I take a series of passes at Herbert's poetry, developing later what is at the beginning only sketched, seeing one movement or tone or image in terms of another, and so on.

If you imagined yourself asked to think and write about an experience of language-learning, a fundamental problem would quickly present itself: how much attention should you give to the particular way in which you yourself learned the language, how much to the language you learned? One danger is that you would focus exclusively on the language as an external object, erasing your own experience, and in doing so create the pretense that what you saw and learned was simply there, and that it would, or should, be the same for everyone. Working in this way you would pretend to disappear into a transparent pane of glass through which this reality could be seen. But the knower is always part of the known; the language that you learn is always different from the language I learn; my Herbert can never be exactly the same as yours. Meaning does not lie in the text, or in the culture, to be picked up like a stone, but in an experience of interaction, which is naturally different for each of us.

Yet this perception can be carried too far, to the point of conceiving of the text or culture as having no reality beyond the one we give it, to thinking of the reader, or traveler or anthropologist, as the only real actor in the universe, the only intelligible speaker. While your experience and mine of a new language, or of Herbert, will not be identical, they should have important similarities and overlaps, and this should be true not only of particular phrases or poems, but of the process by which they are learned. If we both succeed in learning French, we shall, after all, be able to speak to one another in a new way, and to others as well, for our respective versions of that language will be to some degree mutually intelligible.

In writing about my experience of Herbert's language, then, my task is neither to pretend to erase myself nor to claim that my experience is the only relevant reality, but to find a way to do two partly inconsistent things: to recognize my constant presence in everything that is seen or said, and at the same time to keep attention focused on what matters most, the language and the poems as they are seen from this point of view. We ought not deny the objective reality of the poetry, but we should recognize that this same reality is perceived differently by different people, just as a landscape or a flower is. This book is directed not so much at Herbert's poetry, then, as if it could be simply seen for what it is, but at our respective experiences of that poetry, which after all exist for us only as we participate in their making. I shall speak out of my own experience, to the reader's experience, telling her or him not "what is there" so much as what one traveler's sense of it has been. I hope you will recognize the place I describe, but I know it will—and should—be different for you.

In the opening section of the book I am explicitly autobiographical, suggesting in some detail how I worked my way into Herbert's poetry and language. My hope is to define a position from which, and something of a method by which, his poetry can be thought about more thoroughly. Thereafter I am gradually less intrusive, focusing attention on the texts themselves as they are seen from the position I have earlier defined.

Herbert's poetry has a single subject, his own religious life, and this presents the modern American reader with special difficulties. We live, if not in a secular nation or age, in a public intellectual world that has for some time represented itself as resolutely secular, and many people regard religious belief as silly or superstitious or otherwise beneath them. Even when it is respected it is often regarded as personal or private, not to be talked about. What is one to do with this poetry, then: simply disregard its subject matter and focus on its form, voice, and feeling? Or is the subject matter part of its appeal and meaning? If this is so— and I think it is—how is one to think and speak sensibly about this poetry, particularly in a culture that seems to be divided between the secular and religious, and indeed among different religions, in such a way as to preclude any conversation across the lines of separation?

I think that these questions cannot be evaded. This is religious poetry, and to understand it one must in some sense learn the religious language in which it is composed. This means that one must face the question how this language works, and what it means, in two ways: what it means in the hands of Herbert, or one of his contemporaries, and—to the extent this is a separable question—what it means to us, as we even briefly inhabit it. In reading Herbert we shall thus need to think about the nature of religious belief and language, both in Herbert's world and in our own. In fact, as I shall say at length later on, I think that one cannot really read Herbert, or Milton either, whatever one's own beliefs and disbeliefs may be, without engaging in something that looks very much like the practice of theology. If I am right, this is a circumstance full of interest, and perhaps peril.

These are matters as to which we are somewhat differently situated from each other, differences that require, I think, reflection in the way we talk. For me, Herbert's religious language and beliefs have a particular set of associations, arising from the fact that I was raised in the American branch of his church and thus find his modes of thought, including his religious aesthetics, in a rough way familiar—though at the same time dramatically strange. But it is also true that I have found the language of that church deeply problematic, both as a young man and now, in late middle age. At one time I left it behind entirely, feeling that I simply could no longer say the creed in which the fundamental articles of belief are articulated: it was not so much that I did not believe them, as that I could not understand what many of these sentences could possibly mean. Yet I also discovered that a purely secular life was for me impossible, a kind of despair. For many years I regularly attended Quaker meetings, which were systematically—to me, blessedly—silent on all doctrinal matters, an experience that has I think helped me to understand somewhat better Herbert's own attitudes both towards doctrine and towards silence. Years later I find myself once again in the church in which I was raised, but still continuing to find its language problematic. In this way I bring to my own reading of Herbert a set of concerns about the character of his religious beliefs, and the language in which they are expressed, that another might not have, and may on that account find uncongenial; on the other hand, this very fact may enable me to be helpful to those to whom this discourse, and the way of life it involves, are more completely foreign than they are to me.

As I said above, I shall begin by speaking of the ways in which Herbert's poetry came to my attention in the different places that I inhabited, as a way of explaining the perspective from which I finally turned to this work in a systematic way. This part of the book is not only autobiographical, but a tiny fragment of cultural history, since the places I inhabited were of course also held by others. This is especially true of the education in reading I received at Amherst College, distinguished for its teaching of English.

In part 1, I shall discuss a series of rather well-known poems, with the thought that these are likely to be among those with which the reader is already most familiar. In this way I hope to recapitulate not only my own beginnings with Herbert but something of the reader's as well. Then in part 2 I start again, at the beginning of *The Temple*, working through several sequences of poems in the order in which Herbert presents them. Here I mean to show how the poems can be read in light of each other, both as one poem responds to those that precede it and as each set of poems creates a series of themes, like musical ideas, that will carry through the rest of the book. Finally, in part 3, I consider first two sets of poems that deal with certain central themes of Herbert's verse, especially the definition of God and self, and then the sequence that brings Herbert's book to a close. The three parts are written somewhat differently, for they are meant to reflect different stages in the process of learning Herbert's language, and they accordingly make different demands on the reader. In particular, the reader will notice that as I proceed the tempo of the book gradually picks up: I read more selectively, leaving a larger number of poems to the reader's future attention, and at the same time my own observations become shorter. By the end I assume the sort of shared understanding that permits real brevity of remark.

I shall make rather little reference to what other people have said about these poems, for my aim is not so much to contribute to a conversation with other critics, however corrective and enlightening that might be, as to find a way to express what it has meant for me to read my way into this poetry. When I am aware of someone else's ideas, of course I do refer to them; what I mean is that I have not canvassed the literature in order to contrast my reading of each poem with those of others. This means that on particular points I have no doubt been anticipated by others and, more seriously, that my own readings may in one way or another be significantly incomplete. But it has seemed to me important to proceed in this way, with all of its costs.[1] My

---

1. I say more on this subject in the Note on Method at the end of the book. In

imagined audience is accordingly not so much the expert on Herbert, though I hope such a person can read this book with interest and attention, as any reader who has a general interest in poetry, and in what reading poetry involves—and all the better if he or she finds the poetry of Herbert at once appealing and problematic.

In talking about the experiences these poems offer their reader, I frequently use the first-person plural: "we see," "we learn," "surprises us," and so forth. This is an old-fashioned locution that some people dislike because they feel that it asserts a kind of cultural or attitudinal unity that they wish, often rightly, to deny. I know of no better way to talk, however, and hope it can be understood by my reader that I am not claiming that all of us somehow respond in exactly the same way—this book is in fact built on the opposite principle—but that this is my way of talking about how a poem works. I use the first-person plural to express a hope, not to dictate a result, and I want my own reader constantly to ask whether a particular use of "we" or "us" does speak for her or him. My aspiration is not that you will agree with everything I say, but that you will find this performance of what Herbert means useful in shaping your own understanding of his poetry.

The poems are printed in larger type than the rest of the book. This is meant both to make the poems easier to read and as a typographical expression of the importance of Herbert's poems compared to what I say about them. My hope is that after reading this book the reader will say, not that I am a good critic but that Herbert is an extraordinary poet, who has become both more accessible and more important as a result of this reading.

For the most part I reproduce in full the poems I talk about. This is partly because I do not want to assume the reader's familiarity with the poetry, partly because I want to invite the reader to slow down and pay real attention to the verse, which will itself do much to teach us how it should be read. The reader will thus be asked to shift repeatedly back and forth between two modes of reading, the kind appropriate for discursive prose and the kind required for dense and difficult poetry. This is a book that asks to be read slowly.

Another reason for reproducing entire poems is that selective quotation, always dangerous, is in Herbert's case especially so. The speakers

---

the Note on Bibliography I describe some recent books on Herbert, both as a way of locating what I have done in the context they define and as a way of inviting the reader to turn to those that seem interesting to him or her.

of Herbert's poems, while in a sense all of course aspects of the author, are not, I believe, mouthpieces for a central and secure self whose utterances can be quoted as representing what Herbert believed. It is in fact the peculiar genius of this poetry to throw every single utterance, without exception, into question, as it is poised in sequence with others or set against them, and in the process to render uncertain as well the identity and stability of the speaking person. This verse, more than any I know, makes simultaneously problematic both the self and its language. For Herbert, truth lies not in what is or can be said at any one moment, but in the relations that can be established among various things that can be said at different times—among the statements, gestures, and voices that make up his verse. The meaning of his poetry accordingly lies not in particular utterances but in its iridescent movements from point to point.

The door of the church at Bemerton, through which Herbert passed
daily during the last three years of his life

Attunements

Chapter 1

Slow Reading: An Introduction to George Herbert

The first time I remember hearing the words of George Herbert it was not in a classroom but as an incident in life, a social gesture, at the boarding school that it was one of the peculiarities of my life to attend. One bright May morning, soft and still cool from the night, I met on the paths of the school grounds one of my teachers, James Satterthwaite—tall, lean as a board, severe and elegant in manner, with a preternaturally deep and formal voice—who looked piercingly at me, then gazed out at the day and declaimed: "Sweet day, so cool, so calm, so bright, The bridal of the earth and sky." He walked on without another word, leaving me stunned with this wonderful image, this way of talking about a miraculous day. If I had never heard another line of Herbert's poetry, this would have lived in my mind as a miniature poetic gesture.

What is one, after all, to feel on such a morning, which seems like the dawn of the universe reborn? Herbert's way is to see the day as a "bridall," the union of two elements, "earth" and "sky," which are thus personified, made human and sexual, as they join to make a third thing, the "day," different from either and consisting of the relation between them. A bridal is not a state of being but a moment of irreversible change, as virginity gives way to sexuality and procreation, a moment of fecundity and hope. Yet it is a ceremony or ritual as well, and as such has a kind of permanence: though occurring only once in the life of any two people, it is repeated indefinitely in the lives of many. In marriage, as in poetry, it is not only the elements themselves but the manner of their joining that counts. My first impression of Herbert was the affirmation of the value and beauty of nature, a gesture of praise like a psalm, directed not to the Maker of the world but to the world itself.

This fragment was given part of its meaning for me by the institutional context in which it was uttered. Groton School, for that is where I

3

was, had been founded in the nineteenth century on the model of the English public schools with the aim of recreating in America something of the ideal of the English gentleman. In a rather sentimental way it idealized England, Episcopalian Christianity, genteel country life, and high culture, and was thus connected with tendencies of feeling, both in England and America, that sentimentalized Herbert too, who was seen, as by some he still is, as the sweet and saintly poet of the English church. This view of Herbert was promulgated by Isaak Walton's *Life of Mr. George Herbert,* our major source for his biography,[1] which described him, especially during his last three years when he was a rural parish priest, as a model of perfect piety. He was so beloved of his parishioners that for his sake they would leave their ploughs in the field and come to daily service. At Groton we were schooled in a sense of class and style, of which an important element was our relation to certain cultural icons, including the great English poets. To allude to Herbert in this way on a May morning was at once to introduce a boy, in a lovely way, to one of these poets and to affirm a view of life that placed that poet, and poetry itself, comfortably in control of the culture of the School.

Learning to Read "Vertue"

But this poem, perhaps Herbert's most famous, went on in quite another vein, of which I was wholly unaware:

Vertue

Sweet day, so cool, so calm, so bright,
The bridall of the earth and skie:
The dew shall weep thy fall to night;
      For thou must die.

Sweet rose, whose hue angrie and brave
Bids the rash gazer wipe his eye:
Thy root is ever in its grave,
      And thou must die.

---

1. This was published in 1670. The standard modern biography is Amy M. Charles, *A Life of George Herbert* (Ithaca, N.Y.: Cornell University Press, 1977). On Walton's biographical aims and methods, see David Novarr, *The Making of Walton's "Lives"* (Ithaca, N.Y.: Cornell University Press, 1958).

Sweet spring, full of sweet dayes and roses,
A box where sweets compacted lie;
My musick shows ye have your closes,
      And all must die.

Onely a sweet and vertuous soul,
Like season'd timber, never gives;
But though the whole world turn to coal,
      Then chiefly lives.

In a gesture of poignant sympathy ("the dew shall weep"), the poem makes us feel the impending death of the day, and not only of the day, but of the rose, of the spring, of all organic life. This is done in something of an antiphonal style, with voice answering voice. Suppose, for example, I had responded to my teacher's utterance of the first two lines by declaiming the next two: there would have been on one side an assertion of the beauty of the morning, followed by an answer, admonitory, in another key; and so too in the next stanza, about the rose, and in the third, about the spring. A poetry not of statement alone, then, but of statement and response.

As the second voice proceeds it becomes less sympathetic with the world it talks about, more simply assertive or doctrinal in character; more like a voice of doom: "And all must die." But in the final stanza it seems to answer its own grimness, with the promise that "the sweet and vertuous soul" will, like nothing else, "chiefly live," even though the whole world "turn to coal." The bleakness of death is faced and overcome by the promise of eternal life. The poem thus fits after all into the comfortable scheme of things that Groton existed to maintain, and had I been taught the poem at school, I think this would have been the emphasis.

But this is still too cozy a reading, and by far. Think first of the death that the day and rose and spring must suffer: this is actually not a real death, like ours, but a stage in a cycle, the cycle of regeneration that marks the organic world that the poem glorifies. Tomorrow will be a new day; the rose bush will in fact live for years, creating new blossoms every spring—its root in the soil is a source of life, not death— and the spring too will return. The particular day or flower or season does of course die, just as any moment fades instantly into the past, but these particulars are all defined as part of a process that is as permanent as anything could be. Their life is like the "bridall" that happens once to any one couple, but repeatedly and forever in the life of a community. This sense of regeneration after "death" is in fact a large part of the beauty of the day and the rose: they are at once impermanent and permanent, one fact contrasted with the other. They die but do not die. But this cannot be said of us, in our organic lives, for each of us is simply particular, living in linear time, with a beginning and an end, moving from birth to death, not in the cyclical or circular time of day, season, and flower.

The poem creates both of these senses of time, for it at once proceeds in a linear fashion, from beginning to end, in time, and is capable of endless repetition, as it is read and reread. This is in fact a feature of all poetry with a stable form, and indeed an important part of the meaning of form in every temporal art, including drama and music and dance, for they likewise take place in the stream of time, and thus disappear into the past, yet normally have much the same form every time they are performed. In this sense they are at once evanescent, disappearing instantly into the past, and permanent, outside time. Here the phrase "My musick shows ye have your closes" invokes both senses of time simultaneously, the ineluctable process from point to point by which music works, and the repeatable and hence cyclical character of the form.

By its nature every poem raises the question of transience and permanence, of death and immortality: some, like this one and Keats's odes and many of Emily Dickinson's poems, make dramatically meaningful use of the fact, calling the reader's attention to his or her engagement in the very processes of mortality about which the poem speaks.[2] "Vertue" thus enacts the double sense of life it talks about, both linear and cyclical, attributing this doubleness to nature and denying it to us. As we read ourselves into the poem, then, we will hear its "thou must

---

2. I think here especially of Keats's "Ode on a Grecian Urn," which itself creates the kind of frozen and repeatable life that it sees and criticizes in the scenes on the imagined urn. For Dickinson see Sharon Cameron, *Lyric Time: Dickinson and the Limits of Genre* (Baltimore: Johns Hopkins University Press, 1979), especially chapter 5.

Here is another poem by Herbert that makes its dual temporality meaningful:

Sinnes round

Sorrie I am, my God, sorrie I am,
That my offences course it in a ring.

die" speaking to us, as well as to the day and the rose and the spring, directly and even more bleakly, for our death is forever. The effect is like a sudden giving way underfoot, as we first realize that things are bad, then that they are even worse than that. As Edgar says in *King Lear*, "The worst is not / So long as we can say 'This is the worst.'"

At the end of "Vertue" we are told that even the natural world, the cyclical repetition of day and rose, will ultimately die too, really die, as we do: "though the whole world turn to coal." This is a second giving way underfoot, for the poem has up to now held out to us the prospect that while we do die, something else that we love, the process of life itself, goes on forever. This, we now learn, is not true. But is the effect of this bleakness only to intensify the significance of the promise of eternal life? We really do die, unlike the day and rose; yet we really are the beneficiaries of the assertion that we shall "chiefly

---

My thoughts are working like a busie flame,
Untill their cockatrice they hatch and bring:
And when they once have perfected their draughts,
My words take fire from my inflamed thoughts.

My words take fire from my inflamed thoughts,
Which spit it forth like the Sicilian Hill.
They vent the wares, and passe them with their faults,
And by their breathing ventilate the ill.
But words suffice not, where are lewd intentions:
My hands do joyn to finish the inventions.

My hands do joyn to finish the inventions:
And so my sinnes ascend three stories high,
As Babel grew, before there were dissensions.
Yet ill deeds loyter not: for they supplie
New thoughts of sinning: wherefore, to my shame,
Sorrie I am, my God, sorrie I am.

The speaker's idea is that sin involves him in a round, or circle, in which he repeats his movement from one point to another. But in fact, whenever the round begins again, it does so from a lower point, established by the sequence from stanza to stanza, which moves in linear time to "new thoughts of sinning." The poem as a whole thus creates the effect of an unending downward spiral, reinforced by a shift in the meaning of the word "sorrie." At first the speaker uses the word as the equivalent of sorrowful or repentant: "sorrie I am that . . ." But by the end he sees that he is "sorrie" in another, absolute sense: vile, wretched, worthless. Yet at the same time something counters this downward movement, namely the fact that in it he comes to recognize more fully the truth of his condition.

live," and this not only after our own deaths but after the end of the
entire organic process of which the day, the rose, and the spring are a
part. All this bleakness just makes the future brighter.

But does it? There is still another stage to reading this poem, which
can be suggested by the question: What kind of life is it that perishes,
what kind of life goes on forever? The life that perishes is that of the
day; of the "bridall" that unites opposing elements in sexual generation;
of one element or person—here the "dew"—weeping for another; the
life of love, and sex, and sympathy, and beauty. And it is the life of
the rose too, boldly assertive, challenging: a life of rashness and bravery
and anger, of bright colors. Against this we are offered the kind of life
that the disembodied soul will "chiefly live," in a world that has turned
to coal, and it is to say the least not appealing. The living thing is
itself no longer really alive at all, but "seasoned timber," and unlike
the weeping dew, or the bold flower, it "never gives," in either sense
of the term: it never yields, and it never makes a gift of itself, a fact
the poem reinforces with its rhyme, "never gives" and "chiefly lives."
The image of the soul as timber in fact undermines the promise itself,
for timber does ultimately decay, or "turn to coal" (which for Herbert
meant charcoal). And behind it all, a threat worse than any, is the
negative condition, implied but never stated, that only the "sweet and
vertuous soul" will enjoy this future life, such as it is; and who is the
reader to think he qualifies? First we learn that the promise of eternal
life this poem makes is not so attractive after all; then that even this
may not be ours.

In "Vertue" Herbert thus addresses with remarkable particularity
a question of enormous generality, natural versus supernatural life,
seeing in one the merit of eternity, in the other everything else of
value. From one perspective, the question the poem addresses is how
much "vertue"—that is, elemental force, endurance, distinctive char-
acter—virtue in the moral sense actually has. The answer is, enough
to endure forever, to bear it out even to the edge of doom—if you
are lucky enough to have it in the first place.

Based on this example, then, Herbert's mind is very far indeed from
the religious sentimentality often attributed to him. Sentimentality con-
sists, I think, mainly in seeing part of the truth, or one kind of truth,
and erasing the rest; usually a pleasing part, but one can be sentimental
in despair or gloom as well. Herbert's mind is the opposite of this:
comprehensive, combining, and contrastive.

He is not a debunking ironist, however, rejecting what he seems to assert in order to assert its opposite. Like Shakespeare, he is on both sides of his dramatic opposition, and believes in eternity as deeply as he values the life of this world. It is not that he casts doubt on the fact of eternal life; rather, he finds a way of reflecting on what it is, and what it means, in a kind of writing that is a mode of thought. His subject is the truth of our situation, which is neither that we shall simply live forever in the same way and with the same meaning that we live now, nor that we shall simply perish with the rose. The truth is in neither position, but in the comprehension of both, and more. The poem's topic could be the subject of philosophy, or systematic theology; but its achievement is a kind of thought not available to those disciplines, or to any expository prose, for it is indelibly united with its form, and with the kind of life that form creates.

In thinking about this aspect of Herbert's poetry I am reminded again and again of Shakespeare, who likewise thought by opposition. The sonnet that deplores lust—"The expense of spirit in a waste of shame / Is lust in action"—ends up calling lust "heaven" as well as "hell"; the poem written to praise a lover's beauty—"Shall I compare thee to a summer's day?"—ends up praising not the beauty of the lover, of which in fact we hear almost nothing, but the "eternal lines" of the verse itself; and the apparent paean to marital bliss—"Let me not to the marriage of true minds / Admit impediments"—goes on to represent love as deeply grim, for example in the line I alluded to above: "But bears it out even to the edge of doom." The same impulse here concentrated into the glass of his sonnets also animates Shakespeare's plays. He seems to be incapable of saying how things are to one person without instantly bringing on someone else to represent an opposed view—sometimes one against one, as Richard against Henry, sometimes in a cluster or array, as in *Hamlet,* which can be seen to give first one speaker then another, through the whole cast of major characters, a moment in the sun. In Herbert's case the opposition is not externalized, in the form of imagined actors different from the author, but internalized, in the form of different aspects or versions of the self, competing for the right to speak in the name of the author.

Or so I say now. For a long time I knew of "Vertue" only the splendid image of the first two lines—I had no idea even who the author was; then, when I read the poem, I saw something of the certainty of death and loss against which hope is claimed at the end. But it was only when I began to teach it, a few years ago, that I could see it as the sort of composition I describe, made up of countering voices and appeals and aiming at a truth not statable in any single phrase or gesture.

A Poetry of Voices

Here is a poem built like "Vertue" upon an opposition, this time in the extreme form of explicit rebellion:

The Collar

I Struck the board, and cry'd, No more.
                    I will abroad.
         What? shall I ever sigh and pine?
My lines and life are free; free as the rode,
         Loose as the winde, as large as store.
             Shall I be still in suit?
         Have I no harvest but a thorn
         To let me bloud, and not restore
         What I have lost with cordiall fruit?
                    Sure there was wine
Before my sighs did drie it: there was corn
             Before my tears did drown it.
         Is the yeare onely lost to me?
             Have I no bayes to crown it?
No flowers, no garlands gay? all blasted?
                    All wasted?
         Not so, my heart: but there is fruit,
                    And thou hast hands.
         Recover all thy sigh-blown age
On double pleasures: leave thy cold dispute
Of what is fit, and not. Forsake thy cage,
                    Thy rope of sands,
Which pettie thoughts have made, and made to thee
         Good cable, to enforce and draw,
                    And be thy law,
         While thou didst wink and wouldst not see.
                    Away, Take Heed,
                    I will abroad.

Call in thy deaths head there: tie up thy fears.
                    He that forbears
           To suit and serve his need,
                    Deserves his load.
But as I rav'd and grew more fierce and wilde
                    At every word,
      Me thoughts I heard one calling, *Child!*
           And I reply'd, *My Lord.*[3]

At college I no doubt read some of Herbert's poems, including "Vertue," but what I most remember of Herbert's work is an account of the way one teacher, Benjamin DeMott, himself notable for self-dramatization, read this poem to his class: the rebellious portion with his voice full of vitality and force, the closing quatrain with his palms pressed together in front of his chest, his eyes turned heavenward, and the final words uttered in a quiet chant. This was an explicit performance of what the poem itself makes plain, that this is a poetry of voices. The poem is in fact a dramatic monologue, rather like one of Browning's,

---

3. Notes:

1. *Rode* means both "road" and, undercutting it, "rood," or cross. To be as "free as the cross" is to be completely unfree, except in the crucial and paradoxical sense articulated in Augustine's famous prayer: "O God, . . . whose service is perfect freedom." (In the Book of Common Prayer in use in Herbert's time this prayer was part of the service for Morning Prayer, presumably said by Herbert on a daily basis.)

2. *Away, Take Heed.* This is the reading of the Bodleian manuscript, in which the speaker is addressing a personified admonitor, "Take Heed." Most editors follow the first edition, "away; take heed:". I am persuaded to follow the Bodleian manuscript by the reasons advanced in *The Bodleian Manuscript of George Herbert's Poems: A Facsimile of Tanner 307,* ed. Amy M. Charles and Mario Di Cesare (Delmar, N.Y.: Scholars' Facsimiles and Reprints, 1984), xxxvi. Herbert may be alluding here particularly to Mark 13:23 and 33: "But take ye heed: behold, I have foretold you all things" and "Take ye heed, watch and pray: for ye know not when the time is."

3. *Me thoughts* is the past form of the now archaic, but then current, "methinks."

4. *One calling:* the term *call* was a powerful one in the language of Protestant theology of the time, including the sense of calling a person to a ministry. See, e.g., Barbara Lewalski, *Protestant Poetics and the Seventeenth-Century Religious Lyric* (Princeton: Princeton University Press, 1979), 16, and Peter Lake, *Moderate Puritans and the Elizabethan Church* (Cambridge: Cambridge University Press, 1982), 28–30. Compare Herbert's poem, "The Call."

in which the "speaker" is obviously not in any simple sense the poet himself;[4] or, perhaps more accurately, like one of Robert Frost's poems, for his voices, like Herbert's, are mainly internal ones, different versions of himself.

The first voice here is that of a rebel, a person who has given up much for his religion—perhaps he is a priest—and now feels the cost too much to bear. In his choler he wants to slip that other collar, which restrains him. He will set forth into the world, he says, full of freedom and capacity and complaint. Others have harvests; for him life is thorns that make him bleed, without recompense. He too could have wine and bread, true restoratives, like other people. Is he the only one whose life is to be ruined, and ruined totally?

This rebellious voice is answered by another: "Not so, my heart." Our initial expectation might be that the second voice will be adverse to the first, and deny what it has said or complicate it, but this voice surprises us by doing the opposite: it affirms rebellion in even stronger terms, casting it in another register, more serious and sinister. It is a bit as if a person were blustering away ineffectually, blowing off steam, half expecting his good angel to answer the bad one he was half pretending to be, when the devil himself suddenly appeared and spoke, saying to him: "You can really mean it, you know; you can really do it; take the chance!" In this case it really is the devil, too, speaking as he did in the Garden of Eden: "there is fruit, / And thou hast hands." This voice has the power of the intellect, breaking in on a moment of passion and rationalizing it, creating as it were an ideology of rebellion. The poem does not place emotion against reason, as we might have expected, with emotion in rebellion, reason correcting it; reason itself is the agent of revolt. There thus emerges within the self a rebel that is far more serious than the voice that seemed to itself to be so extreme and radical, but now proves by comparison to be posturing and self-dramatizing. This has some of the effect, described in "Vertue," of ground giving way under foot. "I thought I was daringly expressing my most rebellious and dangerous thoughts, but I discover: 'Not so, my heart.'"

---

4. I am thinking of his famous poems, "My Last Duchess," or "Soliloquy of the Spanish Cloister," or "The Bishop Orders His Tomb at Saint Praxed's Church," or, better, his masterpiece, *The Ring and the Book,* which is entirely constructed out of contrasting voices yet leads to a vision of the truth not statable in any of them.

It is not out of simple piety, then, but in response to this disturbing appearance of a reality within him that the speaker concludes as he does, hearing or imagining another voice, outside of himself, that calls him "*Child!*"—this Caller too is perhaps meant by the title—to which he responds in a new voice of his own, with words of acceptance and submission.[5] The speaker is moved to this by fear of his own capacity for serious revolt, suddenly revealed beneath the surface of a rebelliousness he could tolerate. After all, the first voice actually departs from the "board"—in the language of the English church a term referring to the Communion table—rather little: what he yearns for is described as "wine" and (in the English sense) "corn," which are the elements of the Eucharist itself. Similarly the "thorns" of which he complains could take the form not only of a bed, in the usual locution, but of a crown, recalling Jesus' own; and when he says his life is free as "the rode," he unconsciously invokes Christ's "rood" or cross, thus denying what he claims. What the speaker really wants here is not freedom, which is seen mainly in negative terms as a kind of escape, but restoration, and restoration specifically by bread and wine—the "harvest"—which is what the church has promised him but, he feels, not delivered. Small wonder he is ready to hear one calling "*Child!*"

This movement of return is enacted in the form of the verse itself, for after a sea of what feels like random rhymes and line lengths, the end of the poem is marked by the gradual emergence of firmer measures and rhyme patterns, especially in the closing quatrain.[6] But this restoration

---

5. Notice how precisely the two quoted phrases, "*Child!*" and "*My Lord*," call for particular intonations. Compare Robert Frost's view, discussed below, that every sentence has its unique sound; and the similar precision with which we can hear the tone with which, in the King James version, Jesus speaks to Mary Magdalene after his Resurrection: "She, supposing him to be the gardener, saith unto him, 'Sir, if thou have borne him hence, tell me where thou hast laid him, and I will take him away.' Jesus saith unto her, 'Mary'" (John 20:15–16).

6. To see some of the significance of this, look at John Wesley's rewriting of this poem, which is entirely regular from beginning to end:

> No more, I cried, shall grief be mine,
> I will throw off the load;
> No longer weep, and sigh, and pine
> To find an absent God.
>
> Free as the Muse, my wishes move,
> Through Nature's wilds they roam:

to order is partial at best: the recognition of the capacities within the self that motivate it cannot so easily be erased, and the closing gesture itself seems to lack the force of the earlier rebellion.[7] The quatrain is

> Loose as the wind, ye wanderers, rove,
>   And bring me pleasure home!
>
> Still shall I urge, with endless toil,
>   Yet not obtain my suit?
> Still shall I plant the' ungrateful soil,
>   Yet never taste the fruit?
>
> Not so, my heart!—for fruit there is:
>   Seize it with eager haste;
> Riot in joys, dissolve in bliss,
>   And pamper every taste.
>
> On right and wrong thy thoughts no more
>   In cold dispute employ;
> Forsake thy cell, the bounds pass o'er,
>   And give a loose to joy.
>
> Conscience and Reason's power deride,
>   Let stronger Nature draw;
> Self be thy end, and Sense thy guide,
>   And Appetite thy law.
>
> Away, ye shades, while light I rise,
>   I tread you all beneath!
> Grasp the dear hours my youth supplies,
>   Nor idly dream of death.
>
> Whoe'er enslaved to grief and pain,
>   Yet starts from pleasure's road,
> Still let him weep, and still complain,
>   And sink beneath his load.—
>
> But as I raved, and grew more wild
>   And fierce at every word,
> Methought I heard One calling, "Child!"
>   And I replied, "My Lord!"

The Poetical Works of John and Charles Wesley, ed. G. Osborn (London, 1868), 1:38–39. In her book on Herbert, Helen Vendler makes good use of Wesley's rewriting of several of Herbert's poems. On "The Collar," for example, see Helen Vendler, *The Poetry of George Herbert* (Cambridge, Mass.: Harvard University Press, 1975), 131–35.

7. This is one reading. It is also possible to read the simplicity and brevity of the act of submission as a kind of emphasis upon it, a way of marking its depth and sincerity. This uncertainty of meaning expresses an ambivalence about simplicity itself, and the value of such a gesture, that, as we shall see, runs deep in Herbert's poetry.

itself imperfect, containing four different line lengths, and perhaps the closing rhyme is itself slightly off.[8] Doubt is even raised as to whether the speaker actually heard one calling him or just imagined it: "Me thoughts I heard one calling . . ."

Notice that the responding voice does not counter but in a sense repeats, and in repeating rewrites, what the first voice says. Throughout his work Herbert proceeds this way, rewriting and transforming what he has done. The first three quatrains of "Vertue," for example, rewrite the same theme, but with important variations, first in the direction of intensity in life—the angry rose—then away from it. Transformation will in fact be a deep theme of this poetry, both as Herbert sees it happen in the world, where human life is transformed by grace, and as he achieves it in his poems.

We naturally read any poem, and any poet, in light of what we have already read, the other poems that have formed our expectations, trained our attention, and in this way shaped our responses and our tastes. To bring to Herbert a sense of poetry derived from Pope, say, would produce a very different experience of his texts from one based on Shelley or Browning. In my own case, the poet who most shaped my sense of what poetry was, and could do, was Robert Frost, and in reading Herbert I found illuminating parallels, especially in the fact that both seemed to build so much of their poetry out of voices. Frost's art and teaching are thus at work in my own reading, and it may be worth saying, at least in a sketchy way, how this is so.

In saying that Herbert's poetry of voices is in an important way like Frost's I of course reverse the proper sequence, for any influence went the other way.[9] But to one educated at Amherst College, as I was, it did not quite feel like that, for at Amherst Frost was the model of what

8. So Russell Fraser argues in "George Herbert's Poetry," *Sewanee Review* 95 (1987): 560, 573. But I think not: elsewhere Herbert rhymes "Lord" and "stirr'd" ("Submission") and "sword" and "blurr'd" ("The Church-porch," stanza 15). From these uses I assume the existence of a true rhyme in "The Collar," though of course all the instances could be equally imperfect.

9. For possible parallels, compare the rhyming in "After Apple-Picking" and "The Collar"; the basic images of "The Storm" and "Tree at My Window"; and the similar endings of "Prayer" (I)—"something understood"—and of Frost's sonnet, "For once, then, something." Also, Frost often expressed his indebtedness to Emerson, whose poetry is in many ways Herbertian and whose journals reveal that he had read Herbert extensively and well.

a poet could be, and much of his excellence was seen to lie in his capacity to manage his voices.[10] Reuben Brower, in particular, a great figure in English at Amherst and later at Harvard, focused in both teaching and writing on the way Frost was a poet of voices; and in the wonderful literature and writing courses taught by Theodore Baird and others "voice" and "tone of voice" were central items in our critical vocabulary, helping to shape the way we responded to other writers and thought about our own use of language. Reading Frost, whose voices are closer to our own than Herbert's, helped me to understand how a poetry could be built on voice as a general matter and also, I think, to hear Herbert's voices better when I came to read his poetry.

How was Frost a poet of voices? One may think of overtly dramatic poems, like "Mending Wall," in which one speaker rests on one sentence—"Something there is that doesn't love a wall"—and the other, on another—"Good fences make good neighbors." Each of these sentences has, as Frost insisted every English sentence had, its own cadence and music, or what he called its "sentence-sound." His poetry was created, he said, by casting the sound of the sentence against the regularities of meter and rhythm to create a music of its own.[11] Part of the sentence sound is that of the distinct speaking voice it creates, and here the poem is made of the contrast between these two voices. Or think of "West-Running Brook," where a husband and wife speak to each other about the brook they find on their new property, she imaginatively, full of play and fun, he ponderously, full of pretension and theory and claims of importance, together making a conversation that seems to be no conversation at all; but perhaps it is just the way this married couple accept their differences, by disregarding them and each other.

Just as often the conversation is between voices imagined to be internal. In particular Frost repeatedly exhibits a conflict between two impulses,

---

10. See Reuben Brower, *The Poetry of Robert Frost: Constellations of Intention* (New York: Oxford University Press, 1963), and compare two other fine books by his former Amherst students: Richard Poirier, *Robert Frost: The Work of Knowing* (New York: Oxford University Press, 1977) and William Pritchard, *Frost: A Literary Life Reconsidered* (New York: Oxford University Press, 1984).

11. See, e.g., his letters to John Bartlett, 4 July 1913, to Sidney Cox, 19 January 1914, and to John Cournos, 8 July 1914 in *Selected Letters of Robert Frost*, ed. L. Thompson (New York: Holt, Rinehart and Winston, 1964), 79, 107, 128, and "The Figure a Poem Makes," written in 1939 as a preface to the first edition of his collected poems, and also available in *Robert Frost on Writing*, ed. E. Barry (New Brunswick, N.J.: Rutgers University Press, 1973), 125.

one that struggles to see in the natural world actors like ourselves, with motives and sympathies and moral capacities, and another, responding, that sees either malevolence or nothing. Consider this early poem:

Range-Finding

The battle rent a cobweb diamond-strung
And cut a flower beside a ground bird's nest
Before it stained a single human breast.
The stricken flower bent double and so hung.
And still the bird revisited her young.
A butterfly its fall had dispossessed,
A moment sought in air his flower of rest,
Then lightly stooped to it and fluttering clung.
On the bare upland pasture there had spread
O'ernight 'twixt mullein stalks a wheel of thread
And straining cables wet with silver dew.
A sudden passing bullet shook it dry.
The indwelling spider ran to greet the fly,
But finding nothing, sullenly withdrew.

There are two voices at work here: the first wants to describe the flower and bird and butterfly as essentially human, at once the proper objects of sympathy and themselves capable of it, the second undermines all that. Thus we are first told that the flower is "stricken"; then that the bird is perhaps disturbed by this, but, it turns out not for long, and not at all for the flower's sake; the butterfly likewise adjusts readily to its loss and is without sympathy for the flower, let alone for the human suffering soon to come. Despite the hopes implied in much of the language, then, this is not the natural world of Wordsworth, resonating to the human heart, but one of cold indifference and remoteness, essentially unknowable.

Or is it? The last lines suggest another possibility, that nature is indeed like us, not in sympathy but in malevolence and selfishness; even the cold indifference is human too. One is reminded of Frost's famous poem "Design," which begins with the image of the white spider on a white heal-all capturing a white moth, and then asks what made this strange pattern: "What brought the kindred spider to that height, / Then steered the white moth thither in the night?" The first possibility is: "What but design of darkness to appall?" But this is followed by an even bleaker one; namely that there is no order at all, not even a malign one: "If design govern in a thing so small."[12] Or think of his poem, "The Most of It," in which the speaking voice, hungering for a response from the world, for the possibility of meaning, sees what he thinks is a fellow creature coming through the woods and into the lake to swim towards him; but it is only a deer, who crashes into the underbrush and disappears: "And that was all."

There is a shift across these poems: in "Range-Finding" the two competing possibilities are that nature is either cozy and cute, and thus subject to our imaginative appropriation, or malign and ugly, and unfortunately still like us. This is the point at which "Design" begins, with its spider that is "dimpled, fat, and white," combining both aspects at once; but the poem goes on to suggest a third possibility, that of sheer meaninglessness. To see nature as evil is still to subject it to appropriation too, after all. "The Most of It" faces the last possibility even more expressly, seeing in the act of writing, even of description, a necessary claim of meaning that in some sense will always be false. To speak is to risk the sentimental attribution of significance to the world; one function of poetic speech in this poet is to make this danger explicit and to qualify it by the articulation of other, bleaker, possibilities. This poetry of voices thus brings itself in the end to ask whether anything can be said or done, in any voice.

I say all this partly because I think there is something of Herbert showing up in Frost, partly because it may be easier for us to hear these things in Frost than it is in Herbert. After all, the capacity to hear tones of voice, of irony or skepticism, of detachment or earnest engagement, is one of the last things one acquires in learning a language, and we can use all the help we can get.

To return for a moment to "Vertue," is that also a poem of voices? There is only one speaker, and from beginning to end his gesture is declamation: first upon the world of nature and death, then upon eternal "life." He is not in doubt, nor engaged in a process of self-transformation or self-criticism. This is the right voice for the assertion of doctrine with which the poem ends, a kind of preaching. Yet he begins by expressing something else, a love of the natural world, with its life and

---

12. For a development of this reading see Randall Jarrell, *Poetry and the Age* (New York: Vintage Books, 1955), 34, 45.

its death, and he does this in a poet's way, by contrast and complexity, admiration and sympathy. But this gradually disappears. By the third stanza the speaker is unable to imagine the spring with the same sort of particularity and vitality that he imagined the day and the rose. The spring unites days and roses and multiplies them, so conceptually speaking this stanza should have the force of the first two many times over; but poetically, much of the vigor is drained from the image: spring is reduced to a "box where sweets compacted lie." "Sweets" are good things, no doubt, but they are not independent sources of life, and the repetition of this word has begun to cloy. The speaker cannot himself express, or invite in the reader, the sort of admiration and sympathy he had achieved in his earlier apostrophe to the day and the rose; it is as though his own imagination has become washed out. He moves in the direction of generalization, away from imagined particulars towards the sort of assertive and conclusory talk that one might expect in a sermon. And to the extent he still thinks in images, they don't work: think of the "season'd timber," supposed to be immune from turning to coal when that is a fate to which it is peculiarly liable.

The declamatory style the speaker adopts from the beginning places him outside of the processes he speaks about, in a position of essential superiority, and this will in Herbert nearly always be a sign that there is something wrong; here, most seriously, the failure to contemplate the possibility that neither his soul nor his reader's may be "vertuous." The voice propounds its truths with recognizing the implied conditional, which if unrealized will lead to a very different end indeed. In this way the speaker reveals that he does not know the full meaning of what he says, to his reader or to himself. The sermon voice against the poet's voice: the logic of the poem asserts the former against the latter, but its life reverses these allegiances.

I say that reading Frost helped to prepare me for Herbert, but this is no doubt also a consequence of the way I learned to read poetry in general. English was the queen of the disciplines at Amherst, the center of intellectual life and the source of the highest standards, or so I felt, and not I alone, judging by those who went on to become teachers of English. We were trained in "New Criticism," which meant in practice the close analysis of texts without much attention to authorial intention or biography. This school of criticism is widely derided now by those who think in terms of theoretical systems, but I think sometimes in ignorance of the quality of intellectual life achieved at Amherst and places like it. Attention was focused on the text, where I still think it belongs, and on its language. If some of us inclined too far in the direction of seeing each poem as a discrete art object, as its own well-wrought urn, others found the mysteries of language undoing such schematic readings. We did learn to focus, as I still do, on the tensions or contrasts that give life to a text, on its movements and transformations, its restorations and irresolutions. At best we were invited to see that the poem was about the adequacies and inadequacies of the language in which it was composed, the connections and expectations by which it worked. Insofar as we focused especially on voice, this taught us that all writing had a natural ethical dimension, for in her voices any writer defines both herself and her audience, and those she speaks about as well. This is how we were taught to think of our own writing too, in the freshman writing course, English 1–2, that shaped much of the life of the college: we learned that in our writing we spoke in voices that defined us, and our readers, and the relation between us. Writing is the creation of a self, as one of the teachers put it,[13] and of no writer have I found this to be more true than Herbert.

Think of "The Collar" itself: one voice, of exasperated rebellion; another voice, confirming the rebellion with reason; a third, imagining the father calling "*Child!*" and enacting the child's response; and among them all not a stable set of relations, but a drama. The life of the poem lies in no one voice but in the sequence or pattern by which it moves from one to the other, in its performed shifts in definition and relation.

The fact that Herbert's poetry is restlessly dramatic, often built upon a tension between opposed voices, means among other things that one simply cannot take a phrase or sentence out of context and represent it as what "Herbert believed." Part of the meaning of this poetry is the very fact that "Herbert" is not one voice or self, but several; much of his life, and much of the life of his poetry, lies in the articulation of various relations among these selves and voices and states of feeling. Likewise "belief" for Herbert is not a simple credal affirmation, reducible to doctrinal terms, but a field of contest and uncertainty, including various forms of disbelief. We should resist the tendency to try to explicate Herbert's work

---

13. For an account of a course based on English 1–2 see William E. Coles, Jr., *Teaching Composing: A Guide to Teaching Writing as a Self-Creating Process* (Rochelle Park, N.J.: Hayden Book Company, 1974).

in doctrinal terms, as though it were based upon a propositional scheme and written to give that scheme expression. It is not: it is based upon his own experience of life, including his life with his language, a very different thing. For him, after all, this language of doctrine was not one he chose from an array of possibilities, but in its essentials the only way someone in his world could possibly talk. Disbelief would have been as impossible for him as many people find belief to be in our own age. Herbert's poetry is a way of struggling both with that language and with its inescapability.

Stripping the Self to Its Core

One of the central puzzles to the religious mind, at least in the Jewish and Christian traditions, is how to reconcile the pains and injustices of this world, often horrible, with the goodness and omnipotence of God. This is the specific subject of the Book of Job, which may be thought to give an answer not comforting, and it is a central concern of the entire Hebrew Bible: How are the sufferings of God's people to be explained? How can they be alleviated? To find the answer in our own misconduct, as that text does, is appealing only if we believe, as some in the Jewish tradition do, that we can conform our conduct to divine standards. If we maintain our side of the covenant, God will maintain his. But if one holds to the Christian, and especially Protestant, belief in the radically fallen nature of human beings, this is impossible. It is of the essence of grace that it is not deserved. Affliction, then, may be random and unjust; or it may be just, because it is deserved; but in neither case can Christian doctrine comfortably accommodate it.

Herbert's verse is much occupied with this subject, no doubt in part because he had his own share of loss and suffering. Raised as a younger son in a branch of a noble family, he lost his own father when he was only three. His mother, a person of great capacity, kept the family together and arranged for his education at Cambridge, where he flourished intellectually, despite his relatively narrow resources, becoming first a Fellow of Trinity College and then University Orator, in the last position coming to the notice of King James himself, from whom he hoped for preferment to an important national position. But all the while he was in Cambridge he was repeatedly subject to severe and wearing illnesses, which he perhaps rightly attributed to the noxious climate of the fens; as a student he did not have enough money to live in comfort, or to buy the books he needed; and King James died without having advanced him.

One great blessing of Herbert's life was his friendship with Nicholas Ferrar, the person to whom he sent his poems at his death. Ferrar was the founder, in 1626, of the religious community at Little Gidding, later to be commemorated by T. S. Eliot in *Four Quartets*. It was at Ferrar's urging that Herbert undertook the restoration of the parish church of Leighton Bromswold, near Little Gidding, of which he had recently been appointed prebend. This was an expensive matter, taxing not only his own resources but those of his family, but it was done beautifully, and the church remains unspoiled: its tower a very early example of seventeenth-century classicism, its largely wooden interior severe and plain, with the twin pulpit and reading desk expressing Herbert's sense of the equality of prayer and Scripture on the one hand and of preaching on the other.[14] He never seems to have found a public or official employment adequate to his capacities, and during much of his life after Cambridge he was in effect dependent upon his relatives and connections. In 1630 he became rector of Bemerton, a small church near Salisbury, where he spent the last three years of his life—according to Walton, as a model of what a parish priest could be, a view that is supported by his own prose description, in *A Priest to the Temple,* of the tasks and qualities that belong to that office. But his diseases continued, and he died in his thirty-ninth year, in 1633.

Several of his poems deal with affliction, many of them bearing that

---

14. This according to Walton, who says:

> He liv'd to see it so Wainscoated, as to be exceeded by none; and, by his order, the Reading Pew, and Pulpit, were a little distant from each other, and both of an equal height; for, he would often say, "They should neither have a precedency or priority of the other; but, that *Prayer* and *Preaching* being equally useful, might agree like Brethren, and have an equal honour and estimation."

Izaak Walton, *The Lives of Dr. John Donne, Sir Henry Wotton, Mr. Richard Hooker, Mr. George Herbert* (1670; Menston, England: Scolar Press, 1969), 4:33. But in "The Church-porch," stanza 69, Herbert's speaker says: "Resort to sermons, but to prayers most: Praying's the end of preaching." On the construction of the church at Leighton Bromswold, see Herbert's poem "The Crosse," discussed on pages 240–42. For an explanation of Walton's remark here about wainscotting, which seems wrong, and his even odder remark on the same page that the work was "a costly *Mosaick,*" see Novarr, *Making of Walton's "Lives,"* 342.

Interior of church at Leighton Bromswold, showing its twin pulpits

title, others—such as "The Crosse"—under different names. Here is the most famous, an explicit piece of autobiography, in which Herbert tells what seems to be the core of his life's story and does so in such a way as to draw into question both his language—What is it possible to say?—and his identity—What is it possible to be?

Affliction (I)

When first thou didst entice to thee my heart,
                  I thought the service brave:
So many joyes I writ down for my part,
                  Besides what I might have
Out of my stock of naturall delights,
Augmented with thy gracious benefits.

I looked on thy furniture so fine,
                  And made it fine to me:

Thy glorious houshold-stuffe did me entwine,
              And 'tice me unto thee.
Such starres I counted mine: both heav'n and earth
Payd me my wages in a world of mirth.

What pleasures could I want, whose King I served,
              Where joyes my fellows were?
Thus argu'd into hopes, my thoughts reserved
              No place for grief or fear.
Therefore my sudden soul caught at the place,
And made her youth and fiercenesse seek thy face.

At first thou gav'st me milk and sweetnesses;
              I had my wish and way:
My dayes were straw'd with flow'rs and happinesse;
              There was no moneth but May.
But with my yeares sorrow did twist and grow,
And made a partie unawares for wo.

My flesh began unto my soul in pain,
              "Sicknesses cleave my bones;
Consuming agues dwell in ev'ry vein,
              And tune my breath to grones."
Sorrow was all my soul; I scarce beleeved,
Till grief did tell me roundly, that I lived.

When I got health, thou took'st away my life,
              And more; for my friends die:
My mirth and edge was lost; a blunted knife
              Was of more use then I.
Thus thinne and lean without a fence or friend,
I was blown through with ev'ry storm and winde.

Whereas my birth and spirit rather took
              The way that takes the town;
Thou didst betray me to a lingring book,
              And wrap me in a gown.
I was entangled in the world of strife,
Before I had the power to change my life.

Yet, for I threatned oft the siege to raise,
              Not simpring all mine age,

Thou often didst with Academick praise
           Melt and dissolve my rage.
I took thy sweetned pill, till I came where
I could not go away, nor persevere.

Yet lest perchance I should too happie be
           In my unhappinesse,
Turning my purge to food, thou throwest me
           Into more sicknesses.
Thus doth thy power crosse-bias me, not making
Thine own gift good, yet me from my wayes taking.

Now I am here, what thou wilt do with me
           None of my books will show:
I reade, and sigh, and wish I were a tree;
           For sure then I should grow
To fruit or shade: at least some bird would trust
Her houshold to me, and I should be just.

Yet, though thou troublest me, I must be meek;
           In weaknesse must be stout.
Well, I will change the service, and go seek
           Some other master out.
Ah my deare God! Though I am clean forgot,
Let me not love thee, if I love thee not.[15]

Two stories are told in this formally autobiographical poem, the first
of the speaker's own felt experience, moving from "milk and sweet-

---

15. Notes:

1. *Caught at the place* means, among other things, "took the position offered."

2. *Made a partie unawares for wo* means something like "gradually came to support woe."

3. *My flesh began unto* means "my flesh spoke to," as the quotation marks, which I have added, indicate.

4. *I should be just* includes the Protestant term of art, "justified," as in the phrase "justified by faith."

5. *Crosse-bias* means at once "cross my will" and do so with Christ's cross.

6. With "[I] wish I were a tree" compare "Oh that I were an Orenge-tree" in "Employment" (II); "we are the trees, whom shaking fastens more" in "Affliction" (V); "[man] is a tree yet bears more fruit" in "Man"; and "Man stole the fruit, but I must climbe the tree" in "The Sacrifice" (where Christ is the speaker).

nesses" to pain, loss, and illness, the second that of his movement from one way of imagining himself and his world to another. It is the second transformation, as we shall see, that makes the first one tolerable.

The first story is plain enough: "I" began in thy "service," thinking it "brave," full of "joyes" and "pleasures"—"both heav'n and earth / Payd me my wages in a world of mirth." But, with years, came "sorrow" and "pain," the death of friends, a dull life in an academic "gown" rather than the pursuit of ambition in the "town," still more illnesses, and a general wretchedness: "not making / Thine own gift good, yet me from my wayes taking." The narrative line is simple, from happiness to misery, all down hill.

But against this movement, and transforming its significance, is another, a gradual metamorphosis in the way the speaker imagines himself and his world, achieved in the very process of speaking his thoughts. At the beginning the speaker is not only happy, he is confident that he knows what happiness is: "natural delights" and "gracious benefits," "mirth" and "joyes," "milk and sweetnesses." Who would not want such things and be glad to have them? Our very language requires it of us: these are good things. Yet notice how completely this way of talking focuses upon the self, and its blessings, which are themselves imagined as acquisitions: furniture, wages, pleasures. This is the voice of natural man, liking what pleases, disliking what displeases. He speaks confidently of his own identity and its desires, which are at the center of his universe: his "stock of naturall delights" is somehow simply his, as if by right and without cause; God's action is merely to supplement or augment these, with his "gracious benefits," which are themselves reduced by the very politeness of the phrase to the world of human court language, and devalued as well by the off-rhyme with "delights." His manner of "looking" at the "furniture" is to claim it for himself; his benefits are thought of as "wages," hence earned; he imagines himself lucky in just the way a courtier is lucky who is accepted by a powerful and generous patron.

By the end this voice has been transformed: "Now I am here, what thou wilt do with me / None of my books will show." No longer does he assert his own claims to characterize experience ("thought it brave"), or to plan confidently for the future ("writ down for my part"), or to appropriate what is in the world outside him ("made it fine to me"), or to add up his assets ("counted mine"). Instead, stripped of all these capacities, he feels able to do nothing beyond acknowledging that he is simply "here"—this is the biblical "here," recalling Abraham's "Here

I am," in the presence of God[16]—and, in addition, wishing that he could be something of value, if only a tree, whose "fruit and shade" would benefit someone else, if only a bird. The earlier claim, "I had my wish and way" rings very differently now, as an expression not of bliss but of moral ignorance and worse, an instinctive selfishness that has, through these very afflictions, been ground away. The afflictions are no longer seen simply as impediments or burdens but as the source of the change, which is not, after all, from a good state to a bad one, but—against much of our nature—the other way round.[17] The effect of the afflictions he describes is to reduce him to a bare soul, which is at once a process of painful loss and a kind of movement into truth. The speaker is incompletely aware of this transformation, but it is performed before our eyes in the poem, which moves by stages, from one version of the self, centered on its own pleasures and desires—"There was no moneth but May"—to another, which can accept its place in the world, including its own necessary ignorances and silences. When it hopes, it hopes to be of value to another.

The fact that the speaker does not wholly know the meaning of the story he tells explains the treble ending: first, resignation—but expressed in terms that show no real understanding of his situation, taking the form instead of submission to an authoritarian rule ("I must be meek"); second, rebellion, as in "The Collar," but this time weakly, perhaps with a touch of self-depreciating humor, and only for a moment ("Well, I will change the service"); then, at the end, a new stage of knowledge and acceptance, in which the speaker contemplates the possibility that he is "clean forgot" and this in two ways: forgotten by God and forgetful of God; that is, without any contact with God at all of the sort contemplated throughout the poem, whether by the conferral of gracious benefits or the infliction of pains. Yet even here, at the edge of silence and the mind, something is possible: the speaker can love God, or at least imagine doing so; in hope, at least, this is the core of his being, all that is left when everything else is stripped away. "Let me not love thee, if I love thee not." It may seem like nothing; but in a sense it is all that a human being can aspire to. The point to which this speaker

---

16. Genesis 22:1. See also Isaiah 6:8: "Also I heard the voice of the Lord, saying, Whom shall I send, and who will go for us? Then said I, Here am I; send me."

17. With "thinne and lean without a fence or friend" compare "A Christians state and case / Is not a corpulent, but a thinne and spare, / Yet active strength" ("The Size").

brings himself is the simultaneous recognition that this is as deep a need as he has in his being, the last thing he could give up, and that the God he needs to love is not the God of comfort and support alone, but of pain and affliction too. This gives new and bitter meaning to the Christian's "first and great commandment," that "thou shalt love the Lord thy God with all thy heart, and with all thy soul, and with all thy mind" (Matthew 22:30).

Like "Vertue," then, this poem implicitly contrasts two ways of being, but not so much the organic and temporal against the spiritual and timeless as the selfish and controlling against the trusting and giving. Yet, again as with "Vertue," both have their undeniable appeals, and this means that the story of the poem as I have summed it up above is too simple. Some of the afflictions themselves, however in one sense beneficial, are indeed terrible: "My friends die." And who could possibly want to become "thinne and leane without a fence or friend"? The good things of which he has been deprived—friends, and health, and comfort, and pleasure—are truly good things. One could not strip oneself of desire for them. And still another level of complication is suggested by the fact that his selfish desire for the more trivial items, the "furniture" and "houshold stuffe," did have the good effect of drawing him into "service": the enticement of which he complains was in fact the work of grace. Against the benign side of affliction, then, is not only its pain but the human fact that the optimistic story, the one that makes bad things good, also makes human life impossible on the only terms on which we can live it, for it makes the principle by which we organize everything, that of pain and pleasure, utterly unreliable. Theologically necessary, perhaps, but impossible: as though, at sea under a gray sky, we suddenly saw our compass card spinning aimlessly in its box, having lost its magnetic charge. This explains the speaker's wish to be a tree, less than human, without a will and without language: a tree makes no choices, yet is good. This is a wish for the state prior to the Fall, in the garden of Eden; yet even this wish is undermined when we recall what fruit that tree produced.

It is Herbert's great achievement, here and elsewhere, to write a poetry that calls into question both himself, as he realizes the unreliability of his own impulses, and the language by which he defines himself and his world, as he comes to see that too as a source of delusion. "Milk and sweetnesses" must be good things; the point at which one "chiefly lives" must be a good one; "joyes" are necessarily good things, "griefs" are bad ones, and so on; yet the opposites of these things are also true.

On these conditions satisfactory speech is impossible, and for two reasons: the failings of the self, the failings of language. In such a context, what may be valued most is not quite speech at all, but what Herbert calls a "grone," a cry from a suffering heart that is stripped of all its accidents, all its hopes and confidences: "Ah my deare God! Though I am clean forgot, / Let me not love thee, if I love thee not."

I said earlier that Robert Frost's poetry is built out of the sense that whenever we speak we sentimentalize our world and ourselves—the flower and the butterfly; the deer in the lake—and that one function of his poetry is to expose and counteract that tendency. George Herbert writes out of an analogous sense, that to speak is to sin, and in a radical way, for it is to assert our will against God's will and the validity of our perceptions against the fact that we cannot accurately perceive or understand what is good and bad. One of the functions of Herbert's poetry is to make this sense conscious, and to counteract it. This counteraction is paradoxically but necessarily in words—how else could it be done?—but often (in a sense always) it concludes in silence, a silence given meaning by the words that have come before.

"Affliction" has two such moments, of increasing intensity: when the speaker says, "Now I am here," acknowledging that his "books"— his language—tell him nothing any more, and aspiring to the utter silence of a tree; and at the close, when he affirms his humanity, against the tree, by claiming not a power to speak but a capacity to love—or, more bleakly, a need to love, which is in the nature of things mute: a feeling, a gesture, not sayable; at most a "grone."

The story of "Affliction" has a shape similar to that of a classic tragedy, such as Sophocles' *Oedipus*: the hero starts off in felicity, having everything a person could want, and through a series of events that are only partly, if at all, his own fault, is reduced to an essential core, stripped of his accidents of wealth and office and position and competence, a bare and naked human soul, "without a fence or friend." For the audience this is a terrifying thing to watch, for we see that we are as vulnerable as those whose catastrophes we pity, and we come to realize, a little at least, how unstable is everything that we ourselves habitually rely upon, from health to wealth, perhaps including the very language in which we construct our worlds and selves. Yet at the same time tragedy of this sort is reassuring and confirming, for it shows that the human spirit can maintain its identity and integrity even in the face of its own dissolution. Prometheus, asserting himself against the force of Zeus, even as he is devoured by vultures, is a model of this sort of tragic figure, as is Oedipus at Colonus, asserting his integrity and innocence.[18]

It is hard to see *Lear* in such terms, with its ending so random and cruel—Samuel Johnson could not bear to reread it—and hard to see Herbert's poem that way either. It comes out against the assertion of the self, with the knowledge that its ineradicable impulses, and the language by which it organizes its world, are alike impossibly ignorant and rooted in distortion. Instead of the defiant and integrated self intrepidly facing its dissolution, we have a poetically induced brokenness of the self enacted in the story and in the form, a kind of disintegration out of which can come, almost like a croak, a simple gesture of need, without past or future, part of no story, without an imagined world— the next thing in fact to silence. Or so it seems until you realize that all this takes place in beautifully ordered language, and by an art that necessarily affirms the power and value of its maker.

Preaching and Poetry

"Affliction" (I) has at its center Herbert's sense that the very activity in which he is engaged, writing a poem, is impossible, both because the language he is given distorts and misleads at every stage, and because his own nature calls upon him to assert his will constantly against that of his God, including in the act of poetic composition itself. How can one possibly say anything that is true or valuable?

This issue, difficult enough in any context, has additional and distressing complications as soon as the poet imagines himself trying to speak for religious truth, as Herbert does. The first line of our next poem, "The Windows," puts it in the form of an explicit question: "Lord, how can man preach thy eternall word?" But before examining the rest of the poem I want to say something about the nature of the question itself, especially about "preaching."[19]

---

18. See generally Michelle Gellrich, *Tragedy and Theory: The Problem of Conflict Since Aristotle* (Princeton: Princeton University Press, 1988); Martha Nussbaum, *The Fragility of Goodness: Luck and Ethics in Greek Tragedy* (Cambridge: Cambridge University Press, 1986).

19. Herbert here uses the word "man" to mean not only men, but human beings generally. This is a feature of the religious discourse of his time which naturally recurs throughout his verse, for example in the opening lines of his well-known poem, "The Pulley": "When God at first made man." Most people today take some pains to avoid

"Thy Eternall Word"

At one level the difficulty is plain enough, and runs through all of Western religious discourse: how can a finite and culturally located human creature possibly reflect in human language the infinite, the omnipotent, the eternal, the ineffable? "Thy word" is "eternall," we are not: how then can we possibly express it in our language? The entire project of the theological use of language, indeed of the religious life, not only in Herbert but virtually everywhere, is threatened from the beginning by this question. This may indeed help explain the drive of so many religious thinkers and writers, including Herbert himself, towards music, art, and architecture, and towards silence itself.

To take a familiar example, think of Augustine's *Confessions*—in many ways a model for Herbert's *Temple*[20]—which begins with a sense of the impossibility of its own existence and activity. Augustine starts by quoting words of praise from the Psalms—"Magnus es, Domine"—and then acknowledges, as a kind of prior but previously unarticulated fact, the desire to praise that he has just expressed in these borrowed words. Yet he recognizes too that in a sense he cannot really praise, for he does not know and understand that which, or He Whom, he would praise. So can I call upon you? he asks. But how can I do that, without knowing you? And how can I know you? This is the gift of faith, he says, to call without knowing. But when I do call, how should I do it: should I ask you to be within me? But there is no place within me, who am finite, that can contain you, who are infinite; and, since I am created by you, you are here within me already. Who are you then?

> Most high, utterly good, utterly powerful, most omnipotent, most merciful and most just, deeply hidden yet most intimately present, perfection of both beauty and strength, stable and incomprehensible, immutable and yet changing all things, never new, never old, making everything new and "leading" the proud "to be old without their

---

such locutions, for reasons that are to us obvious. But this is how Herbert thought and spoke, and if we are to learn his language we must accept that fact about it. From time to time I will accordingly use "man" as he does, particularly when summarizing either what he says or a contemporary position to which he is responding.

20. Augustine's *Works* is one book we know he owned, for he refers to it in his will. See *The Works of George Herbert*, ed. F. E. Hutchinson (Oxford: Clarendon Press, 1941), 382.

knowledge" (Job 9:5, Old Latin version); always active, always in repose, gathering to yourself but not in need, supporting and filling and protecting, creating and nurturing and bringing to maturity, searching even though to you nothing is lacking: you love without burning, you are jealous in a way that is free of anxiety, you "repent" (Gen. 6:6) without the pain of regret, you are wrathful and remain tranquil. You will a change without any change in your design. You recover what you find, yet have never lost. Never in any need, you rejoice in your gains (Luke 15:7); you are never avaricious, yet you require interest (Matt. 25:27). We pay you more than you require so as to make you our debtor, yet who has anything which does not belong to you? (I Cor. 4:7). You pay off debts, though owing nothing to anyone; you cancel debts and incur no loss. But in these words what have I said, my God, my life, my holy sweetness? What has anyone achieved in words when he speaks about you?[21]

Augustine here locates himself and his reader in a world and a relation in which language cannot do what we are likely to think of as its usual job: it cannot describe, or name, or work as a set of adequate gestures of communication, because what the speaking self confronts is not comprehensible by us or expressible in our language. He expresses this by breaking down and both his own and his reader's confidence in language itself, creating directly in the reader a sense of dislocation that is rather like his own as he confronts his God. Augustine thus reduces himself to an essential human core, consisting of an impulse to praise, which he calls faith; an active sense of the inadequacy of his mind and language; and the capacity to speak not about but to another, whom he can address as "thou." Herbert's poetry often works in a similar way, speaking out of a sense, sharply felt, of the infinity of God and his own finiteness, and a corresponding sense of the impossibility of the poetry itself.[22] And like Augustine, Herbert often finds his solution, such as it is, in his capacity to address the "thou" he cannot know.

All theology must face the question made vivid by Herbert and Augustine, namely what connection there can be between the words

---

21. *Saint Augustine: Confessions,* trans. H. Chadwick (New York: Oxford University Press, 1991), 4–5.

22. See, e.g., the closing lines of "Artillerie"—"There is no articling with thee: / I am but finite, yet thine infinitely"—and compare "The Search."

we say and the reality we seek to address or describe. Here above all, one would think, language should be open and polyphonic, conscious of its limits, or what I like to think of as "literary"; here least of all, should it be reduced to dogma, doctrine, or flat assertion. Indeed— against our experience—we should expect religious people to be exemplary as pluralists, ready to see the beauty and truth of other languages, other rituals, since they should be so continually aware of the incompleteness of their own.[23] Here, for example, is Emerson on the subject:[24]

Brahma

If the red slayer thinks he slays,
Or if the slain thinks he is slain,
They know not well the subtle ways
I keep, and pass, and turn again.

Far or forgot to me is near,
Shadow and sunlight are the same;
The vanished gods to me appear;
And one to me are shame and fame.

They reckon ill who leave me out;
When me they fly, I am the wings;
I am the doubter and the doubt,
And I the hymn the Brahmin sings.

The strong gods pine for my abode,
And pine in vain the sacred Seven;
But thou, meek lover of the good!
Find me, and turn thy back on heaven.

On such assumptions as these there could be no place for an authoritarian

---

23. David Tracy is a modern theologian who works out of just such a pluralist sensibility. See especially *The Analogical Imagination: Christian Theology and the Culture of Pluralism* (New York: Crossroad, 1981).

24. This poem may well have been influenced by Emerson's reading of Herbert, as may "Uriel" too, discussed at page 34 below. Emerson's prose style is even more religiously poetic, for it induces in its reader a kind of detachment from "reality"— that is, from our confidence that our language reproduces reality without difficulty— and thus works an immersion in another kind of imagined and felt space. See Faith Morrow Williams, "Young Emerson as a Religious Writer," Ph.D. diss., Columbia University, 1973. For further discussion, see pages 184–87.

language of dogma and doctrine. Yet of course the field of Christian theology, and not only Christian, has been deeply marked for centuries by dogmatic assertion and claims.

Is this to be explained in part as a kind of collective resistance, a refusal to acknowledge the all too evident inadequacy of doctrinal language itself? Dogmatism would then be a manifestation of our incapacity to tolerate the breakdown of language to which theological reflection and religious experience naturally lead.[25] For there is a strain running counter to such dogmatism, not only in writers like Herbert and Emerson and Augustine, but in the gospels themselves, which are full of the cryptic, the paradoxical, the impossible. A parable of Jesus, for example, will often lead its audience from what they comprehend, cast in the terms of their own culture and its values, to what cannot be comprehended. This is perhaps the nature of all good theological discourse: to acknowledge the impossibility, yet claim the necessity, of its own endeavor.[26]

But if one cannot capture the divine in descriptive or doctrinal speech, what kind of theological language-uses can there sensibly be? This is a question to which Herbert's poetry is an extended answer. He must face the difficulty in two ways, as it affects his power to speak to God and as it bears on his relation to his own reader, for both are in different ways problematic. With respect to God what is most nearly possible for him is prayer, and Herbert's poems can be read that way; not as assertions of truth but as gestures towards another, of praise or thanksgiving, say; or, more accurately—since his attempts at prayer are themselves inherently flawed—as a series of repeated and partial attempts to pray, struggles to

---

25. Gnosticism is another response to that breakdown, a claim of special knowledge of God. See Philip Lee, *Against the Protestant Gnostics* (New York: Oxford University Press, 1987).

26. Here again I think of Emerson and in particular of "Uriel," which, in verse that has a kinship to Herbert's own, tells the story of the angel who told intolerable truths. (Robert Frost said that this was "the best Western poem yet." See M. R. Konvitz and S. E. Whicher, eds., *Emerson: A Collection of Critical Essays*, [Englewood Cliffs, N.J.: Prentice-Hall, 1962], 16.) Uriel's offense was to give his "sentiment divine / Against the being of a line":

> "Line in nature is not found;
> Unit and universe are round;
> In vain produced, all rays return;
> Evil will bless and ice will burn."

move into right relation with the other. Like Augustine, he thus turns from attempted description and definition to the creation of an enacted relation with another, addressed as "Thou."

But how is this to be done, or done well, when he himself is not an integer or unit, but a set of inconsistent voices; when the "Thou" he addresses cannot be understood; and when the experience of life, its pains and afflictions, seems so inconsistent with what he has been told and believes to be true of that God? For example, if one tries to praise God, for what attributes or actions is one to do this? To attempt to praise is to claim to know what is worthy of praise in Him, and this we cannot know. Or: for what events or actions should we give thanks? Even to attempt to give thanks is to claim to know what things have been good for us, what things have not, and this is impossible. There is no point of view available to us from which truth, including the experience of others, can simply be observed and comprehended. Everything we say or do proceeds from the radically limited spot of consciousness that is the individual person, and this spot is marked by an essential, and natural, self-centeredness. Every utterance, not just descriptions and statements of doctrine but every gesture and performance, is in this sense imperfect through and through. Herbert knows all this and makes it plain; and his verse is consequently less a series of prayers than a series of poems exploring and enacting the impossibility of prayer. With respect to his reader, this works less as the elaboration or affirmation of doctrine than as the creation of experiences—including those of contradiction and complexity, of the breakdown of language and mind—that offer his reader something of his own sense of the intractable difficulty of life in relation to his language, to his many selves, and to his God.

"How Can Man Preach?"

Both the question with which "The Windows" begins—"How can man preach?"—and Herbert's performed response to it have general implications, for the difficulties I have mentioned attend to every speech-act in relation to God—prayer and praise, thanksgiving and confession, submission and acceptance—and indeed to the making of poems as well. But Herbert's question and response have particular as well as general force: "Lord, how can man *preach* thy eternall word?" It is the specific practice of "preaching," and his own relation as a "preacher" to the "eternall word," that particularly concerns him here. What was the form of language and life that he called "preaching," and what was especially problematic about it?

It is significant that Herbert was a Protestant, and an English one, for preaching had a role under Protestantism, and in England, different from that in the Catholic tradition. Protestantism began with a call for a return to Scripture as the sole theological authority, against the Roman insistence upon the authority of the tradition of the church, and with a call to preaching too, against the more ceremonial or sacramental functions of the priest. The prominence of preaching among Protestants may seem inconsistent with the emphasis upon the importance of Scripture—Why not just read the sacred text aloud?—but in fact it was not. The Scripture needed interpretation, not only in its difficult passages, but in its larger design; the translation of the text into the vernacular, which was the natural consequence of the Protestant position, drew attention to difficulties in the text that required explication; and the great theological controversies of the era, coupled with the expanded role of the layman in Protestant church government, naturally led to preaching as a form of argument and instruction.

There was also a shift in the conception both of the individual person and of the church itself that gave a new importance to preaching. The central theological principle of Protestantism was that we are "justified by faith alone," rather than by merit, or good works, or right behavior. It is ultimately not our conduct or goodness but God's action that saves us, for which the term is "grace"; but there must also be a human correlative, consisting at root of a trusting willingness to receive what God offers, for which the term is "faith." The purpose of preaching is to bring people to faith. The poet and preacher John Donne said, for example: "There is no salvation but by faith, nor faith but by hearing, nor hearing but by preaching."[27] The church thus became not merely a

---

27. Quoted in Horton Davies, *Worship and Theology in England: From Andrewes to Baxter and Fox, 1603–1690* (Princeton: Princeton University Press, 1975), 148. Donne himself may have been alluding to Romans 10:17: "So then faith cometh by hearing, and hearing by the word of God." See the discussions of preaching more generally in Davies at 133–86, and in Davies's earlier volume in the same series, *Worship and Theology in England: From Cranmer to Hooker, 1534–1603* (Princeton: Princeton University Press, 1970), 227–54, 294–324. See also Patrick Collinson, *The Elizabethan Puritan Movement* (Berkeley: University of California Press, 1967), 41–42, 49–51, 106, and Peter Lake, *Moderate Puritans,* especially 16, where he quotes one preacher, Dering, as saying: "We cannot believe except we hear, [nor] can we hear without a preacher." One fact Dering

place for the celebration of ritual, but an active community bent on its own redemption. Thus the call among English reformers to move from a mere reading ministry—where the priest read the Scriptures and the liturgy, as this was prescribed in the Book of Common Prayer, and perhaps also a homily, prepared by others and mass-produced for the purpose—to a preaching ministry, in which the priest undertook as well to expound the word of God in his own language. The central task of the preacher was to "edify" his community; this was a term of art, derived from Paul's Epistles, that meant building a living spiritual community, a church, just as one builds a physical structure. This way of thinking is reflected explicitly in the title to Herbert's own book, *The Temple*.[28]

All of these features of Protestantism intensify the demands on the priest. He is to preach about rather than simply read the "eternall word," which is both uniquely divine and imperfectly comprehensible; to do this it is not enough that he be learned or intelligent, a competent expounder of a difficult text; he must himself be inspired, capable of speaking, as well as hearing, the Word.[29] His preaching must itself be

---

and Donne both have in mind is the illiteracy of much of the congregation and the scarcity of books for those who could read.

28. In a famous passage—to which the title of Herbert's book may in fact be an allusion—the Apostle Paul said, "Know ye not that ye are the temple of God, and that the Spirit of God dwelleth in you?" (I Corinthians 3:16). And the title page, both in the Bodleian manuscript and the first edition of 1633 has this quotation from Psalm 29: "In his Temple doth every man speak of his honour."

See also John Coolidge, *The Pauline Renaissance in England: Puritanism and the Bible* (Oxford: Clarendon Press, 1970), especially at 23–54, and Peter Lake, *Anglicans and Puritans? Presbyterianism and English Conformist Thought from Whitgift to Hooker* (London: Unwin Hyman, 1988), 29–31, 45–59, 120–26, 164–69. For a very brief but magisterial account of the Puritan movement see G. R. Elton, *The Tudor Constitution: Documents and Commentary*, 2d ed. (Cambridge: Cambridge University Press, 1982), 442–48. See also Debora Kuller Shuger, *Habits of Thought in the English Renaissance: Religion, Politics, and the Dominant Culture* (Berkeley and Los Angeles: University of California Press, 1990), which deals particularly with sermons.

29. This remains a difference between Catholic and Protestant churches to this day: the former, including the Anglican, rely far more on ritual than preaching, the latter to a large degree reverse the process. A friend of mine, a Methodist minister, once explained his own anxiety of preaching before a particularly distinguished congregation: "It is not enough that I be right," he said: "I must convince them." Compared to this the usual Catholic homily is informal, for the pressure in that service is on the celebration of the Mass.

a source of conviction and regeneration in others, a vehicle for the direct action of the Holy Spirit. He must become a center at which the Holy Spirit lives and speaks, for the Word is not merely the scriptural text but, as the opening of John's Gospel makes plain, God himself: "In the beginning was the Word . . ." How are these things possibly to be done? Small wonder that Herbert's speaker begins with such a question.

Things are made even worse by the Protestant sense, which Herbert fully shared, of the radical sinfulness of all human beings. It is not only as an intellectual or linguistic matter that preaching is impossible; the impossibility arises from our very nature, our character as human beings, and it reaches not only preaching but any good speech, any good action, none of which is possible to us as a matter of our own capacity and merit, but only as an act of grace. By his watchword, "justification by faith alone," Luther meant that there was nothing one could do oneself to ensure or even affect one's salvation: no works of piety, no acts of merit. It is faith alone by which you are saved, and this is an act of God's grace, not your will or character.[30]

Such in general terms are the beliefs that make preaching, and much else, seem impossible. But it is important to say at once that what matters here is not the mere fact that we are fallen, God infinite, our language inadequate, or even that God suffered for us, but what Herbert in his poetry makes these things mean. These beliefs are not final statements of position, that is, nor premises from which deductions follow, but the roughly formed material for thought and life made available by this culture to those who inhabited it (as our own culture provides us, say, with notions of popular sovereignty, constitutional government, and a consumer economy). These are general elements of the language Herbert inherited and found himself inhabiting, and upon which he worked in making his own version of it, his own language of meaning, in his poetry. Ultimately these beliefs are for Herbert not matters of doctrine but of life, and especially of the life of his poetry.

---

30. In Calvin this led to a doctrine of predestination, which seems not to have been a large part of Herbert's conception of the world. But see the conclusion of "The Water-course":

Who gives to man, as he sees fit, $\begin{cases} \text{Salvation.} \\ \text{Damnation.} \end{cases}$

A Poem on Preaching

The Windows

L ord, how can man preach thy eternall word?
   He is a brittle crazie glasse:
Yet in thy temple thou dost him afford
    This glorious and transcendent place,
    To be a window, through thy grace.

But when thou dost anneal in glasse thy storie,
   Making thy life to shine within
The holy Preachers; then the light and glorie
    More rev'rend grows, & more doth win:
    Which else shows watrish, bleak, & thin.

Doctrine and life, colours and light, in one
   When they combine and mingle, bring
A strong regard and aw: but speech alone
    Doth vanish like a flaring thing,
    And in the eare, not conscience ring.[31]

Herbert's speaker first asks his question, then focuses upon the particular impediment to "preaching" last referred to above, our fallen nature: man is "a brittle crazie glass." What does this image mean? Of course part of it is a general sense of fragility and disorder, and perhaps of vanity too, since "glass" means "mirror." But my own sense of it is more specific, and it is suggested by what happens next, namely that God affords this window a "glorious and transcendent place" in his temple. The glass preexists its place, to which God, like a workman,

---

31. Notes:

1. *Glasse* is at first a mirror, as well as a pane of glass; then it becomes what the title promises us, a window. This metamorphosis reflects the larger one that is the poem's subject.

2. *Anneal* is a technical term, meaning in general to transform by heat, in particular to fix colors in glass or ceramics by such a process.

3. *Win*, which here means something like "achieve," is also related to our adjective "winning," as well as (by a pun) to "windows." Compare "The Foil": "As if grief were not foul, nor vertue winning."

raises it. In speaking of a "brittle crazie glasse," then, I think that Herbert is imagining what a church window would look like lying in the shop or on the ground: the lead lines that hold its pieces together would make no pattern at all, but seem, as he says, crazed, as we sometimes say the cracked surface of porcelain is "crazed," or "crazy." This is an expression of the sense of man's inherent worthlessness and flaw, his need for the "grace" that God indeed now shows by raising him up and placing him in a church, as a window. (The church is of course both the imagined physical edifice and the spiritual community of human souls.)

Notice that the poem could simply stop here: its thought and versification are both in a sense complete, and the message he is "preaching" in the poem is plain, and beautiful too. Why, then, does he go on? And why does the next stanza begin with a "But"? Part of it is that the poetic imagination cannot let go of what it has once begun; part of it, I think, that there is something unsatisfactory in the first stanza, something too neat, too conclusory. What actually is our condition, more fully imagined, and what is this "grace" that rescues us? How does becoming a "window" get us to "preaching"?

The second stanza responds to these questions by an act of imagination, in which man is now transformed into a stained-glass window, full of color and telling a story; before this, he is "watrish, bleak, & thin"— that is, a grisaille window, as yet uncolored, unstained, whose pale gray-green light tells no story. It is not enough for us simply to be moved from one place to another, then, as the first stanza suggests; the work of grace is not simply to relocate the preacher in the building, but to transform him through and through by heat—annealing him—which it does by creating within him the sacred story. Just as the pieces that make up a glass window are first stained, under heat, then arrayed to tell a story, the preacher is both transformed by a story and tells one too. In both cases the light comes from outside. The window (or preacher) receives its color, and its character as story, from the metamorphosis that it has undergone; but this is the work of someone else, for it is "thy life" that "shines within." This—the gracious action of Another—is the answer to the question how one can "preach thy eternall word," and it is important to see that the transformation is a real one: the light can make a kind of beauty shining through the window that it could not achieve alone. This metamorphosis is in a sense enacted for us in the form of the poem, as the simplicity of the first stanza is transformed—annealed—by the complexity and richness of the second.

The third stanza responds in general terms to the first two, using them as a kind of text for its own sermon: it tells us that what counts in preaching, and in prayer and poetry too, is not the words alone but the life behind the words, the life the words make possible—"Doctrine and life, colours and light." This would of course in a practical way be true of a typical parish priest, well known to his parishioners: it is his character, as they know it, upon which they will draw in hearing his words, in interpreting them and in weighing them. The real meaning of his words will lie not in his words alone but in the contexts in which they are uttered, in the human relations of which they are a part. "Doctrine" is given meaning by the "life" of the speaker, and vice versa, and this must be true not only of the preacher but of any person.

But all this is to cast doubt on the value of the poem itself, which is "speech alone" if anything is, for we know it only on a printed page. Must it then "vanish like a flaring thing"? Or can we read the poem, like the preaching, for the life that lies behind it, for the life that it creates?

In this case the life of the poem lies in a series of transformations, enacted in imitation and definition of the central transformation it describes, that of the preacher. It begins with a tension between two distinct modes of thought, the conceptually explicit and the imagistic. The opening question is asked in the first mode—"How can man?"— and supported in the second: "He is a brittle crazie glass." The response continues the image—"To be a window"—but then explains it conceptually: "through thy grace." In the second stanza the imagistic mode predominates, as we are asked to imagine glass being annealed to tell a story, within the window and the preacher both at once, and "light and glorie" shining through. We are told that this is being said of the preacher, but we are given no language other than that of the metaphor itself in which to talk about it, no language of doctrine or theory. Nothing is said here, that is, about conversion, say, as there was in stanza one about grace. The window's transformation and that of the preacher are merged in our minds, not separated; one does not serve as an analogy for the other.

The third stanza shifts back in the direction of the conceptually explicit, for here the speaker is commenting, telling us what the meaning of the preceding stanzas really is, as though in a sermon. He makes the analogies overt: "Doctrine and life, colours and light." But this does not quite work: is the "doctrine" the "colour," for example, or the "light?" Which is the "life"? Instead of a one-to-one analogy, what we have here is a set of images of combination itself, and, more than that, of the kind of combination that leads to transformation. This is marked for us by it being this stanza in which color is first mentioned, a gesture that itself transforms what has gone before. But this voice, the same voice that asked the question that began the poem in the first place, will not rest with an image but requires a conclusion. His assertions may pale against the force of the earlier images, but they do have a place: image and exposition combine, like colors and light.

The poem begins with a specific reference to speech—"How can man preach?"—and concludes by speaking of "speech alone"; in between is the glorious visual imagery, to which and from which the poem leads. Yet there is a paradox here: the visual imagery is itself verbally created—there is no actual painting or stained glass before us—and this enacts the kind of combination, of colors and light, doctrine and life, here of real sound and imagined sight, that the poem praises. The last image captures this beautifully: "flaring" is an image of fire, something seen; "vanish" too is primarily visual; yet the speaker is talking about "speech alone" and the last word, "ring," makes sound predominant, as a kind of counterpoint to the visual. "Speech alone" may indeed "vanish," but it does "ring," and this poem is in any event not speech alone, far from it; it combines the visual and conceptual—windows and colors and light—and sound too.

This poem is in effect a performance of the kind of "preaching" that is possible for Herbert: not didactic and expository, but imagistic, transformative, and poetic in kind. The performance itself responds to the doubts that the speaker raises about the value of preaching, and of poetry too. As the doctrine of grace is first expressed in the image of the glass made a window, and then recast in the second stanza, when the glass is annealed to tell a story, it is given life of a kind radically different from any utterance in explicitly doctrinal terms.

Think of it this way: the speaker first doubts the possibility of preaching, but then affirms it, at least when God has acted on the preacher in the wonderful way he describes. But there remains the question: what is the relation of this particular speaker to the process he is celebrating? There is no claim that he is transformed; like the speaker in "Vertue," he is outside of these events, describing them to others. His positive conclusion, then, can as such have little weight; what we need is testimony or demonstration. It is this that the poem gives us, supplying the defect in the speaker, in much the same way that "Vertue" acted on its speaker to another end, undermining his claims and assertions.

I suggested earlier that in reading Herbert we shall have to face the meaning to us of his religious language, which is certain to be different for different people reading his work today.[32] This is an issue that will occupy us throughout this book, but perhaps I can now pose this question, which many readers will find troubling: how far is it possible to read Herbert's poetry, cast as it is in religious language, and with a theologically defined audience, without ourselves in some sense sharing the beliefs that that language expresses? This may seem an odd question, but I think it raises a real issue, one that provides a suitable context for further thought about what we mean both by reading and by belief. I wish to ask, that is: What are the beliefs implied in reading George Herbert?[33]

There is one rather obvious sense in which we must believe what he says, for this is how we read anything with which we actually engage, as Coleridge said when he spoke of the "willing suspension of disbelief" entailed in all poetic reading. We are normally not troubled by this fact at all. To read *Winnie-the-Pooh,* for example, you must in some sense believe, or pretend to believe, that these stuffed animals can talk, or to read *The Wind in the Willows,* that Mole and Ratty have characters like human characters, or to read the *Iliad,* that gods can make themselves invisible, dive deep into the sea, affect the course of battles, and so forth. But we don't really believe these things, one might say, for when we turn from the fictional to the real world we know that stuffed animals don't talk, real animals are not human, and that there are no gods at all.

Or do we? Do not these fictions in fact furnish our minds and shape our expectations, giving us things to say to ourselves or to others on

---

32. Notice that the differences are not only among groups but between individuals: two High Church Anglicans, for example, might respond very differently indeed to this language, as might two members of a conservative reformed church, or two atheists. In our rush to acknowledge the importance of groups or cultures we often leave out the significance of individual variation.

33. This question was suggested to me by Joseph Vining, *The Authoritative and the Authoritarian* (Chicago: University of Chicago Press, 1985), which works out a vision of the beliefs that are implied in the practices of reading authoritative texts that lie at the heart of American law.

occasion after occasion? The little girl is bouncy, just like Tigger; or is wholly excited by learning something new, like Mole; or is at a moment so alive with grace and charm that she must have been touched by a goddess.

Herbert's language, if actually engaged with, will come I think to play at least this much of a role in the reader's life, as will Milton's say, or Donne's too; indeed, without this kind of engagement reading is impossible. Think of reading once more by analogy to travel: to read Herbert is like spending a year, say, in Morocco or Bangkok. Having lived that way for a time it becomes part of one's experience, part of what Kenneth Burke called one's "equipment for life." To protect yourself by staying in the Hilton Hotel would be simply to insulate yourself from that experience and to give yourself another, that of hotel life. To engage with a text or culture means to accept something other, provisionally but really, and this works changes in the self. Suppose, to take the analogy one further stage, that your travels take you to a place where you learn the local language, not only intellectually but actually, by which I mean that you learn to use it to make the gestures, to engage in the practices, that constitute life in that world. Belief is now no longer an issue. Language and practice are things that people do, and we have done them: prayed for the gods to bring rain, exorcised a witch, built our house with a barrier at the door to exclude demons, bowed low to a holy man, and so on. To say we disbelieve the meaning of all these things is a somewhat thin remark against the actuality of our conduct and experience, our engagement with a way of imagining the world and ourselves. To speak a language is in an important sense to believe it.

What I say is of course not only true of Christian language, or theological language, but of any. The language of the Talmud, for example, to one who has actually engaged in its processes of thought and imagination, will always have a kind of reality that cannot be erased by an assertion of disbelief; the same is true of the language of modern law, or of Homer's poetry.

Outside the field of religion we are so comfortable with this fact as not even to notice it; but religious belief is such a charged topic for many of us that we want to deny it. Here I want only to say—or to warn—first, that to engage with this poetry is to engage with the language in which it is written, and this requires a momentary acceptance of it, an acceptance that will in some sense live in the mind thereafter, even if one ultimately rejects it wholeheartedly, as disgusting or vile, just as the experience of Morocco or Paris lives in the mind even if it is later rejected. But one cannot reject it while one is reading it, for that is no longer reading. We must engage with the mind and imagination on the terms that it offers us, or not at all; and even if we later reject these terms, our experience of them will nonetheless have been a real one. Second, I want to say that this experience may affect our own sense of what religious belief is in the first place, both for us, in our pluralistic world in which every construction of reality is poised against others, and for Herbert himself.

In speaking of the religious beliefs of other people our habit is often to describe a set of propositions, largely meaningless to us, which they accept as true: that the Old One made man out of an otter and gave him the sea and the land; that every grove and stream has its tutelary deity; or that Zeus, having dismembered his father and shut the other Titans up underground, rules all the other gods on Mt. Olympus. Christianity, to which formal credal statements are so important, naturally invites such a treatment. But how much of the life of belief is captured that way? To think of the beliefs of others as a set of propositions affirmed may seriously misstate things, partly because doubt is as much a part of the life of faith as is belief, partly because this view seems to suppose either that the person simply believes in some automatic way what everyone else does or that she chooses one set of propositions or another from some array, a selection we could expect her to be able to explain. But neither image fits, I think, the religious life of most people. For a person growing up in a world, the religion she is offered by her culture and her family offers her one of the languages she can use to make sense of life, one set of practices by which she can engage with it. Choice has often rather little to do with it; the language simply is a part of one's life. On the other hand, one's response to this inheritance is one's own, different from that of others, and it is one's own responsibility too.[34]

As theology, and as poetry too, Herbert's verse is not inherently propositional or doctrinal in kind, but an art of language, the meaning of which lies less in the doctrines that underlie it than in the experience the text reflects and creates. To say that the life of poetry is not in

---

34. One could think of the theological world in which Herbert grew up as being like a landscape: it is there; it can be described; but it is somewhat different to each observer; and, for the artist at least, what matters most is not what is there but what he makes of it.

statement, but in experience, is of course familiar enough; here it needs to be repeated because when we confront religious poetry we tend to switch modes of thought and think in doctrinal or propositional terms. The second point is perhaps less familiar: that the life of the religion of which Herbert speaks is not doctrinal or propositional either, but experiential. What this means for us is that in participating in the aesthetic experience offered by the poetry we are necessarily engaging in its religious aspect as well. Indeed there is a sense in which one cannot read it well without engaging in the practice of theology. It would be a mistake to try to distance oneself from this fact or to deny it,[35] I think; but to accept it is not free of difficulty, for, as I suggest above, the reader who does participate in this language, on these terms, will actually experience a construction of the world, a set of feelings and meanings too, that are religious in character, and this is so even if he or she is inclined to be hostile to religion in general.

Suppose that instead of looking for the nature of religious belief in particular propositions affirmed or denied, we looked to the religious practices that people engage in and ask what they seem to mean. Jaroslav Pelikan in *The Vindication of Tradition* takes such a line when he says that what really defines the Christian community is the Eucharist, the gathering together to share the mystic meal.[36] This is what Christians have done, somewhere in the world every day, for almost two thousand years. Their various creeds and other doctrinal assertions are attempts to explain, to themselves, what it is that they are doing; they make

---

35. Helen Vendler moves in this direction. Vendler, *Poetry of George Herbert*, 4–5.

36. *The Vindication of Tradition* (New Haven, Conn.: Yale University Press, 1984), 48–49. This is a rather Catholic view. A Protestant position can be put equally strongly, as Harnack does at the end of his monumental *History of Dogma:*

> The Gospel entered into the world, not as a doctrine, but as a joyful message and as a power of the Spirit of God. . . . [The doctrine that Luther restored, centuries later,] was the Gospel as a glad message and *as a power of God.* That this was what it was, he also pronounced to be the chief, nay the only, principle of theology. What the Gospel is must be ascertained from Holy Scripture; the power of God cannot be construed by thought, it must be experienced; the *faith* in God as the Father of Jesus Christ, which answers to this power, cannot be enticed forth by reason or authority; it must become a part of one's life.

Adolph Harnack, *History of Dogma,* trans. W. M'Gilchrist (London: Williams & Norgate, 1899), 7: 272–74.

and repeat them knowing that they will be imperfect, incomplete, distorted. The life of the church is the life of community and ritual, of prayer and conversation, not the creed in which we try to explain and order that life. The language of the creed, like the language of doctrine more generally, is secondary not primary. When we seek to describe the religion of other people by restating their cardinal points of belief, as propositions, we commit ourselves to a particular and limited view of what religion itself is. It may not mainly be the beliefs in such a sense that divided the Protestants and Catholics, and still do, or separate the orthodox and the heretics in any religion, but other matters, far harder to capture in language: the tone and spirit of the communal religious life, the attitudes and feelings with which practices are performed, the sense of self, community, and deity that are enacted in every interchange. One could put it this way: When two groups go to war over a matter of doctrine, the question is presented Why do they care so very much about this particular issue? To say that it is fundamental, or something like that, simply begs the question: why is it fundamental? The answer must be found elsewhere, in the community's sense of identity, in the character and quality of its life.

I am suggesting here a way of thinking of language uses, including theological ones, not simply as the affirmation of propositions, but as gestures, or what Wittgenstein called language games, whose meaning cannot be restated in propositional terms. The question this suggests is one not of truth or falsity, but of meaning: what do these practices mean, to the primary participants, and to us when we participate as visitors? This question in turn suggests a different criterion of evaluation, namely how fully these practices cohere with our deepest experience of life and each other. Think, for example, of the story of Adam and Eve in the Garden of Eden. As a story meant to be historically true, in the sense that once there were two such people in a garden, it is unacceptable to most people today, including most Christians and Jews; but as a story that accounts for and thus identifies and brings to consciousness deep features of our moral and imaginative life, it is wonderful, and perhaps terrible too. If not the truth of historical factuality, it has the truth of coherence, comprehensiveness, and fidelity to experience—though its image of woman as created out of the rib of man may be rejected on these grounds as well as historical ones, as perhaps a manifestation of parturition envy.

This is not to say that for either the modern Christian or for Herbert the fundamental theological propositions are irrelevant; but they do not exhaust the meaning of religious discourse and practice and indeed are not primary to it. Just as the life of the church lies not in its dogmatic assertions, but in experience or practice, so too the meaning of George Herbert's poems lies not in the doctrines or propositions they assert or assume, but in the life he makes on such terms. But this has its own consequences: to the extent that Herbert's poetry works for us at all it works as a validation of this language, and of these practices, for it could not exist without them. If you accept and admire this poetry, you are entangled in an affirmation of its language. This poetry teaches us how to imagine the experience of the self living on such terms, a self that must establish a relation with this language, which, like all language, is inherently unsatisfactory and imperfect; in doing so, it also teaches a theological lesson, to focus on life and experience, not upon mere doctrine or dogma.

The Limits and Blessings of Language

It is not only the sermon, or "preaching," that Herbert's view of language and the self makes problematic, in some sense impossible, but our every act of language, including—indeed especially—the poem.

Jordan (I)

Who sayes that fictions onely and false hair
    Become a verse? Is there in truth no beautie?
Is all good structure in a winding stair?
May no lines passe, except they do their dutie
    Not to a true, but painted chair?

Is it no verse, except enchanted groves
And sudden arbours shadow course-spunne lines?
Must purling streams refresh a lovers loves?
Must all be vail'd, while he that reades, divines,
    Catching the sense at two removes?

Shepherds are honest people; let them sing:
Riddle who list, for me, and pull for Prime:
I envie no mans nightingale or spring;

> Nor let them punish me with losse of rime,
> Who plainly say, *My God, My King.*[37]

This poem twists two lines of thought together: one asserts the speaker's right to his religious subject matter, namely "truth" against "fictions"; the other asserts the value of plain and simple speech, on whatever subject, against the ornate, the conventional, and the obscure: "Must all be vail'd?" The conclusion to the first line of thought is that he is entitled to write poems, perhaps highly complex ones, the burden of which is religious: "*My God, My King.*" The conclusion of the second is that the proper form for such a poem is no poem at all, but the bare simplicity itself: again, "*My God, My King.*" The truth that he means to make his subject matter is inconsistent not only with conventional love poetry, and its cliché-ridden style, but with the inherent complications of poetry itself. Like "Affliction," the poem resolves itself into a gesture.

In its insistence on simplicity the poem seems to be written against itself, against all poetry in fact, all artificiality, and in favor of the plain and true. In this it is part of a tradition that will later include Words-worth and Frost, both of whom sought to use words and sentences that came from ordinary life, in apparent affirmance of naturalness and sim-plicity. For Herbert the impulse to speak this way—"*My God, My King*"—has a religious dimension as well, for it was a Protestant article of faith that everything essential for us to know or to do is incontro-vertibly set forth in the Scriptures with clarity and simplicity. As the speaker of his poem "Divinitie" puts it:

> *Love God, and love your neighbour. Watch and pray.*
> *Do as ye would be done unto.*

---

37. Notes:

1. The title of course refers to the River Jordan, but its significance is obscure, at least to me. To the extent it invokes Baptism, it may be taken to affirm the value of a sacramental act against doctrine, preaching, and poetry alike.
2. Notice that the right answer to the question "Who sayes . . . ?" is "No one," for nobody argues the position the speaker resists. This speaker is thus struggling with a construction of his own.
3. *Riddle* means to propound riddles, an occupation as trivial as card-playing.
4. According to the OED *prime* was a hand in the card game Primero, consisting of one card from each suit. *Pull* means "draw" a card. "Pull for prime" thus means to draw for the winning hand.

> O dark instructions; ev'n as dark as day!
> Who can these Gordian knots undo?

This being so, what remains for one to do, either as preacher or as poet? What, beyond the repetition of simple truths, are the possibilities of good speech?

The logic of this poem recommends simplicity of utterance: *My God, My King* is as good as any poem could possibly be.[38] But its performance works the other way, for the poem itself is complex, elegant, and ornate, and—with special relevance given what he says at the end—carefully rhymed. The very moment at which Herbert casts off the shackles of rhyme, he rhymes. A poem against poetry then, a complex text written to affirm the value of plain simplicity. Are we to read these tensions as simply irreconcilable, or is the poem in a sense to disappear now that it has done its work, to be shuffled off like a dead skin?[39] Neither of those readings is quite right, I think, for the poem's work continues even in its close, not only in the rhyme but more importantly by providing a context of complex language against which this simple phrase—*"My God, My King"*—can sound like the clear bell of simplicity it has thus become.

Suppose that the rest of the poem simply were not there, and the whole utterance consisted of *"My God, My King."* Would that do? It would sound like a ritualized or even a banal remark; and even if it were in the best way heartfelt, the emotion would find dramatically incomplete expression in such language. Perhaps it would still be good—as good as a poem—if properly meant and felt, but how is one to know

---

38. Compare "A True Hymn," where the speaker says that "my heart" has been trying to say something all day, but can only find this phrase: *"My joy, my life, my crown."*

> Yet slight not these few words:
> If truly said, they may take part
> Among the best in art.

The test suggested is not the beauty of the verse, but the sincerity of the feelings or attitudes that lie behind it. But how is one to know these, even in oneself? And this poem too shows that the simplicity it advocates is not enough; the poet must make this complex utterance in praise of it.

39. Stanley Fish has constructed a theory not only of Herbert's poetry but of a great deal more out of this possibility. See Fish, *Self-Consuming Artifacts: The Experience of Seventeenth-Century Literature* (Berkeley and Los Angeles: University of California Press, 1972), especially chap. 3 on Herbert.

that, whether it is said by oneself or by another? If we were to take the closing recommendation seriously and reduce all speech to this level, the danger would be an extreme Protestant version of empty ritual, consisting of the mere repetition of pious phrases, and this, as a psychological matter, could not be meant in a heartfelt way very long.

Something more is needed to give the gesture the meaning claimed for it: the simplicity, to be real simplicity, must be achieved, and here this is done by the creation of a context against which it can appear indeed as simple truth, and not merely as a dead phrase or cliché. The very simplicity praised here thus depends for its existence upon its opposite. Complexity and simplicity are not opposed after all, but necessary to each other's existence. The poem in fact acts on the simplicity of the closing phrase rather as preaching acts on Scripture: it gives the permanent and general text a context against which it can have a new and particular meaning. The poem itself values neither simplicity nor complexity alone, but this peculiar and apparently self-contradictory combination of two incompatible elements, each of which achieves its definition, and its value, only in relation to the other: like "doctrine and life, colours and light."

There is another dimension to this poem, as I said above, for the speaker resists not only complexity but the kind of verse that is riddled with formulas and clichés: "enchanted groves" and "purling streams," "nightingale" and "spring," which are all a kind of idolatrous obeisance to the "painted."[40] It is thus upon vacuity as well as complexity that the speaker turns his back at the end, in favor of the great simplicity, *"My God, My King."*

But the clichés used here are not representative of this poem, or the kind of poetry it represents, since they are used ironically. The speaker seems to confuse two points, complexity and tired repetition, rejecting both; the poem, by contrast, asserts the value of complexity (when joined with simplicity) and repudiates tired repetition, not only of the

---

40. I am reminded of Alexander Pope's lines in "An Essay on Criticism":

> Wher-e'er you find *the cooling Western Breeze,*
> In the next Line *it whispers thro' the Trees;*
> If *Chrystal Streams with pleasing Murmurs creep,*
> The Reader's threaten'd (not in vain) with *Sleep.*

But Herbert's verse is characteristically more complex: "sudden arbours" has a freshness and immediacy the other phrases lack.

"poetic" kind but, by implication, even of phrases that are both simple and true—and thus undermines the apparent claim for the sufficiency of the closing phrase, which would itself, in another context, be like a poetic cliché that carried no energy, no matter how deeply it was meant. What the poem ultimately affirms is the kind of complex and conflicted life it achieves and offers to its reader.

One way to think of this poem—and indeed of the whole body of Herbert's work—is to say, as I suggested earlier, that he is perpetually asking: What are the possibilities of true speech? The response suggested here is: not in poeticisms nor in bare simplicities, not in clichés of either kind—which is after all what we are mainly given by our culture to speak—but in a poetry that creates a way of speaking that works negatively, by casting the impossibilities and defects of one form of speech against those of another. The miracle achieved here is that in the context so created the last phrase of the poem does sound with clear and simple force. The function of the rest of the poem, as Frost might say, is to define with precision its "sentence sound," and thus the feelings and relationships it expresses.

To shift fields dramatically for a moment, there is a perhaps surprising analogy in the constitutional opinions of the Supreme Court, where complexity and simplicity seem to require one another. One judicial tendency, the more scholarly and lawyerlike, is to complicate and refine: to see each case in full institutional context; to be sensitive to the competing claims of state and citizen; and to think about the present case in the terms established by prior cases, which, as they multiply, produce a discourse of great complexity. This is the activity of legal analysis, and it is important that it be done well. But if that were all, it would lead to a sense of constitutional law as technical only: Where, one would ask, are the great ideas and principles upon which it is all founded? The reciprocal impulse is to look to these very truths: to utter them with simplicity and to apply them as if their meaning were plain. The danger here is the kind of simplicity that becomes simplemindedness, and has the vice as well of arrogating power to oneself. In a good opinion, it is the context established by the complex and detailed attention to the competing claims of the parties and texts that creates the occasion for simplicity, the context in which it can have the force of truth and generality and not that of a mere slogan or cliché.[41]

---

41. Or think of the way the opening paragraph of the Declaration of Independence

What "Jordan," "Affliction," and "The Windows" in different ways bring to the center of consciousness is the sense that the very act of writing, whether as preacher or as poet, is perilous or impossible. The dangers against which the poet must work are many: the emptiness of "speech alone," and its apparent irrelevance to what really matters, which is the life of the heart—it is the preacher's inner transformation that counts, or the quality of feeling and understanding with which one says *"My God, My King"*; the insistent self-centeredness of the speaker (a fact to which we shall see Herbert repeatedly return); the structural inadequacy of any statement of doctrine—if it were not inadequate, after all, there would be no need for poetry and not much for preaching; and the very ornateness of what one makes in language, and its beauty, which may be a source of false pride, as well as false occupation. The danger is that the art of poetry—or preaching—may become an art of self-centered vanity, of what another of Herbert's speakers, in "Vanitie" (II), calls "false embroyderies." Or, to put it another way, the human actor alone, until transformed by forces outside of the self, can by reason of our inherently fallen state say nothing of value at all: only the empty clichés of "Jordan," or speech that becomes a "flaring thing."

Is poetry, then, even when it is written as a hymn of praise, inherently untrustworthy, a kind of misleading of the self, compared with the true emanations of a true heart? Yet what would the true emanations of a true heart be, or be like? They too are impossible to know. "Thy word is all, if we could spell": thus says the speaker in "The Flower," but part of his point is that we cannot spell.

Against the dangers, then, of ornamentation, show, elaboration for its own sake, inauthenticity, a fundamental misleading of the soul into falsity, are arrayed another set: the impossibility of life without language, the danger of mindlessness, and another form of the inauthentic. This is indeed one point of the second "Jordan" poem:

Jordan (II)

When first my lines of heav'nly joyes made mention,
Such was their lustre, they did so excell,

---

provides a context of civility and complexity that makes its assertions of fundamental rights seem reasonable and natural. For further analysis in these terms, see my book *When Words Lose Their Meaning* (Chicago: University of Chicago Press, 1984), chap. 9.

That I sought out quaint words, and trim invention;
My thoughts began to burnish, sprout, and swell,
Curling with metaphors a plain intention,
Decking the sense, as if it were to sell.

Thousands of notions in my brain did runne,
Off'ring their service, if I were not sped:
I often blotted what I had begunne;
This was not quick enough, and that was dead.
Nothing could seem too rich to clothe the sunne,
Much lesse those joyes which trample on his head.

As flames do work and winde, when they ascend,
So did I weave my self into the sense.
But while I bustled, I might heare a friend
Whisper, *How wide is all this long pretence!*
There is in love a sweetnesse readie penn'd:
Copie out onely that, and save expense.[42]

This poem recalls "Jordan" (I), in that the speaker seems to reject the kind of verse that is full of "quaint words, and trim invention." Here, however, he is rejecting not the work of others but that of his own earlier self.[43] He began with a "plain intention," he says, but that was not enough for him; he had to deck it out with imagery, as if he were presenting wares for sale or, as we would say, as if he were advertising it. The process was intoxicating, as he wrote and rewrote, trying to produce verse rich enough "to clothe the sunne"—an aspiration

---

42. Notes:

1. *Quick* means "alive."

2. *The sunne* includes both sun and Son.

3. *Those joyes which trample on his head:* I am not sure of this line. Perhaps it means: nothing of ours is good enough to clothe the sun, or the Son, even our best; and certainly not those literary performances, here called "joyes," that purport to serve and praise but are in fact egocentric, and thus hostile to him and his love for us.

43. As a claim about Herbert's own work this is most suspect: he is not given to "quaint words" and his intentions are almost never plain but demonstrably complex. And when has he spoken of "heav'nly joyes"?

at once grand and crazy, for neither the sun nor the Son need clothes from us. Like every artist consumed by his work, he wove himself "into the sense." All this the speaker now sees as mere "bustle," as he imagines his friend's advice to "copie out onely" love, and "save expense." The speaker thus rejects his art in favor of simplicity both of idea and of expression.

But this reading, invited though it is by the speaker, will hardly do. Like the earlier "Jordan," this poem is itself an exercise of the art it rejects, defining the context against which the appeal to simplicity of feeling and expression has its force. The process of writing and revising he describes is a fundamentally good one—are we instead simply to write down whatever comes first to our minds?—and the aspiration "to clothe the sunne," while immense, is not ethically grandiose, for it is not centered on the glory of the artist but of his subject. "There is in love a sweetnesse readie penn'd" is a lovely thought, but "copie out onley that" is an impossible directive, "and save expense" is a good-humored joke that acknowledges this impossibility.[44] This poem, written in apparent rejection of "metaphors," thus ends with one, and a metaphor full of novelty and vividness to boot. And while the speaker begins by suggesting that the poet's ambition "to clothe the sunne" is too high and egotistical, he ends with a direction—"copie out onely that"—that is no less demanding than the imitation of Christ.

Herbert knows that what matters most is the life of the preacher or poet or reader, and that the value of poetry, like that of preaching, must lie in the way it affects that life. But there is no obvious or ready way to do this well; indeed the attempt is full of peril, whether one moves in the direction of simplicity and silence or in the opposite direction of complex speech. Herbert's poetry is written out of the recognition that simplicity and complexity require each other, as do "doctrine and life, colours and light," as do indeed the world of words and the world beyond words. Poetry, like preaching and prayer, is at once necessary and impossible.

In the following poem Herbert suggests that the life of his poetry for

---

44. An echo is sometimes heard here to Sir Philip Sidney's famous lines, in the first sonnet in *Astrophel and Stella,* "Fool, said my muse to me, look in thy heart and write." But the image and the feeling are rather different: Herbert's speaker looks not to his own heart but to love itself, and does not write but "copie."

him, as a writer, lies in what he feels and imagines as he writes, his sense of contact with his audience, divine but unseen.

The Quidditie

My God, a verse is not a crown,
No point of honour, or gay suit,
No hawk, or banquet, or renown,
Nor a good sword, nor yet a lute:

It cannot vault, or dance, or play;
It never was in *France* or *Spain;*
Nor can it entertain the day
With my great stable or demain:

It is no office, art, or news,
Nor the Exchange, or busie Hall;
But it is that which while I use
I am with thee, and *most take all.*[45]

Here the speaker purports to disparage his verse—it is "not a crown"— but he does this in terms that seem to be unconsciously self-disparaging, for we know that the standards by which his poetry is said to fail are themselves trivial. But what if we attribute to the speaker an awareness of the falseness of the values he invokes? There is after all a comic quality here—"it never was in *France* or *Spain*"—that points in this direction. On such a reading, this part of the poem becomes a way in which the speaker distances himself from others, who accept what he rejects. But this would in turn undermine his serious statement, in the last line, which works only if these things have real value. This uncertainty leads us to mistrust the speaker, and the poet too, in a new way, to doubt the very claim of distance made here, at least on behalf of the poet, for it is inconsistent with the trope of comparison upon

---

45. Notes:

1. *Quiddity* means both "the essence of a thing" and "trifling point" or "quibble." Both aspects are in play here, as the speaker contrasts the essential thing —"I am with thee"—with a list of trifles.

2. *Demain* means "domain."

3. *Most take all* is a proverbial expression meaning something like "the most powerful person gets everything."

which the poem turns. This instability is part of the meaning of the poem, for it involves us in the awareness that these standards, in some sense represented as trivial, are in other ways more deeply meant than the speaker, or we, want to recognize. We first reject them quickly; then see that the comparison by which the poem works requires their affirmance.

The phrase with which the poem concludes is crude and proverbial, perhaps in tone a bit like our own "winner take all" or "that's the bottom line." It asserts that the value just stated sweeps the board of others, rather than each getting its proportionate due. But sandwiched between these various locutions is a simple statement, cast in plain speech—"it is that which while I use / I am with thee"—that to me at least rings with authenticity, an authenticity created in part by the surrounding text that seems so artlessly self-revealing, in part by the inherent credibility and appeal of the claim itself. Herbert would not be the only one to find the meaning of his writing in the kind of self he made in doing it, and in the kind of relation he could thus establish with another.[46]

Herbert knows that to commit oneself to a particular language is to become exposed to its force. It can be a source of falseness and emptiness, as we have seen for example in the clichés of "Jordan" (I); but it may also be a source of beauty and strength. Think of the way the rhyme works in "Jordan" (I), for example, to counter the message; or of the force of the phrase in "Vertue," "My musick shows ye have your closes." In both cases the form has real power. Or consider this:

Deniall

When my devotions could not pierce
           Thy silent eares;
Then was my heart broken, as was my verse:
        My breast was full of fears
          And disorder:

My bent thoughts, like a brittle bow,
         Did flie asunder:

---

46. Notice however that the plainness of the monosyllabic diction in the central statement—"it is that which while I use / I am with thee"—carries over to the rather crude conclusion, "and *most take all*," thus equally emphasizing both.

Each took his way; some would to pleasures go,
　　Some to the warres and thunder
　　　　Of alarms.

As good go any where, they say,
　　　As to benumme
Both knees and heart, in crying night and day,
　　Come, come, my God, O come,
　　　　But no hearing.

O that thou shouldst give dust a tongue
　　　To crie to thee,
And then not heare it crying! all day long
　　My heart was in my knee,
　　　　But no hearing.

Therefore my soul lay out of sight,
　　　Untun'd, unstrung:
My feeble spirit, unable to look right,
　　Like a nipt blossome, hung
　　　　Discontented.

O cheer and tune my heartlesse breast,
　　　Deferre no time;
That so thy favours granting my request,
　　They and my minde may chime,
　　　　And mend my ryme.

This poem is composed in stanzas of five lines, of varying lengths, the first four of which conclude with heavily marked rhymes, leaving the last, a short one, dangling with no tune—though, since it has the same number of feet as line two, we sense that it has a place. Indeed it should have the force of conclusion that the lack of rhyme denies it. This awkward lack of closure expresses in the music the speaker's sense of disconnection and dislocation, which is reinforced by the diction: "And disorder," "Of alarms," "But no hearing," "Discontented." The effect is cumulative, through five stanzas (matching the five lines of the verse) until the very last word of the sixth, where the rhyme works a kind of magic, to perform a hope, a gesture of wholeness and completion.[47]

---

47. "Grief" goes the other way, working by heavily marked alternating rhymes

The irregular stanza form reinforces this effect: when we first see it, the shape of the stanza seems to enact the disorder of which the poet speaks. The four lines that rhyme regularly—*a b a b*—are respectively of four, two, five, and three iambic feet. This at first looks wild, almost random; but, as often in Herbert—whose formal inventiveness is unmatched in English poetry—when the stanza is repeated we come to see it as a form indeed, with its own pattern, working its own constraints and making its own music. The heavy emphasis given the dangling, unrhymed tags in the first five stanzas works at the end in just the other way, to make the rhyme chime.

It is not only in poetic form but in the language itself, hidden until made manifest by the poetry, that Herbert sometimes sees surprising significances that suggest a source of meaning outside of the speaker and his audience. "Paradise," for example, consists of stanzas of three lines, each of which ends in a diminished version of the word ending the preceding line, thus:

Paradise

I blesse thee, Lord, because I GROW
  Among thy trees, which in a ROW
To thee both fruit and order OW.

What open force, or hidden CHARM
Can blast my fruit, or bring me HARM,
While the inclosure is thine ARM?

Inclose me still for fear I START.
Be to me rather sharp and TART,
Then let me want thy hand & ART.

---

until this:

Verses, ye are too fine a thing, too wise
For my rough sorrows: cease, be dumbe and mute,
Give up your feet and running to mine eyes,
And keep your measures for some lovers lute,
Whose grief allows him musick and a ryme:
For mine excludes both measure, tune, and time.
                    Alas, my God!

But notice that this poem about the inadequacy of rhyme itself rhymes regularly throughout.

> When thou does greater judgements SPARE,
> And with thy knife but prune and PARE,
> Ev'n fruitfull trees more fruitfull ARE.
>
> Such sharpnes shows the sweetest FREND:
> Such cuttings rather heal then REND:
> And such beginnings touch their END.

The pattern in each case (after the first stanza anyway, though "row" can mean altercation) is the same—first something good, then something bad, then something neutral—and an important part of the point is that this pattern is not made by the poet but found in the language, in the very words themselves. This sense of the language itself as a source of meaning and beauty outside the speaker, and of the similarly mysterious significance of poetic form itself, counteracts the consciousness, so explicit in the "Jordan" poems, of the deep inadequacy of all language and art. Language is not only a source of limit and danger, it is a miraculous resource. When meaning of this kind appears in the text it seems to come from somewhere else, not from the speaker or poet, as the light comes from outside the window and shines through it: it is an act of grace. This is perhaps most beautifully made plain in "Heaven," near the end of *The Temple,* where an echo converts the questioning words of the speaker into promises of hope:

Heaven

O Who will show me those delights on high?
           Echo.   I.
Thou Echo, thou art mortall, all men know.
           Echo.   No.
Wert thou not born among the trees and leaves?
           Echo.   Leaves.
And are there any leaves, that still abide?
           Echo.   Bide.
What leaves are they? impart the matter wholly.
           Echo.   Holy.
Are holy leaves the Echo then of blisse?
           Echo.   Yes.
Then tell me, what is that supreme delight?
           Echo.   Light.

Light to the minde: what shall the will enjoy?
    Echo.   Joy.
But are there cares and businesse with the pleasure?
    Echo.   Leisure.
Light, joy, and leisure; but shall they persever?
    Echo.   Ever.

This poem draws attention not to the breakdown of language and mind that any attempt to speak seems to precipitate, but to the world outside the self, here the very language that has before proved so impossible, which now speaks to us with love and reassurance. God is present here, in the fabric of our thought and imagination.

It is no accident that this poem of hope and confidence comes at the end of Herbert's book of lyrics: together with "Love" (III), which follows it to conclude the book, it marks a point of achievement or success, towards which the whole preceding series of poems is a struggle. But, like nearly everything in Herbert, even this point has a shadow side: one could see the speaker as a kind of Narcissus—remember, Echo was part of his story—getting false reassurance from what is after all only the tail ends of his own words coming back to him. Is the world full of meaning and response, or is it ultimately remote or empty? Herbert here addresses the question Frost raised, in "Range-Finding," "Design," and "The Most of It," and does so very much in Frost's manner, though I think, at last, with greater hope and confidence. In the myth he invokes, after all, Echo was a real being who—so far as it was possible for a nymph to do so, that is by gradually wasting away until only her voice remained—died for the love of another, thus prefiguring Herbert's own theological story, where another being died out of love for others. On this reading, the myth suggests not a narcissistic emptiness, but the opposite: that it is Christ who speaks to us through the echoes.

We have now begun to learn the language of Herbert's poetry, not by listing or defining terms, nor by seeking to discover a grammar, but by reading a handful of poems as examples of what he does with words. In just such a way one might start off to learn a foreign language by studying a small sample of sentences, using that experience as a way of orienting oneself towards the more intense work to follow. We may ask now: What have we begun to learn from these instances about the way

The church at Leighton Bromswold

Herbert works? What expectations for the future can we properly have begun to form?

Certainly that Herbert is not the simple pious poet he is traditionally said to be, but almost the opposite of that: his is a mind that works by comprising contraries to throw everything in doubt. He writes in voices, contrasting one possible utterance against another, and—like Shakespeare—finds the truth not in any one voice or phrase but in the tension, life, and movement among them. He simultaneously casts into doubt both his various languages and his own identity, for his languages counteract each other and his voices, all internal ones, present not a single coherent self but an array of disharmonious possibilities. Herbert has nothing to learn from postmodern critics about the instabilities either of language or of the self.

His religion complicates things still further, in at least two ways. First, every impulse of the self is just that, an impulse of the self, an asserted center of value against the Christian's duty to pray that "thy will, not mine" be done. The very act of writing a sentence runs against this duty, for it is an assertion of the will. But Herbert cannot give up the claims of the self, however much he may want to do so, and for him this is original sin. Second, religious doctrine itself works in a way deeply uncongenial to his poetry, by declaiming universal truths in a language that asserts its own adequacy. Not that what is said in this language is not true; for Herbert it is a language of truth. This is what makes it so difficult for him; the didactic and authoritarian character of this discourse is at once wholly uncongenial to his poet's mind and expressive of a deep streak in his own nature.

Reading the Poems
in Light of Each Other

Chapter 2

Beginnings

This brings to an end the first stage of this book, the object of which has been to work our way slowly into Herbert's verse, drawing on a range of contexts and comparisons in order to establish some sense of its characteristic concerns, methods, and movements. In the present part of this book I shall proceed quite differently, examining the poems in the order in which Herbert presents them and moving, as I earlier said I would, somewhat faster through them, with gradually less and less background material. The idea is that a large part of the meaning of these poems lies in their interaction with each other, and specifically in the experience they offer when they are read in sequence, as one poem answers or complicates or revises what has gone before.

You might say that we have made two intertwined beginnings on Herbert's poetry, one following my own particular experience, the other tracing the way most readers would naturally begin, with some of his best-known and most widely anthologized poems. Now we begin again, this time as Herbert invites us to do, with the long poem that opens his book, "The Church-porch."[1]

---

1. It is preceded by this:

The Dedication

Lord, my first fruits present themselves to thee;
Yet not mine neither: for from thee they came,
And must return. Accept of them and me,
And make us strive, who shall sing best thy name.
Turn their eyes hither, who shall make a gain:
Theirs, who shall hurt themselves or me, refrain.

This poem—really a prayer—is not Herbert's most important composition, but it does start certain lines of poetic thought that will continue throughout *The Temple:* the distinction he constantly wants to draw between "me" and "thee," "mine" and "thine," which—like "gain" and "loss," also present here—will in the end collapse into a kind of meaninglessness; his sense of life as a kind of striving, often competitive

"The Church-porch"

"The Church-porch" is the first of three sections of *The Temple*—the second being "The Church," which contains all of Herbert's great short verse, the third "The Church Militant," a long historical poem, very different in quality and feeling from the rest[2]—and it is a most difficult and disturbing beginning to this book. It seems at first to exemplify none of the virtues of Herbert's poetry as we have begun to identify them, for from beginning to end it is written in a didactic, self-assured voice of moral and worldly experience. It is explicitly said to be a kind of sermon, instructing its youthful (and male) reader on questions of conduct and manners, but one that is meant to be cast, the speaker tells us, in a more than usually pleasing way:

> Thou, whose sweet youth and early hopes inhance
>   Thy rate and price, and mark thee for a treasure;
> Harken unto a Verser, who may chance
> Ryme thee to good, and make a bait of pleasure.
>   A verse may finde him, who a sermon flies,
>   And turn delight into a sacrifice.   (stanza 1)

The promised instruction takes the form of arguments to virtue, on the apparent assumption that to become good we need only choose rightly:

> Beware of lust: it doth pollute and foul
> Whom God in Baptisme washt with his own blood.
> It blots thy lesson written in thy soul;
> The holy lines cannot be understood.
>   How dare those eyes upon a Bible look,
>   Much lesse towards God, whose lust is all their book?
>
> Abstain wholly, or wed. Thy bounteous Lord
> Allows thee choise of paths: take no by-wayes;

(here he imagines himself competing with his own poems!); and the characteristic turn of self-correction, as he first says something, then revises it—"yet not mine neither."

2. Except for this brief section on "The Church-porch," all of our attention will be given to the poems of the central section, "The Church." For a good analysis of "The Church Militant," see Shuger, *Habits of Thought,* 105–12.

But gladly welcome what he doth afford;
Not grudging, that thy lust hath bounds and staies.
   Continence hath his joy: weigh both; and so
   If rottennesse have more, let Heaven go.   (stanzas 2–3)

The poem goes on in this way for seventy-seven stanzas, which begin with such phrases as these: "Drink not the third glasse"; "Take not his name, who made thy mouth, in vain"; "Lie not"; "Flie idleness"; "Doe all things like a man, not sneakingly"; "Be thriftie, but not covetous"; "Never exceed thy income"; "By no means runne in debt"; "Spend not on hopes"; "Play not for gain but sport"; "Be sweet to all"; "Catch not at quarrels"; "Laugh not too much"; "Envie not greatnesse"; "Be calme in arguing"; "Scorn no mans love"; "Affect in things about thee cleanlinesse"; "Resort to sermons but to prayers most"; "Judge not the preacher"; "Jest not at preachers language, or expression." Unlike the speaker of "The Windows," this one obviously finds no difficulty whatever in preaching. The whole concludes as follows:

In brief, acquit thee bravely; play the man.
Look not on pleasures as they come, but go.
Deferre not the least vertue: lifes poore span
Make not an ell, by trifling in thy wo.
   If thou do ill; the joy fades, not the pains:
   If well; the pain doth fade, the joy remains.   (stanza 77)

I find this an impossible poem to read through without a rebellion of my own at this didactic voice, telling the reader what to do in a language assumed to be adequate, and as if right living were really as easy as this kind of talking. "Lie not; but let thy heart be true to God, / Thy mouth to it, thy actions to them both" (stanza 13); "Be thriftie, but not covetous: therefore give / Thy need, thine honour, and thy friend his due" (stanza 26). It is not that what is said is untrue, but that, like Polonius's similar speech in *Hamlet*, it is all too true, and boring; or in another sense not true, after all, for it is false to one's experience of moral life.

There is some life and variety in the way in which the directions quoted above are supported by argument and thus given content, but this is sometimes of a disturbing kind. For example, the intensity of the speaker's remark about the "rottennesse" of lust in the third stanza, quoted above, expresses a simultaneous loathing and fascination, which is reinforced by his view that marriage does not convert "lust" into something else, but merely gives it "bounds and staies." More generally he assumes—on what warrant other than his own desire?—that the young man he addresses is a potential rake, much tempted by sex and drunkenness and gambling, and in need of arguments based on self-interest. Here he is for example on swearing: "It gets thee nothing, and hath no excuse. / Lust and wine plead a pleasure, avarice gain" (stanza 10), inviting his young listener to act as a calculator of interests, and to include in his accounting the real pleasures that certain vices bring. Or, more trivially: "When thou dost tell anothers jest" (stanza 11). Cynical is too strong a word for this speaker, as perhaps it is for Polonius; but both of them at times assume a kind of radical selfishness in their audience that undoes their more aspirational moral claims.

Here the speaker says, of one who boasts: "He makes flat warre with God, and doth defie / With his poore clod of earth the spacious sky" (stanza 9), an image that makes somewhat heroic the very action it condemns. And here he is in an argument against drunkenness: "He that is drunken, may his mother kill / Bigge with his sister" (stanza 6). If a patient on a couch spoke of the evils of drunkenness in such terms, the analyst would have something to say about the desires he was unconsciously manifesting, and they are not attractive. Compare the unstated feelings that lie behind these remarks: "Art thou a Magistrate? then be severe" (15); "Oh, England! Full of sinne, but most of sloth" (16); "The way to make thy sonne rich" (19); "Look to thy mouth; diseases enter there" (22); "Look on meat, think it dirt, then eat a bit" (22). Behind the moral commonplaces we thus observe an individual speaker, manifesting his own disturbances, posturings, and self-righteousness, in a way that is not subject to much poetic or imaginative control.

My own reading of the poem is this: that this is the best that Herbert can do in a certain voice and mode of thought—call it the sermon—and sometimes it is quite good. If one tried to sum up one's own wisdom, such as it is, one would not do nearly as well. "Pitch thy behaviour low, thy projects high; / So shalt thou humble and magnanimous be" (56); "Laugh not too much: the wittie man laughs least: / For wit is newes only to ignorance" (39); "By all means use sometimes to be alone" (25); "Yet be not surety, if thou be a father" (47); "Towards great persons use respective boldnesse" (43); "A civil guest / Will no more talk all, then eat all the feast" (51); "Scorn no mans love, though of a mean degree" (59); "Give to all something; to a good poore man, /

Till thou change names, and be where he began" (63). This is the aspect of the self that likes to think by maxim or proverb, and it certainly has its uses. Yet the performance is also deeply flawed: by banality, by the emergence of destructive and selfish impulses, and by blindness to its own nature. What the speaker says is mostly true, though in a limited way, sometimes wise or witty, occasionally disturbing, or manifesting disturbance, and not because of the tensions and inconsistencies I mention— they will later be the very stuff of Herbert's poetry—but because they are never made the subject of critical attention or the focus of poetic thought. In this poem Herbert presents the material of his poetry but does not quite know what to do with it. He thus creates in his reader a need for what his real poetry, in the long section that follows, will offer us.

It is true that a significant transformation starts to take place in the course of this poem: the speaker meanders from topic to topic in a kind of random way, revealing the aspects of his personality suggested above, until almost by accident he hits upon the subject of alms, which suggests Sundays, which suggests prayer, which suggests decorum in church, to which subject he devotes the last several stanzas. In writing these, he seems gradually to imagine himself in the physical and spiritual place of the church. Before, he was located nowhere, except in relation to the young man; by a process of association he has now moved to a place with a shape or structure, and a character too, and this acts upon him, making him more coherent, less punitive and self-sure. We have thus experienced at least a beginning of a transformation of ordinary thought and ordinary life into something else; this in turn promises the reader another, when he or she enters the church that is composed of the poems that follow, and appropriately called "The Church." But that is not yet achieved, and the speaker concludes with a couplet that affirms just the language, of joy and pain, that Herbert's later poems, "Affliction" among them, will entirely undo:

> If thou do ill; the joy fades, not the pains:
> If well; the pain doth fade, the joy remains.

The poem as a whole has the function of defining where we are before we undertake the process of thought and reflection in which it is the purpose of the poems of "The Church" to engage us.[3]

---

3. For me this poem reads rather like Herbert's great prose work, *A Priest to the*

I have spoken critically of the didactic voice in which "The Church-porch" was written in, yet I imagine that if you asked Herbert to disown it, he would have been shocked. For an essential part of him, what is said this way is the truth and the only truth; it is his sacred task as a priest to tell us these things, so that we shall do and be what we ought. But at the same time, perhaps unknown to his conscious mind, this way of talking is inadequate to the reality of his own character and experience. His need for it nonetheless, his sense that this is the proper or necessary way to talk, is I think a terrible problem, almost a curse, from which he cannot escape; yet he must escape it if he is to be true to his own experience of uncertainty, to his own doubleness of thought, and ultimately—though it is too early to do more than suggest this—to his own sense of his God. This means that the spiritual struggle captured in *The Temple* is not, as often imagined, a simple struggle between a good side of Herbert against a bad side, as the speaker of "The Church-porch" might conceive of it: the side that is doctrinally and didactically "good" can be humanly "bad," and the other way round as well.[4] Rebellion has its good aspect, submission its bad one, a fact that redoubles the already intolerable uncertainties of "Affliction."

"The Church-porch" can be read, then, as a rather full expression of a certain expository habit of mind, didactic and imperfect, that it will be Herbert's effort in the poems that follow, collectively called "The Church," not so much to deny as to use, to subvert, and to transform.

Temple, usually known as *The Country Parson,* in which Herbert describes how an ideal rural priest would live. Many readers have loved and admired this work, from Isaak Walton to Stanley Fish, but for me it is hard to like: written assertively, full of certainty, and so far as I can tell with hardly a break in its didactic voice. Once again, the problem is not that what Herbert says is untrue, or foolish, or articulates bad moral principles, but that the performance itself feels to me at least reductive and authoritarian, and in that sense false to the complexity and difficulty of life as Herbert elsewhere shows that he experienced it.

The same side of Herbert's mind led him to make a collection of proverbs, over one thousand, published after his death in 1640. As these examples suggest, Herbert's sententiousness is a quality deep in his mind, and we shall see him struggle with it throughout "The Church."

4. Herbert's own description of his book, as Walton reports his deathbed words, supports the simpler vision: he says that it contains "a picture of the many spiritual Conflicts that have past betwixt God and my Soul," as if all good were on one side (God's), all bad on another (his own). But we know, from our reading of "Vertue" and the other poems reproduced above, that this is not so. Walton, *Life of Herbert,* 74.

In his invocation to "The Church," which follows directly, he as much as says this, telling us that he will now leave behind what he calls "precepts" and move to a different level of intensity and mystery:

Superliminare

Thou, whom the former precepts have
Sprinkled and taught, how to behave
Thy self in church; approach, and taste
The churches mysticall repast.

Avoid, Profanenesse; come not here:
Nothing but holy, pure, and cleare,
Or that which groneth to be so,
May at his perill further go.[5]

As its title makes plain—it means "over the threshold"—this poem marks the dividing line between two spaces or two worlds, that of "The Church-porch" and that of "The Church," across which, in retrospect at least, we can see Herbert moving from his sermon voice, public and official and intellectual, the claims of which he felt so strongly and in a way so properly, to another mode of thought and life, far more private and uncertain, expressed in the poems that follow.

It is relevant here that Herbert's English poems, though written down and preserved, were never published during his lifetime, nor perhaps even read by others, except as some few of them may have been put to

---

5. Notes:

1. In the early manuscript book *W*, discussed on pages 75–76, this poem appears as two separate poems, the first entitled "Perirrhanterium" (which refers to the instrument used for sprinkling holy water on entry to the church itself), the second "Superliminare." Herbert apparently later combined the two into one.

2. *Superliminare* is a noun, found not in classical Latin but in the Vulgate, that refers to the lintel, the space over the door where such a poem might be inscribed.

3. I think *avoid* is best read as a command not to the reader but to "profanenesse," meaning, as he goes on to say, "come not here."

4. *Groneth:* later poems will enrich this term enormously.

5. *At his perill* repeats Herbert's sense, found also in "The Dedication," that engagement in the experience of this poetry can be dangerous. This gives the poem something of the character of a warning, in an allusion perhaps to the sign over the gate of Dante's Inferno: "Abandon all hope, ye who enter here."

music (also of his composition) to be sung by the small choir in Salisbury with which he sang and played in the evenings during the last three years of his life.[6] He did collect his poems, twice in his life, and had them transcribed by another hand, the second time in the form of the manuscript book that he sent to his friend Nicholas Ferrar shortly before his death, leaving the decision about publication to him. ("[I]f he can think it may turn to the advantage of any dejected poor Soul, let it be made publick; if not, let him burn it.")[7] This reinforces the impression that the audience of these poems is double: first, and immediately, a wholly private one, consisting of Herbert's "Lord," to whom so many poems are explicitly addressed,[8] and perhaps Herbert himself, or a part of him; second, any particular human beings who may discover that these poems speak to them, and act upon them, in a good way, including, no doubt, his friend Ferrar as well as the unknown reader to whom they speak as to a friend. But even this audience is private too, personal and intimate; not the public world to which his orations and Latin poems, much more full of display, were addressed, nor even the world he spoke to in his sermons, in *The Country Parson* or in "The Church-porch" itself. Herbert hoped his poems would be discovered and valued by others, not as connoisseurs of art, but as souls, engaged in their own versions of the internal life represented here. In reading them one thus feels at once admitted to the private life of another and called upon to attend to one's own internal life as well.

One might imagine it this way: Herbert was one for whom the public world was a field of ambition and combat, aggression and defense,

---

6. Hutchinson thinks that his poems must have circulated in manuscript, "as he enjoyed some reputation as a poet many years before his death." *Works of George Herbert,* xxxix. But it is impossible to know how far this was so, or how much his reputation rested on his Latin poems. Bacon dedicated his *Translation of Certain Psalmes into English Verse* (1625) to Herbert, saying that "in respect of Divinitie, and Poesie" he "could not make better choice." *Works of George Herbert,* xl.

For Herbert's musical life at Salisbury see Amy Charles, *George Herbert,* 163–64.

7. So says Isaak Walton, apparently on the authority of Edmund Duncon, by whom the manuscript was taken to Ferrar. Walton, *Life of Herbert,* 74.

8. To some degree Herbert creates this God by the way he addresses him, just as all writers create their audiences. Of any theological poet or writer we can in fact ask not only how she defines the God she talks *about,* in doctrinal terms, but how she defines the God she talks *to,* as a person addressed. Herbert's poetry recreates and transforms the religious and doctrinal tradition of which it is a part as much, or more, by the way he defines the God to whom he speaks as in any statement of theological position.

in which he held positions of either secular or religious authority, particularly as University Orator. These *Sacred Poems and Private Ejaculations,* as he called them, were private, a way of reflecting on himself, to himself. He may have felt them too self-exposing to be safe to publish, or, even more deeply, that as expressions of an inner rather than an outer self they were of no value, for, as we shall see, one of the central issues of "The Church" is whether the speaker can imagine himself the object of love.

Finally, notice the extraordinary grandiosity of the speaker's claim at the end of "Superliminare": to represent "the churches mysticall repast." Who can he be to do such a thing? The office of priest entitles one to preach, or celebrate the Eucharist, but what can authorize such a claim as this? Against the righteousness and self-certainty of the sermon voice, then, is poised not merely doubt and uncertainty, an insistence on limits and the inherent doubleness of experience, but another kind of claim for the self, even more expansive and potentially unlimited than righteous doctrinal and moral assertion, namely to be a poet of the sacred. The meaning of this tension will be one of Herbert's deepest subjects throughout "The Church."[9]

A word about the texts. *The Temple* exists in two manuscripts, one substantially earlier than the other, called respectively *W* and *B* for the Williams and Bodleian libraries where they can be found. Both manuscripts were carefully prepared but under different circumstances: *W* perhaps in the middle of the 1620s and at Herbert's direction, for it has corrections apparently in his own hand; *B* after his death, in 1633, by scribes at Little Gidding who worked from the presumably somewhat rougher manuscript, now lost, that he committed to his friend Nicholas Ferrar just before he died. *B* is a full folio, written in a formal hand, and either this particular manuscript or one very much like it was used in the preparation of the first edition of *The Temple,* published at Cambridge in 1633.[10]

---

9. See especially "Providence," which begins with a justification of poetry: Of all the creatures in the world "Onely to Man thou hast made known thy wayes ... And made him Secretarie of thy praise."

10. Reproductions of pages from each of the manuscripts, representing their respective versions of "The Altar" and "Love" (III), can be found at pages 84–85 and 262–63 below. *W* is written in the secretary hand of the time, *B* in an elaborate hand, used at Little Gidding, that is remarkably similar to that of Nicholas Ferrar, its founder.

The major difference between the two manuscripts is that *W,* as the earlier text, has many fewer poems than appear in *B,* not quite half. Also, several of the poems in *W* were substantially revised in *B* and a handful were omitted. The general plan and sequence of the two manuscripts is much the same, however, and should be taken to represent Herbert's settled view, particularly since most of the additions in *B* appear in a single long sequence (from "Conscience" through "A Parodie"), with other new poems rather carefully placed elsewhere. The closing sequence of seven poems remains the same (except that "The Elixir" is substantially revised).[11]

The arrangement of the poems was important to Herbert and should be seriously attended to by any reader of his poetry. But to explain the meaning, or meanings, of this arrangement—or of these arrangements—is an entirely different matter.[12] In our own reading we should postpone for the present any attempt to reach conclusions but make it our effort

---

For an example of his writing, see A. L. Maycock, *Nicholas Ferrar of Little Gidding* (London and New York: Macmillan, 1938), illustration facing page 118.

11. For discussion of manuscript matters see Amy M. Charles, *The Williams Manuscript of George Herbert's Poems: A Facsimile Reproduction* (Delmar, N.Y.: Scholars' Facsimiles and Reprints, 1977) and Charles and Di Cesare, *Bodleian Manuscript.* See also Note on the Text, below page 275–76.

12. Amy Charles indicates some of the complexities thus:

> Even an experienced reader trying to determine the pattern of *The Temple* must divine and catch the sense at two or more removes. The final arrangement necessarily becomes more complex and more subtle than that of *W,* because the reader must discern and follow several orders at a time: the physical order in which he follows the poet through the preparatory stages into the church; a generally chronological arrangement leading from Holy Week and Easter through Whitsun and Christmas back through Lent; a theological arrangement leading from sin to salvation; and, most important, the spiritual arrangement in which the soul grows in knowledge and understanding of God's love toward man, undergoes trials and discouragement, and is drawn gradually, sometimes haltingly, but inexorably from the point of partial knowledge to that of knowing even as it is known, in Herbert's quiet surrender to divine love in the powerful understatement of "So I did sit and eat."

Williams Manuscript, xxx. See also Louis L. Martz, "George Herbert: The Unity of *The Temple,*" in *The Poetry of Meditation: A Study in English Religious Literature of the Seventeenth Century,* rev. ed. (New Haven, Conn.: Yale University Press, 1962); and Stanley Fish, *The Living Temple: George Herbert and Catechizing* (Berkeley and Los Angeles: University of California Press, 1978), 123, where he says the order is both "random *and* patterned": "patterned because the points of self-examination are finite"

to understand the relation among the poems as they unfold before us. Yet it will give rather little away to say now that while there is in general terms a movement in these poems towards acceptance and trust, we should not expect, from this poet above all, a mechanical or linear order, say from the door of the church to the altar, from prayer to Eucharist, or from despair to hope. Herbert's sense of life as a perpetual struggle to understand, to speak, to be; his sense of the self as fragmented into a variety of voices, each of which is in a different way self-centered; his sense that language and form are at once traps, from which we cannot extricate ourselves, and sources of meaning from beyond the horizon of our knowledge; all these (and more) make any order of that sort unthinkable. Rather, we should expect the book as a whole to have the kind of order, and life, that his individual poems themselves do.

"The Altar"

The first poem in "The Church" is this:

The Altar

A broken ALTAR, Lord, thy servant reares,
Made of a heart, and cemented with teares:
    Whose parts are as thy hand did frame;
    No workmans tool hath touch'd the same.
            A   HEART   alone
            Is   such   a   stone,
            As   nothing   but
            Thy pow'r doth cut.
            Wherefore each part
            Of   my   hard   heart
            Meets in this frame,
            To praise thy Name.
    That, if I chance to hold my peace,
    These stones to praise thee may not cease.
O   let   thy   blessed   SACRIFICE   be   mine,
And   sanctifie   this   ALTAR   to   be   thine.

---

and "random because each point harbors its special danger into which the self-examiner may be falling even as he thinks to satisfy it."

To read this poem requires us to recreate from it a story that lies behind it, as if we were archaeologists trying to figure out how a particular building or other structure—here an altar—came to be built of certain materials and in a certain way. The speaker makes an altar, we are told and shown, out of pieces of his heart. But how did his heart come to be in pieces? It was "broken"; but how, and why? We first surmise, as hearts are usually broken, namely by grief and disappointment; then we learn that it was "cut," and by the only thing that can do this to a heart, "thy power." God is the one ultimately responsible for this heartrending, then, whether its immediate cause was disappointment, grief, or some other experience; this explains why the pieces are "as thy hand did frame," rather than shaped by a "workmans tool."

The poet's effort is to assemble the fragments of his life, or the parts of his life represented by his "heart," into an order that has meaning. The meaning is said to be "praise," but this is problematic to say the least, for how can he possibly praise the One who has cut his heart to pieces? This muted question is a dim foreshadowing of "Affliction" and other poems on that theme. At the end the speaker expresses the hope that this set of fragments will continue to speak after "I" have come to "hold my peace," but this too is odd, since the imagined altar is made of stone, as indeed the heart is too, with all that the image of a stony heart may signify.[13] Herbert here imagines, in the stones of his heart, a kind of mute speech or gesture mirrored by the pure speech of the poems, which are the units out of which his book is built. In this way "The Altar" defines not only itself, as a poem made up of its various parts, but the whole book of poems,

---

13. "These stones to praise thee may not cease" recalls Luke 19:40, where Jesus responds to the Pharisees (who asked him to rebuke his disciples for praising him as "the King that cometh in the name of the Lord") by saying: "I tell you that, if these should hold their peace, the stones would immediately cry out," presumably in praise of him as well. Here Herbert contemplates his own death, and silence, following which these stones, his poems, will continue to speak. Against the dominant humility of the poem is once more an element of real grandiosity as well.

This overtone is reinforced by another possible reference, to Mark 13, where Jesus, responding to one of his disciples who had just marveled at the temple (!) in Jerusalem, said: "Seest thou these great buildings? there shall not be left one stone upon another, that shall not be thrown down." He goes on to describe the future, full of war and earthquake and famine and other affliction, until the Son of man shall return in glory. Then: "Heaven and earth shall pass away: but my words shall not pass away." Mark 13: 2 and 31.

which is also composed of fragments—the poems themselves—for which a claim is made of fundamental authenticity: each of these is a piece of my heart, together they make a kind of altar.

What kind of altar is made, in this poem and in this book? It seems to be an old-fashioned kind, a monument raised to the Lord, as an Old Testament figure might do, not a modern piece of church furniture. And the physical design of the poem tells us that it is ordered, architectural, imitative of established forms. It seems to be perfect. But the second word tells us that it is "broken," and we learn that this is so in several ways: the heart is broken, not whole, and the altar into which it is made, or transformed, is itself fragmented, held together only with tears, not much of a cement. The poem is broken in another way, too, and right at the center: it logically depends on the force of "wherefore," but what is concluded thereafter—especially the "praise"—does not in fact follow from what precedes it. The altar and poem and heart are composed yet broken wholes; hence the call in the last two lines for another stage of transformation, beyond the process of composition by which the heart became an altar, the words a poem, the poems a book: a kind of healing, for which his word is sanctification.

The poem thus at once enacts and calls for the process of edification at the heart of Protestant Christian life, which it is the aim of the book as a whole to achieve: the making of an altar, or a temple or church, and this at once in the physical realm—the poem itself has the shape of an altar—and in the spiritual, as self and community are remade. Here all this is done through words, words arranged by art; but by not the art of the poet alone: grace is required, to make the parts and arrangement both. As was also the case in "The Windows," this poem is thus an invocation of God as a kind of muse: "sanctifie this ALTAR to be thine," says Herbert, speaking of his own poem, and his book of poems. "The Altar" is thus a type or symbol of the book as a whole and will acquire much of its meaning only as we read what follows.

To call this poem "The Altar" is to invoke two rather different sets of associations. The first, and I think dominant one—especially given the shape of this particular altar—derives from the Old Testament tradition in which an altar is first a monument, then a place of propitiatory sacrifice, a type of which Christ's is to be the ultimate version.[14] (Genesis

---

14. Here and elsewhere I speak of the "Old Testament" rather than the "Hebrew

12:7 says that Abram, led by God to the land of Canaan, "there builded an altar unto the Lord.") This is also of course to imagine the Old Testament God as well, as conceived by Herbert and those of his persuasion: He was the God of power and justice, demanding compliance with his law. The poem thus raises, without our really knowing it, a central question that the rest of this book will address: how is God— the "Thou" so often spoken to—to be imagined and thought of? Our starting place is the Old Testament altar; the end, Herbert's version of a New Testament God, will be "Love" (III), the last poem in the book, entirely different in feeling: "Love bade me welcome." By the end of "The Altar", indeed, the altar is no longer imagined as the place where man sacrifices to God but as the place of Christ's sacrifice for man.

A second set of associations arises from the contemporary dispute between the Puritans, who wanted to reform the practices of the Church of England to conform with the severe models of Geneva and Scotland, and the Anglicans, who resisted them. The Puritans wanted a simple habit for the parson, a common table for Communion (at which communicants would sit, not kneel), and the abolition of the altar and of all images, whether in the form of statues, paintings, or windows. The Anglicans, by contrast, wanted to continue traditional ways, including the use of priestly vestments, images, a Communion rail (at which communicants knelt), and an altar before which the Eucharist was celebrated. In calling his book of poems an "altar," then, Herbert seems to speak as a ceremonial conservative, as he also does in "The Windows," when he gives a stained glass window such a central place in his imagined church. But both of these images have significances that work the other way as well: the implied reference in "The Altar" to the Old Testament is congenial to the Puritan sensibility, and the assertion, in "The Windows," that what matters most is the heart and life of the preacher, not appearances, likewise undermines the importance of surface forms. And, to move from verbal to material structures, in designing the church at Leighton Bromswold Herbert gave the preaching pulpit and reading desk equal prominence and an identical design; and it appears that Communion was there celebrated, if not at a table, in rows of seats facing each other

---

Bible," for this is the way in which Herbert and others in his culture would have conceived of it. His Bible was in English, not Hebrew; and for him the "Old Testament" would have been a precursor to the "New" and read as such. For an example of his sense of the relation between these two texts, see "The Bunch of Grapes."

across the sanctuary, like choir stalls, and that there was originally no altar, or only a small one.[15] In both domains these images have, as is so typical in Herbert, wide-ranging and dissonant rays of significance.

It is also important to note, what is so natural to us that it might easily be missed, that the speaker in "The Altar" presents himself not as a unit or integer, but as divided at least into two: the "I" (or "the servant") who acts and speaks, and the "heart," upon which both God and that servant act. This establishes a theme that will run across the whole series of poems in this book, the definition of the self, or more properly selves and voices, of the poet. Here and elsewhere the speaker is conceived of as a voice and being that has a heart, with which it has a relation—the heart is where it suffers; but it can speak to the heart too, and in this poem at least, even arrange its pieces in order; yet, as we shall later see, the heart can have its ways of speaking too, of which the most characteristic is the "grone." Herbert's conception of a person, then, is not as a single thing, but as a place of tension, conversation, conflict, and uncertainty—though here his parts are for the moment united in the poem itself.

It may indeed be that his sense of multiple selves is what makes his kind of poetry possible in the first place, for in it he seeks forms that will give place and expression to the widest variety of internal voices and tensions, creating a kind of homology between his various poems and various selves. It also means that to talk about "the speaker" of this or that poem is not to engage in technical niceties but to focus attention on a central aspect of the meaning of Herbert's verse. As "Vertue" gave significance to the otherwise ordinary fact about poetry, that it exists in

---

15. A Communion rail was added in the nineteenth century, before which Communion was taken at a table in the chancel. See H. B. Malling, "Leighton Bromswold, the Church and the Lordship," in *Transactions of Cambridgeshire and Huntingdonshire Archeological Society*, 2 (1908): 212, 210. See also Robert Van de Weyer, *Little Gidding: Story and Guide* (London: Lamp Press, 1989), 74. A picture of the pulpits can be found at page 23.

For descriptions of this church see Walton's *Life* of Herbert; Malling, "Leighton Bromswold, the Church and the Lordship," 2: 205–19; Royal Commission on Historical Monuments, *An Inventory of the Historical Monuments of Huntingdonshire* (His Majesty's Stationery Office, 1926), 178–80; and *The Victoria History of the Counties of England: A History of Huntingdonshire* (1936), 3: 90–91. Pevsner says that it is "among the most interesting seventeenth-century churches in the whole of England." Sir Nikolaus Pevsner, *The Buildings of England: Bedfordshire and the County of Huntingdon and Peterborough* (London: Penguin Books, 1968), 195.

The communion stalls at Leighton Bromswold

two kinds of time, so *The Temple* as a whole gives intense meaning to what is normally just an ordinary fact of poetry too, namely that each poem is written in a different voice, for Herbert's central aim here is a sustained act of self-definition and self-transformation.

What does it mean, to Herbert or to us, that this poem should have the physical shape that it does? At the very least it means that for Herbert poetry exists for the eye as well as for the ear. It is an art on the page, whether handwritten or printed, and Herbert aggressively employs this mode of meaning, as many poets do not. The fact that it is possible for these words to be arranged in the form of an altar is a testimony to the possibilities for order and significance in the universe, as the echoes in "Heaven" and the nested words in "Paradise" also suggest; though here, as perhaps always, this testimony is qualified by the flaws and imperfections in the structure itself, including the ethical one, that the poem has the form not only of an altar but of a capital "I."

To test the contribution that the physical shape of a poem makes to its meaning one might try the experiment of writing it out as prose. To take as an example a quite different but famous poem by a modern writer, suppose you were to come upon a scrap of paper with these words written on it: "So much depends upon a red wheel barrow glazed with rain water beside the white chickens." We might be forgiven if we thought it a slightly crazy, slightly pretentious utterance: crazy because it seems to have no point standing alone and because there is no readily imaginable larger text of which it could be a part (except maybe a drama); pretentious, by its very gnomic and mysterious quality, which becomes plain if one imagines it as a speech in a play—what character (in a Russian drama, say) would speak such lines?

Recast the words in the form in which they were originally published, by William Carlos Williams, and the whole thing feels different:

> so much depends
> upon
>
> a red wheel
> barrow
>
> glazed with rain
> water
>
> beside the white
> chickens

Now we know it is a poem: this means that it has no larger text of which it is a part, except perhaps a series of poems or other texts by the same author—that is the dramatic production in which it is a single speech—or, in another sense, the poetry, by others, against which it plays by contrast and similarity. And it no longer sounds so pretentious, for we allow our poets to talk in this declaiming and perhaps mysterious way.

More important still, it now has a form of a sort that it did not before, the visual form on the page, and it draws attention to the fact: it is built on the traditional model of form and variation, here into four units—stanzas or "rooms"—each with similar but not identical form. This invites the reader to examine the patterns so created; the poem in turn rewards such examination, with a richness too great to detail here beyond the suggestion that one attend to the patterns made by the

The church.

The Altar.

A broken Altar Lord thy servant reareth
Made of a hart and cimented with teares
    whose parts are as thy hand did frame
    No workmans toole hath touchd y same
        A hart alone
        Is such a stone
        As nothing. but
        Thy powre doth cutt.
        wherefore each part
        Of my hard hart
        Meetes in this frame
        To praise thy name
    That if I chance to hold my peace
    These stones to praise thee may not cease
O lett thy blessed sacrifice bee mine
And sanctifie this Altar to bee thine

"The Altar" as it appears in the manuscript known as *W*, with a
correction perhaps in Herbert's hand: "onely" becomes "blessed"

The Altar

A broken Altar, Lord, thy servant rears
Made of a heart, & cemented with tears.
   Whose parts are as thy hand did frame;
   No workmans tool hath touch'd y̆ same.
      A heart alone
      Is such a stone,
      As nothing but
      Thy power doth cut.
      Wherefore each part
      Of my hard heart
      Meets in this frame,
      To praise thy Name.
   That if I chance to hold my peace,
   These stones to praise thee may not cease.
O let thy blessed sacrifice be mine,
And sanctify this Altar to be thine.

"The Altar" as it appears in the manuscript known as *B*, prepared after Herbert's death at Little Gidding

shifting vowel sounds, and consonants too; to the prominence thus given "glazed with rain"; to the sense of momentary stasis implied by "glazed" and by the poising of red against white, barrow against chickens; to the way the visual aspect of the shape of the poem on the page mirrors its acutely visual imagery, as one thing is placed in contrast to another; and so on.[16]

Something similar could be done with any poem: as we recast it from apparent prose to take its proper form on the page we would suddenly see it invoking expectations, inviting questions, and directing attention to what could now be seen as its parts and to the relations among them. What would it mean to do this with "The Altar"?

A broken ALTAR, Lord, thy servant reares, made of a heart, and cemented with teares: whose parts are as thy hand did frame; no workmans tool hath touch'd the same. A HEART alone is such a stone, as nothing but thy pow'r doth cut. Wherefore each part of my hard heart meets in this frame, to praise thy Name. That, if I chance to hold my peace, these stones to praise thee may not cease. O let thy blessed SACRIFICE be mine, and sanctifie this ALTAR to be thine.

Here the poetic lines are marked by syntactic pauses ("end-stopped"), thus emphasizing the rhymes in a way that the reader would certainly notice even when the poem is written without lines—no one would mistake it for prose. But the rhymes do not come at quite the right places, for the lines they define are of irregular length, and the reader would feel this as a source of disquiet. To cast it again as originally composed is to see the apparent disorder resolved, and resolved in a way one could not readily have imagined, into the shape of an altar itself, almost as if by magic, or—more properly—by grace.

To cast the lines into the shape of the poem is to create a set of relations among them as well: the short lines at the center, intense and

---

16. "The Red Wheel Barrow" is of course not wholly typical, for it has not the rhymes that would tend to give away its character as a poem if written out as prose. But even in its prose form one might have noticed the parallels between "wheel barrow," "rain water," and "white chickens," and the pause in each that marks the end of a line, in this case giving the stanza itself something of the shape of a wheel barrow.

staccato, are indeed the center of the poem, the earlier ones leading up to, the later ones away from this "cutting" and "meeting." The rhymes, now highlighted, connect the "heart alone" and the "stone," and give to "cut," coming after "but" and at the end of a clause, a kind of cutting power itself. "Mine" and "thine" are marked as natural contrasts, confirming a use of language that will be rendered deeply problematic later.[17]

---

17. For example in the following:

Clasping of Hands

Lord, thou art mine, and I am thine,
If mine I am: and thine much more,
Then I or ought, or can be mine.
Yet to be thine, doth me restore;
So that again I now am mine,
And with advantage mine the more,
Since this being mine, brings with it thine,
And thou with me dost thee restore.
    If I without thee would be mine,
    I neither should be mine nor thine.

Lord, I am thine, and thou art mine:
So mine thou art, that something more
I may presume thee mine, then thine.
For thou didst suffer to restore
Not thee, but me, and to be mine,
And with advantage mine the more,
Since thou in death wast none of thine,
Yet then as mine didst me restore.
    O be mine still! still make me thine!
    Or rather make no Thine and Mine!

The central terms of which this poem is built, "mine" and "thine," lose their distinction and significance, not only as a matter of logic but more importantly as a result of their chiming repetitions. Like Kipling's Kim, who repeated his name until it made no sense, these reiterations dissolve the meaning of the terms.

These are not just any two words, but essential to the sense of self and other, as radically necessary to speech of any kind—which always has a speaker, always an audience—as any we could name. What is more, they will be made essential throughout "The Church" from "The Altar" on, for example: "Let me not love thee, if I love thee not" ("Affliction" [I]); "All were thine / And none of mine: / Surely thine alone" ("An Offering"); and "There is no articling with thee: / I am but finite, yet thine infinitely" ("Artillerie," which appears not far before "Clasping of Hands").

The form of "The Altar" draws dramatic attention to a striking feature of all poetry, namely our sense that words that have been chosen to express with maximum precision a particular feeling or idea or perception, or to enact a set of gestures, somehow also fall into patterns of sound, and indeed of vision as well, that have their own force and meaning, which reinforce or undermine the significance claimed in the other dimension. This is as true of a sonnet in its way as it is of "The Altar" itself, but there is nothing in the world that makes this especially likely, for the dimension of sound—rhyme, meter, rhythm—and the dimension of word-meaning are usually thought of as quite different. In fact we speak of onomatopoeia to mark the special occasions where that is not so: "gurgle," "hush," "snap," and so forth. To find one's words, chosen to express a thought or feeling, falling into music, would be as surprising as to find one's words chosen for their sounds somehow achieving striking thoughts and images.

We normally think of the dimensions of sight and meaning as different too. We do not conceive of ourselves as choosing our words with an eye to how they appear on the page, the way they will set up as it were, and it must be deeply surprising to find oneself making an order of this kind too, as in "The Red Wheel Barrow" or "The Altar." That one's words can thus work in ordered ways, creating and confirming and dislodging expectations at once in the two dimensions of sound and sense—and now the third, sight—and do so in ways that mutually interact to create the meaning of the whole, is a kind of miracle, a source of wonder and hope found in the world, outside of ourselves, in our language. "The Altar" draws attention to this aspect of itself, and by extension of all of Herbert's poems; even when they are most despairing, there is thus another sense in which they are full of affirmation.

The whole problem of self-assertion in the poetic act itself depends upon the existence of this distinction, here for the moment erased by the music.

The two stanzas do not work in exactly the same way. The first, which asserts that "I" am "thine," begins to achieve a loss of identity in an imagined merger. But symmetry requires the second, that "thou" art "mine," which necessarily works the other way, as an assertion of the claiming self against the blurring of the distinction otherwise achieved in the poem.

With Herbert's poem compare John 17:10: "And all mine are thine, and thine are mine; and I am glorified in them."

"The Sacrifice"

In "The Sacrifice," the long poem that follows next, Herbert elaborates a topic that was raised in "The Altar" yet not pursued there, namely what it might mean to "let thy blessed SACRIFICE be mine." This could mean what the speaker no doubt thinks it means, that he is asking to be among the beneficiaries of that great act, but the words also carry another hope, far more grandiose, that as a poet he can appropriate that sacrifice and make it his. Here he does just that, imagining Christ suffering on the cross and expressing his feelings of grief and reproach. Here is how the poem begins:

> O*h all ye, who passe by,* whose eyes and minde
> To wordly things are sharp, but to me blinde;
> To me, who took eyes that I might you finde:
>   Was ever grief like mine?

Herbert thus makes (not "lets") the "sacrifice be mine"; and he does this dramatically, by speaking in the voice of Christ throughout, a bold act indeed.

   This poetic move is not in itself original but, as Rosemond Tuve has shown,[18] derives from a liturgical genre developed in the Middle Ages that consisted of Christ's reproaches to his people from the cross, said, or sung, on Good Friday. But Herbert's particular use of this form is original, and daring, for here there is no liturgical context in which the arrogance of claiming to speak for God is dissipated by the character of the ritual itself. Herbert thus appropriates a public form to his private use, and a striking and perhaps dangerous use it is, especially in a poet who will assert again and again his sense of his own unworthiness, or worthlessness, against the power and love and grace of God. For in imagining how Christ might speak—just as, though more mutedly, in imagining elsewhere how God might be spoken to—Herbert's literary performance claims for this part of himself, for his poetic imagination, a stunning set of powers and capacities.

---

18. Rosemond Tuve, *A Reading of George Herbert* (Chicago: University of Chicago Press, 1952), 19–99.

The Meaning of the Sacrifice

To imagine Christ's experience on the cross, as Herbert does, necessarily raises what is perhaps the greatest puzzle of Christian theology, which is why it was necessary for Christ to die at all, and if so, why in this hideous way. Other religions, most relevantly Judaism, have no such act of bloody torture at their center. The very point of the story of Abraham and Isaac is, after all, to reject the idea of human sacrifice. While for some people the cross is ineffably beautiful, a symbol of peace, for others it is a gruesome image of death, and this in relation not only to the suffering, death, and repression that have been inflicted in its name, but to its origins. The crucifixion does not seem to be the act of a God who loves life and the world he has made. "We preach Christ crucified," said the Apostle Paul; rightly adding that this is "unto the Jews a stumbling-block, and unto the Greeks foolishness" (1 Corinthians 1:23).

When one asks of religious authorities why Christ died, one is told—especially by Paul—"for our sins." "In Adam's fall we sinned all," as the old *New England Reader* had it. Justice requires payment or atonement; Christ provides it. But this seems to define a horrible God, one who would kill and torture his own son to satisfy his own abstract demands for justice. There are more than a few overtones of the also horrible story of Abraham and Isaac, but without the palliative of that story, namely that it takes a step away from human sacrifice. Christ is a human sacrifice and more, a divine one. What kind of religion, what kind of life, has this event at its center? Or—as the reader of Herbert is invited to ask—what kind of poetry?

There is in the Scripture another strain of explanation, rooted not in justice but in love. Consider, for example, Jesus' sermon to his disciples in the gospel of John, in which he gives them a single commandment, namely "That ye love one another; as I have loved you, that ye also love one another." He goes on to explain what this love is: "Greater love hath no man than this, that a man lay down his life for his friends" (John 13:34, 15:13). The sacrifice that he is about to suffer or perform is motivated, that is, not by justice but by love. This is an alternative to the vision of God exacting payment from his son, but the question still remains: Why is it necessary for him to die in the first place? Why is it not enough for the God of love to present himself, perhaps like the Buddha, as a Loving Being in the world?

These are questions inescapably presented by the Christian story, and above all by the crucifixion itself. Herbert will address them not by theological argument, nor by the development of doctrine, but in his poetry, as he creates and re-creates both himself—or his selves—and the God he talks about and addresses. What is problematic in Christianity thus becomes problematic in the poetry too. Indeed that is its point: his poetry is a way not of evading but of making visible, and addressing, these difficulties. Herbert is no apologist for Christianity, nor a poet of simple piety, but a mind and soul engaged with the difficulty of his own experience of life and language—including the language of Christianity—sometimes to the point of torment, a torment he here sees shared, and greatly exceeded, by the figure on the cross.

The Authoritarian Language of Religion

It is hard for us to imagine Herbert's situation with respect to religious doctrine, since we tend to regard religious belief as optional in a way that he could not. We think of ourselves as choosing whether or not to be religious at all and as choosing the particular form of religion that suits us. But for Herbert the language of Christianity defined his world in a way that was inescapable: it was not one religion, one language, among many, but simply the way things were. One could argue about specific issues in the terms Christianity provided, indeed for an educated person that was virtually necessary, but one could not reject the language as a whole. This was not legally or socially possible, nor for most people psychologically either: to be an atheist was to take on the whole force of one's culture, an act that could not be fueled by something as mild as disbelief.[19] As Marlowe's *Faustus* shows, it was more easily imaginable to hate God than disbelieve in him, and there are strains of this in Herbert too, as we have seen in "The Collar" and elsewhere.

Herbert's confusion about doctrine runs deep into his being: he is committed to the truths of Christianity, but more than that; he is overcommitted, for a part of him is as didactic, conclusory, and authoritarian as he sometimes imagines the church, or his God, to be. His rebellions and resistances are sometimes against the God with whom he wishes to be reconciled, sometimes against forces of oppression and

---

19. Though the requirement was no doubt often evaded, in England every person was obliged by law to attend the services of the established church. In Europe as a whole, the fragmentation of the church during and after the Reformation naturally intensified the question of allegiance to particular creeds; this was later reinforced by the fact that conflicts between churches came to be conflicts between nations as well.

self-righteousness in himself, and it is impossible for him to be sure which. It is hard to see how the confusion could be clarified, because it is hard to imagine how he could ever establish a self external to his language, from which it could be examined.

One way to think of Herbert's effort in these poems, then, is that he is seeking to define a self, and a relation to his inheritance, that will enable him to do something with this language—this story, these images, this way of talking—other than simply reiterating it; to put himself in a position from which he can accept it, even choose it, as an act of his own, rather than feel perpetually subject to compulsion. But to do such a thing a person would somehow have to work one's way out from underneath this language, at least in part, and this is an almost impossible task for someone who is surrounded, as he was, by people and texts that spoke no other way. Herbert's "somehow" is his poetry.

One might look for an analogy to Milton's *Paradise Lost,* which begins with a speaker who affirms without question an authoritarian language. He tells us of Satan's "foul revolt" and the loss of our "blissful seat" in paradise and so forth, but without giving any content to these terms, which function as labels, imposed in the only way he can imagine. God is "good" by definition, and Satan is "evil"; but what is this goodness or evil? All we really know is that there was "disobedience" on the part of mankind, "revolt" on the part of Satan, but we are given no poetic or imaginative reason to think these things bad. They are bad because they must be; no other alternative is imaginable. The language of religious truth functions here as a purely authoritarian system.

Against it are two forces. One, surprisingly, is Satan's heroic claim to reimagine language and the world, as this appears in his early speeches: "The mind is its own place, and in itself / Can make a Heav'n of Hell, a Hell of Heav'n." The other rebellious force is the ambition, similar in grandiosity to Satan's own, of the speaker himself, who proposes to exceed the achievements of all the poets in the world: his song "with no middle flight intends to soar / Above the Aonian Mount, while it pursues / Things unattempted yet in Prose or Rhyme." His goal is nothing less than to "assert Eternal Providence, / And justify the ways of God to men." It sounds crazy.

The reader is thus spoken to by a narrator who can imagine only one correct way to conceive of reality, the way of the essential doctrines, images, and narratives of Christianity. In *Paradise Lost* the language defining this vision is asserted in a bold, not to say tyrannical manner;

yet it is resisted too, and we must find ourselves, in part at least, on the side of resistance, if not to the language at least to the authoritarian way it necessarily functions. Like Blake or Shelley, we may even see Satan as the true hero of the poem, against the author's presumed intention, with a force and appeal from which the poem never recovers.[20] Short of that, we may find ourselves stirred by Satan's speeches but, at least on rereading, feel less than wholly captured by them, for he proves to be an authoritarian too: "Better to reign in Hell, than Serve in Heav'n" is a motto for himself alone. And in his own way he is just as conclusory as the narrator is: he never gives any content to the claims against God that motivated his rebellion. He calls his revolt a "glorious enterprise," but upon what was it based? The simple fact that God had power and Satan wanted it, no more. This is what was intolerable to him.

Satan and the narrator thus combine to imagine a purely authoritarian God, one for whom disobedience is the worst crime: one affirms, the other denies the authority of this God and in this sense they are opposed; but both agree as to his tyrannical nature, and Satan's denial is in the service of a language, and a figure, just as authoritarian as those the narrator affirms. One aim of the poem as a whole is to move us from this way of imagining and talking about God, and ourselves, to another one, leading us to see that it is ultimately Satan's own definition of God—in which we are at the beginning led to participate—that constitutes his damnation. After all, as he said and we failed to notice, "The mind is its own place" and can make "a Hell of Heav'n."

The importance of all this for the reading of Herbert is that the situation that *Paradise Lost* defines for its reader is a clarified version of the situation of people actually living in seventeenth-century England: there is one language that no one can doubt, everyone affirms, taught to everyone from infancy. To grow up in it, as in any language that makes total and exclusive claims, is to be indoctrinated. Not by choice, but by gradual socialization, it becomes the material of thought and feeling.[21] The question is: how can one come to terms with this language?

---

20. William Blake, "The Marriage of Heaven and Hell" (1793): Milton "was a true poet and of the devil's party without knowing it." Percy Bysshe Shelley, *A Defence of Poetry* (1821): "Nothing can exceed the energy and magnificence of the character of Satan as expressed in *Paradise Lost*. . . . Milton's Devil as a moral being is far superior to his God."

21. This was especially so of the Bible and the Book of Common Prayer, which

The instinct to rebel from the authoritarian aspect of it is a good one; yet to continue to see it as wholly authoritarian in nature may be wrong, or right. What Milton and Herbert in their very different ways do is to use poetry as a way of gaining distance on this set of ways of thinking and imagining the world, so that they may in another sense make it more fully their own; or, perhaps more accurately, come more freely and fully to inhabit the places, and engage in the practices, it defines. For both poets authority in a sense resides not in this most authoritative of discourses, Christian theology, but in the art by which they come to terms with it.

By contrast to Herbert and Milton, most of us in our time are pluralists, who do not believe that the claims of any tradition, including our own, to truth—or beauty or justice—are exclusive. Like Herbert, we must ask what relations we can establish with our traditions, but for us the question is less how to come to terms with an authoritarian language than how to explain our own renewed choices. In our situation the danger seems to be not so much the submission to a totalizing system as the reduction of everything to a set of preferences, none of which can be explained because any language in which we might do this is itself seen as chosen as a matter of preference. You choose your God at a cafeteria, or, to shift the image only slightly, you confect him or her the way you make a salad at a salad bar. Perhaps our totalizing system is the image of the consumer choice.

Another response—and some regard this as a good thing—is to think that religion is simply no longer possible. This may of course be true, either in general or for a particular person, but one still must have some way of imagining the world, and what shall it be? What relation shall one have to the traditions of one's culture? And, to put it in psychological terms, what is one to do with the impulses of thanks and praise and awe and concern for others that we all have and that art itself can be seen to stimulate: are they to be encouraged and nurtured, given a place

---

were read again and again. Think what it would mean to say repeatedly in the litany, for example, "Have mercie upon us miserable sinners," or in a prayer before Communion, "we be not worthy so muche as to gather up the crumbes under thy Table," or in the general confession "there is no health in us"; or to participate in the (presumably uncommon) service called a Commination of Sinners, which begins by reiterating and reaffirming God's curses on sinners. See *The Prayer-Book of Queen Elizabeth 1559* (London: Griffin Farran, 1890).

in which to act and offered a set of gestures and rituals for their expression, or are they to be curtailed and suppressed?

"The Sacrifice"

"The Sacrifice" is too long to reproduce in full, but it is important to understand that each of its sixty-three stanzas follows the pattern of the first: it consists of three rhymed lines followed by a refrain that, with two exceptions to be discussed below, is identical throughout the poem: "Was ever grief like mine?"[22] The poem is written to imagine the character and meaning of this grief itself, which here, as usual in Herbert, includes physical as well as emotional suffering. A large part of it lies in the indifference, hostility, or murderous action of the human beings Christ has come to save:

O*h all ye, who passe by,* whose eyes and minde
To wordly things are sharp, but to me blinde;
To me, who took eyes that I might you finde:
                              Was ever grief like mine?

The Princes of my people make a head
Against their Maker: they do wish me dead,
Who cannot wish, except I give them bread:
                              Was ever grief like mine?

Without me each one, who doth now me brave,
Had to this day been an Egyptian slave.
They use that power against me, which I gave:
                              Was ever grief like mine?

Mine own Apostle, who the bag did beare,
Though he had all I had, did not forbeare
To sell me also, and to put me there:
                              Was ever grief like mine?

---

22. The two exceptions, each heavily marked, come at the central moment when Jesus expires and at the end of the poem. See page 100, below. This refrain may be wearing on the reader, an effect that can be reduced if the refrain is read in a muted voice, different from the stanzas, like a religious chant.

For thirtie pence he did my death devise,
Who at three hundred did the ointment prize,
Not half so sweet as my sweet sacrifice:
> Was ever grief like mine?

Therefore my soul melts, and my hearts deare treasure
Drops bloud (the onely beads) my words to measure:
O let this cup passe, if it be thy pleasure:
> Was ever grief like mine?

These drops being temper'd with a sinners tears,
A Balsome are for both the Hemispheres:
Curing all wounds, but mine; all, but my fears:
> Was ever grief like mine?[23]

As the speaker of this poem, Jesus addresses an audience imagined to be inattentive and nonresponsive: *"all ye, who passe by,"* presumably without noticing, or caring about, who he is. They are "blinde," yet he speaks to them: is this on the assumption that they will hear though they will not see? Or does he believe that human beings will be as inattentive to what he says as to what he suffers? To the extent the latter is the case, the poem has an odd and powerful rhetorical force, because the virtual absence of an audience is a demonstration of his isolation, the frustration of his attempts to reach the human world that lies at the core of his "grief." To the extent he assumes the former, he demonstrates his willingness to reach humanity at any cost, an attempt that is pathetically doomed to fail unless the reader does attend and respond.

---

23. Notes:

1. Stanzas 4 and 5 refer to Judas, who complained when Mary anointed the feet of Jesus, a few days before he died, with a "very costly" ointment. "Why was this ointment not sold for three hundred pence, and given to the poor?" (John 12:5). The text goes on to say that Judas said this not because "he cared for the poor; but because he was a thief, and had the bag, and bare what was put therein." The bag might hold funds specifically for alms, or perhaps just the common funds of the disciples. See John 13:29. Elsewhere it is said that Judas received thirty pieces of silver (not pence) for his betrayal (Matthew 26:15), for which he hanged himself (Matthew 27:5).

2. "O let this cup passe, if it be thy pleasure" refers to Christ's words before his crucifixion: "Father, if thou be willing, remove this cup from me: nevertheless, not my will, but thine, be done" (Luke 22:42). Cf. Mark 14:35, Matthew 26:42. Herbert is not following one gospel here, but combining them.

If that does happen, if the reader does respond, there will be a kind of success for Christ after all: not the first time, not when he was present in the material world, but the second time, as these events are retold in speech, here and now. Perhaps, then, words may do what life cannot, reversing the orientation of "The Windows" and "Jordan"; may, that is, if the reader is able and willing to "let thy blessed sacrifice be mine." This is not doctrine in the negative sense, not dogma or cliché, but doctrine as "The Windows" defined it, a transforming story. In that story the reader has a central role, for she is defined by the poem's mode of address as among those who turn away or "passe by." One question the poem puts to its reader, then, is whether that act can be reversed, whether she can now, at last, attend to what she has thus far ignored.

The reiterated refrain marks this speech as a complaint, and a complaint of a poetically dangerous kind, for it is a claim to suffer uniquely, more than anyone else. This is a kind of speech that as a social matter we commonly, and rightly, mistrust. We say that someone who speaks that way is whining. But this response is at work in the poem in a powerful way: the reader naturally wants to deny the uniqueness of the suffering— we all suffer, after all: who are you to complain so?—but is instantly confronted with the reversal of his expectations. This *is* unique; it is God, not man, speaking.

Yet it is man as well: the sense of injustice, of isolation, of pain, of abandonment, all these are true human sufferings. And we cannot deny them: whatever else one may believe, or not believe, there seems to be no reason for us, and was none for Herbert, to doubt that Jesus existed as a human being and did in fact die in this way, on the cross, and that his suffering was terrible. For Herbert, it was also as God that Jesus did these things; but what that means requires the definition that only art can give. Part of the object of the poem, then, and its achievement, is to present this speaker as both God and man at once, in each capacity suffering more than we could do.

The speaker begins his enactment of the crucifixion with the moment on the Mount of Olives when, while the disciples sleep, he sweats blood in his agony (Luke 22:44). But the grief he feels is a moral, not a primarily physical one, that of totally unjust devaluation: "they do wish me dead, / Who cannot wish, except I give them bread." This is a direct reversal of what should be, gratitude and love returned; instead, the greater the gift, the greater the hatred. More striking even than the reversal itself is the speaker's response to it: "Therefore my soul melts," he says; melts, that is, with grief for the humans who fail and for his own failure to reach them; a melting that is another attempt to reach them, offering now his blood in agony as a gift. This agony is unique not only in its origin and sympathy but in its incurability: "curing all wounds, but mine; all, but my fears." Christ suffers more than anyone else in the history of the world, for he suffers both as man and as God. As man he suffers physical pain, humiliation, abandonment by his friends; as God he suffers morally, for the infinite injustice inflicted upon him— "I him obey who all else commands"—and spiritually too, for he loves those who injure him, and suffers for their sake as well as his own. He experiences, for the moment at least, the worst of both worlds, and does so in order that we may experience the best.

There is here a partial performance of an answer to the question raised above, why Christ must die: it is not Adam's sin, or God's implacable justice that requires this, but our own human obduracy, our refusal to see or hear or respond. If we could hear, words would be enough; if we could see, his presence would be enough: in a literal kind of last-gasp attempt to do everything, the speaker here offers his blood and pain, his life, in the far from certain hope that this at least will reach us. This is one expression of what it means for "a man [to] lay down his life for his friends." It also defines a possible function for poetry, and for preaching too: to tell the story which, in the nature of things, Christ himself cannot tell, that of his suffering, the story that may reach people whom his own words and actions alone cannot reach. It is to make the art of preaching, and of this kind of poetry, a sacred one.

The rest of the poem tells this story in an effort of its own, like a gospel, to reach those "who passe by" with what it is hard indeed to pass by, another person willingly accepting suffering and death for another. This is for Herbert the center of the Christian story, and he returns to it again and again; in the greatest doubt and confusion, this much he can remind himself he knows, that another did die for him, and the knowledge of this act of love is enough to enable him to start again.

The poem works this story out, telling the narrative of human abandonment and assault: abandonment by the disciples, attack by the priests—for blasphemy!—Herod's hostility, the shouts of his "own deare people" for his crucifixion, their choice of Barabbas, his scourging, and buffeting, and beating and mocking.

The souldiers also spit upon that face,
Which Angels did desire to have the grace,
And Prophets, once to see, but found no place:
> Was ever grief like mine?

The grief is not the suffering or insult only, or mainly, but grief at what the soldiers do to themselves. The logic is that it is their very sinfulness, coupled with his love for them, that requires that he die at their hands. "Most true to those, who are my greatest grief." See how he earlier addressed Judas himself:

Judas, dost thou betray me with a kisse?
Canst thou finde hell about my lips? and misse
Of life, just at the gates of life and blisse?
> Was ever grief like mine?

At the central moment, however, the grief is felt as pain of a unique and terrible kind:

And now wearie of sport, glad to ingrosse
All spite in one, counting my life their losse,
They carrie me to my most bitter crosse:
> Was ever grief like mine?

My crosse I bear my self, untill I faint:
Then Simon bears it for me by constraint,
The decreed burden of each mortall Saint:
> Was ever grief like mine?

O all ye who passe by, behold and see;
Man stole the fruit, but I must climbe the tree;
The tree of life to all, but onely me:
> Was ever grief like mine?

Lo, here I hang, charg'd with a world of sinne,
The greater world o' th' two; for that came in
By words, but this by sorrow I must win:
> Was ever grief like mine?

Such sorrow as, if sinfull man could feel,
Or feel his part, he would not cease to kneel,

> Till all were melted, though he were all steel:
>> Was ever grief like mine?
>
> But, *O my God, my God!* why leav'st thou me,
> The sonne, in whom thou dost delight to be?
> *My God, my God—*
>> Never was grief like mine.

Here, at the center of the poem, the speaker begins again with the invocation of the audience that is no audience, "*all ye who passe by,*" and defines with new clarity what it means that he is both God and man: "Man stole the fruit, but I must climbe the tree; / The tree of life to all, but onely me." He suffers, as a man, more than any man could ever suffer, partly because of who he is, what he knows, and how he loves those who kill him; partly because he is here abandoned, as no man will ever be, by God, and shocked and surprised by this more than any man could be.

This is a deprivation that we are told we shall never suffer; yet at the end of the poem we do in a way experience it: Christ's death is portrayed as a real one, as human and complete as if all his talk of divinity were delusive.[24] When he dies there is only silence:

> But now I die; now all is finished.
> My wo, man's weal: and now I bow my head.
> Onely let others say, when I am dead,
>> Never was grief like mine.

Here we ourselves, as readers, experience the deprivation of the presence of Christ that the poem has created for us.

---

24. William Empson observed that the last two lines have a shadow meaning that is full of threat, something like this: "Let them so suffer that each of them will say, in pain, 'Never was grief like mine.'" *Seven Types of Ambiguity* (New York: New Directions, 1947), 228–29.

The phrase "my wo, man's weal" is also ambivalent. The dominant meaning is, I think, "my wo [is] man's weal." But these terms could also be read in joint apposition to the "all" that is the subject of "finished." Then the phrase would mean: "everything is over: my woe and man's weal," suggesting the possibility of terrible retribution to come.

Chapter 3

Sequences

Every poem lays claim to the engaged attention of the reader and in so doing invites a response to what it says and does. But in representing the voice of the suffering Christ, and his death, "The Sacrifice" calls for a response not only to itself but to the event it represents. Of course one possibility is that we can refuse to take that event seriously; this is, in the poem's terms, to be among those who abandon, assault, or "passe by" the suffering Christ. Indeed the poem suggests that this may be all that is possible for us, since in it no human being acts otherwise, except for Simon, who is a saint, and even he bears the cross "by constraint." Yet it is also one aim of the poem to lead us to a different position, for it insists upon attending to this event, in the imagination at least, and in so doing asks us what kind of response to it is possible. This—for Herbert perhaps the central question in life, and in a sense the subject of all of his poetry—is the topic especially of the sequence of the nine poems following "The Sacrifice." One might say that he is beginning to work out what might be meant by the line that closes "The Altar": "And let thy blessed SACRIFICE be mine."

"The Thanksgiving" to "Easter-wings"

The Thanksgiving

Oh King of grief! (a title strange, yet true,
     To thee of all kings only due)
Oh King of wounds! how shall I grieve for thee,
     Who in all grief preventest me?
Shall I weep bloud? why, thou has wept such store
     That all thy body was one doore.
Shall I be scourged, flouted, boxed, sold?
     'Tis but to tell the tale is told.
My God, my God, why dost thou part from me?
     Was such a grief as cannot be.

South door of the church at Leighton Bromswold

Shall I then sing, skipping thy dolefull storie,
    And side with thy triumphant glorie?
Shall thy strokes be my stroking? thorns, my flower?
    Thy rod, my posie? crosse, my bower?

But how then shall I imitate thee, and
    Copie thy fair, though bloudie hand?
Surely I will revenge me on thy love,
    And trie who shall victorious prove.
If thou dost give me wealth, I will restore
    All back unto thee by the poore.
If thou dost give me honour, men shall see,
    The honour doth belong to thee.
I will not marry; or, if she be mine,
    She and her children shall be thine.
My bosome friend, if he blaspheme thy Name,
    I will tear thence his love and fame.
One half of me being gone, the rest I give
    Unto some Chappell, die or live.
As for thy passion—But of that anon,
    When with the other I have done.
For thy predestination I'le contrive,
    That three yeares hence, if I survive,
I'le build a spittle, or mend common wayes,
    But mend mine own without delayes.
Then I will use the works of thy creation,
    As if I us'd them but for fashion.
The world and I will quarrell; and the yeare
    Shall not perceive, that I am here.
My musick shall finde thee, and ev'ry string
    Shall have his attribute to sing;
That all together may accord in thee,
    And prove one God, one harmonie.
If thou shalt give me wit, it shall appeare,
    If thou hast giv'n it me, 'tis here.
Nay, I will reade thy book, and never move
    Till I have found therein thy love,
Thy art of love, which I'le turn back on thee:
    O my deare Saviour, Victorie!
Then for thy passion—I will do for that—
    Alas, my God, I know not what.[1]

---

1. Notes:

1. *Doore* here means doorway, or opening.

Here the speaker directly expresses the sense that he cannot make an adequate response to the Sacrifice. He wants to respond with sympathy, grieving for Christ's grief, but finds himself asking, Is even this, the most fundamental and simple of decent human responses, possible for me? If not, what is?

He begins with a version of Herbert's perpetual question, "How can man...?" But this time it is asked slightly more self-confidently— "How shall I grieve?"—almost as though this were, or should be, a matter within his choice and control. The very question assumes a competence in the speaker that is belied by what follows. While he has the impulse to grieve in response to Christ's grief, he cannot simply act upon it or feel it without at the same time feeling the inadequacy of anything he might say or do. He recognizes a fatal difficulty, which he expresses by saying that Christ "prevents"—that is, "comes before" as well as "balks" or "baffles"—him. But why does the fact that Christ's grief "comes before" interfere either with his feeling itself or with its expression?

The reason is that this speaker measures adequacy by a performative, even a competitive, standard, as though to grieve appropriately for Christ he must suffer what Christ has suffered, or more. The speaker, that is, thinks of himself as an artist in grief, whose work must be the equal of, or superior to, that of his predecessor artist, and he is stymied: even if he could weep blood, that would not be enough, because Christ's whole body did so, and, likewise, to be "scourged, flouted, boxed, sold" would be nothing new. Christ thus slides imperceptibly from the object of sympathetic grief to a competitor who cannot be matched.

Out of this impasse the speaker's inventive mind suggests another route, namely to accept only the triumph of Christ, putting aside the grief. But he quickly sees the impossibility of this as well: first, it would be impossibly paradoxical, he thinks, to make "thy thorns, my flower"— though that is in fact what the Christian is to do; also, it would mean giving up his aim of imitating Christ, that is, copying his "fair, though bloudie hand." This aspiration is itself problematic: meant one way it

---

2. *Spittle* is hospital, or house of the poor; *common wayes* means highways or roads, with perhaps an overtone of "manners" too.

3. *For thy predestination* ... : i.e., to answer your power of predestination I shall make future plans of my own.

is a Christian duty, but if claimed as a realistic hope it is impossible, insane really, a near-sacrilege.

The speaker shifts then from grief and triumph to love and, in a kind of combination of competition and imitation, imagines himself responding to the Sacrifice by becoming exemplary in love. This is the way he will "revenge himself" on Christ. This is an odd phrase, but it makes psychological sense. In heroic cultures especially, though at times in ours as well, it is recognized that a gift is a burden, for it imposes a sense of obligation to reciprocate with a similar gift or at least with appropriate thanks. This is the basis of the "positive reciprocity" that provided the fundamental ethic in heroic cultures, from the Homeric to the Icelandic, mirroring the negative reciprocity for which our term is "feud." And it has its modern analogues, as any university president would say, or anyone for whom a Chicago alderman has done a favor, both of whom might find themselves asking, "What is the price of this gift?" Even in the most intimate relations we see something of this: when the man tells the woman, "I love you," he expects her to respond in kind; silence in the face of such a declaration, or even a mere thanks, is not enough. The debt must be discharged, and if the gift is of infinite love it cannot possibly be; hence the element of good-humored aggression in "revenge me on thy love."

The speaker next makes a lovely speech, in which he imagines all kinds of perfect actions: planning charities, making music, returning love, and so forth. The impulse here is a fine one, in its way as natural and good as that of a flower to thrust itself towards the sun, as was also the speaker's own earlier impulse to grieve in sympathy. But it is also marked by a kind of inherent egotism, both in the impulse to "revenge"—and thus make equal—and in its element of imaginative and poetic display. It is a kind of showing off, made slightly stagy by the end-stopped couplets, and distanced from us by its comic quality: as if a three-year plan for mending the highways could counter divine pre-destination! His response to Christ's love will be to give back wealth, honor, friends, family, all in honor to Christ; yet he cannot do this without claiming credit for the performance, if only by imagining with pleasure how virtuous he will be. Finally, and perhaps best, he will make music, all in praise; but even this entails a claim of artistic adequacy:

> My musick shall finde thee, and ev'ry string
> Shall have his attribute to sing;

> That all together may accord in thee,
> And prove one God, one harmonie.

This is a lovely image, but here too the speaker, like the poet himself, cannot make his artifact without a claim for its beauty, or truth, or adequacy to the occasion. This is at once evidence of our fallen nature—our incapacity to praise another without claiming praise for ourselves—and a strain of hopefulness that runs through Herbert's work in a perpetual note of affirmation.

The poetic display in this poem is of a kind familiar in the Renaissance, where the speaker imagines the world, and himself, anew. One thinks, for example, of Gonzalo's utopian speech in "The Tempest"; or of Romeo and Juliet's poetic redefinition of themselves as lovers, not the enemies they in social fact are; or, for a comic example, the speech of Sir Epicure Mammon in "The Alchemist," speaking thus:

> My meat shall all come in, in Indian shells,
> Dishes of agate set in gold, and studded
> With emeralds, sapphires, hyacinths, and rubies.
> The tongues of carps, dormice, and camels' heels,
> Boiled i' the spirit of Sol, and dissolv'd pearl,
> (Apicius' diet, 'gainst the epilepsy):
> And I will eat these broths with spoons of amber,
> Headed with diamond and carbuncle.
> My foot-boy shall eat pheasants, calver'd salmons,
> Knots, godwits, lampreys: I myself will have
> The beards of barbel serv'd, instead of salads;
> Oiled mushrooms; and the swelling unctuous paps
> Of a fat pregnant sow, newly cut off,
> Drest with an exquisite and poignant sauce;
> For which, I'll say unto my cook, *There's gold,*
> *Go forth, and be a knight.*

In a similar way the speaker in "The Thanksgiving" too is a poet, an artist in imagination. Seeing himself foiled in the expression of grief, and triumph too, he moves to the imitation of Christ, deploying all his talent to imagine it—"thy art of love, which I'le turn back on thee"— yet without success. The poem thus presents us with a voice, an aspect of the self, trying to respond to the Sacrifice and in the process revealing why it cannot do so. One reason is the immensity of the original event;

another is that in its very attempt to respond the imagination will appropriate the central role to itself, as the human and poetic imagination always does, making it "mine" not in the sense of benefitting from it, but in the sense of claiming it, if only as the material of one's art. It is thus a performance of exactly the sort of self-centeredness from which the Passion is intended to save us.

Here, at last, we come to the center of the poem: the speaker's deferred but unavoidable recognition that with respect to the Passion itself he can say or do nothing at all. The best thing that can happen— and it happens before our eyes—is that by frustrating his poetic and emotional efforts the Sacrifice may "prevent" the speaker from making it inappropriately his. The speaker does not, perhaps cannot, know what is happening to him; but in fact it is the very frustration he complains of that saves him, demonstrating, as "Affliction" did too, how unreliable our own preferences are. The poem is thus a performance, in the speaker's life, of the saving force of the Sacrifice, a force that works paradoxically, by confounding and saving him from the success of his own imagination.

All this works as a response to the question implicitly presented by "The Sacrifice": Why, as a theological matter, is Christ's sacrifice necessary in the first place? The answer demonstrated here is that our own nature requires it; the human being's natural self-centeredness, on display in this poetic voice, can be reached only this way. The important gesture here is not the poem of praise with all its art, which the speaker sets out to write, but the acknowledgment of inadequacy, the collapse into silence when language and the mind meet a stumbling block they cannot master. The breakdown of the poem—"Alas, my God, I know not what"—is its highest moment. The silence into which the poet is led at the end, the collapse of speech, is the best possible speech: the speech of a stone, as in "The Altar," or of a heart that is actually moved in ways that "prevent" the poet from making his declamation.

But there is still another level of complexity, for the existence of the poem is necessary to bring us to the point of its own benign failure. As with the "Jordan" poems, then, this is a poem about the limitations of the poetic imagination that is also itself an exercise of the poetic imagination; it brings its own limits—not only those of the speaker— to our attention; and here, in its recognition of its lack of merit, is where its merit lies. But it cannot escape, even that way, from working as an assertion of merit in a context where that is impossible. The poetic act itself makes such a claim by its own nature.

The poems that follow represent a continuing series of attempts to respond to the Sacrifice, each one building on what has gone before. For example:

The Reprisall

I have consider'd it, and finde
 There is no dealing with thy mighty passion:
For though I die for thee, I am behinde;
 My sinnes deserve the condemnation.

O make me innocent, that I
May give a disentangled state and free:
And yet thy wounds still my attempts defie,
 For by thy death I die for thee.

Ah! Was it not enough that thou
By thy eternall glory didst outgo me?
Couldst thou not griefs sad conquests me allow,
 But in all vict'ries overthrow me?

Yet by confession will I come
Into thy conquest: though I can do nought
Against thee, in thee I will overcome
 The man, who once against thee fought.[2]

The speaker here recoils from the experience of the preceding poem, ending as it did in a kind of broken silence, and instead articulates what he has learned as a matter of intellectual principle: "I have consider'd it, and finde / There is no dealing with thy mighty passion." He sees that he cannot even die for Christ, the ultimate gesture—because he,

---

2. Notes:

1. *Reprisall* means both "retaliation" and "reprise," or rewriting.

2. In the line, "For by thy death I die for thee," the speaker seems to be saying that if he were capable of full sympathy, he would die in response to Christ's death, and have nothing left with which to speak or respond. But who could ask for more than that? Not one who asked merely for perfect human sympathy, but one who, like the speaker, felt Christ's death as a challenge that had to be met by an equal response.

3. *Confession* does not refer so much to confession and penance, which the English church did not recognize as sacraments, as to the act of confessing one's faith.

unlike Christ, "deserves the condemnation"—and feels the inadequacy as a defeat. This is an intensification of the competitive aspect of the speaker's voice in "The Thanksgiving," and thus represents not spiritual or intellectual progress, and learning, but a kind of regress—though at the same time his recognition of this very fact is paradoxically a kind of progress too. This tells us that in these poems, as in life, we cannot expect continuous linear movement forward, but a series of slidings back, or to the side, in the universal human effort to evade the truth of our own circumstances.

At the end the speaker is led into an impossible but this time unperceived breakdown of his language: "Yet by confession will I come / Into the conquest." If the confession is a true submission, there is no "conquest"; if there is a conquest, there can be no true submission. The phrase "in thee I will overcome / The man, who once against thee fought" similarly splits the self into impossibly opposed halves; whichever part overcomes, the other part, equally the self, loses. The intellectualizing tendency with which this poem begins in the end breaks down, just as the self-dramatization of "The Thanksgiving" did.

The speaker of both poems is imagining himself engaged in a struggle with Christ: he is thus the one who "once against thee fought"; who then is the "I" who will overcome that self? This paradox, into which the metaphor of competition leads him, is another form of the silence to which this poetry repeatedly leads its reader. Some other language than that of "conquest" and "revenge" will have to be found.

The following poem tries to respond to Christ's suffering and death in another way, by making it the object of human knowledge, in this building on the intellectualizing tendencies of "The Reprisall."

The Agonie

Philosophers have measur'd mountains,
 Fathom'd the depths of seas, of states, and kings,
Walk'd with a staffe to heav'n, and traced fountains:
    But there are two vast, spacious things,
The which to measure it doth more behove:
Yet few there are that sound them; Sinne and Love.

    Who would know Sinne, let him repair
Unto Mount Olivet; there shall he see

> A man so wrung with pains, that all his hair,
>   His skinne, his garments bloudie be.
> Sinne is that presse and vice, which forceth pain
> To hunt his cruell food through ev'ry vein.
>
>   Who knows not Love, let him assay
> And taste that juice, which on the crosse a pike
> Did set again abroach; then let him say
>   If ever he did taste the like.
> Love is that liquour sweet and most divine,
> Which my God feels as bloud; but I, as wine.[3]

This poem first proposes that we should try to "know" both "Sinne and Love," as we know the physical world, by measurement; but then shifts, and defines knowledge not that way at all, but by imaginative participation in Christ's life, or what "The Windows" called "thy storie."[4] After all, neither sin nor love is described as an essence or thing, as "what in itself it actually is" as Aristotle might do it, by a definition of terms. They are given meaning instead by their narrative effects, at the Mount of Olives and Golgotha: sin is what causes this unbelievable agony, when Christ's body sweats blood; love is that very blood itself. It is by the narrative imagination then, not by competition or emulation, or measurement either, that he hopes to make "thy blessed SACRIFICE be mine."

But the story is told only in the briefest way and paradoxically too, for it is really the same story that defines these two radically different things, "Sinne" and "Love," which are in this way made not opposites but correlatives. And there is a dimension of meaning beyond the story, in the extraordinary physicality of this poem, so extreme as to amount to an apparent lapse of basic decorum: "let him assay / And taste that

---

3. Notes:

   1. This poem first imagines the scene at the Mount of Olives, where, while his disciples sleep, Jesus sweats blood in his agony. The second scene is of course the crucifixion, and refers particularly to the wounding of Jesus by a Roman soldier.

   2. The image of the *presse* is specifically that of a wine press.

   4. For the topic of knowledge as measurement in Herbert, see Richard Strier, *Love Known: Theology and Experience in George Herbert's Poetry* (Chicago: University of Chicago Press, 1983), esp. 43, 54.

juice" which the spear did "set abroach," and tell us "if ever he did taste the like." It is not only that the image is physical, our own response is too, as it is say to the delicious description of food in Keats's "Eve of St. Agnes," but this time in an opposite way: here I, at least, feel a physical revulsion, in the mouth, as I imagine myself tasting blood, calling it "juice." By this language the reader is forced to imagine as a physical reality an image that has been reiterated so often as to have lost its life—that the bread is the body and the wine the blood—and the image is in a literal way disgusting. That the speaker should not know this is an embarrassing lapse of linguistic and social decorum.

But, as Christopher Ricks has shown us with respect to the poetry of Keats,[5] such a moment of embarrassment can be central to a poem's experience; and so it is here, for in the last two lines we are released from this imagined tasting and offered another, equally physical, but this time sweet and good:

> Love is that liquour sweet and most divine,
> Which my God feels as bloud; but I, as wine.

As the reader substitutes the imagined and felt taste of wine for the disgusting and tabooed blood, his or her own body becomes a part of the poem. The revulsion and embarrassment are felt physically, and the release is physical too.[6] In this way the poem offers us a direct experience, partly physical, of transformation or metamorphosis. Here in the taste buds, in the mouth, in the tasting of wine, is how love can in the end be known. This is what the Eucharist offers—a movement here reversed, as blood becomes wine—and what poetry can do too.

Once more Herbert turns from words to the world beyond words, from doctrine to life; the poem works in language, but it leads us beyond language. In a world in which sin and love cannot in the usual

---

5. Christopher Ricks, *Keats and Embarrassment* (Oxford: Oxford University Press, 1974).

6. Such physicality, and embarrassment at it, is a feature of much of Herbert's work, culminating in the famous lines of the last poem of "The Church":

> You must sit down, sayes Love, and taste my meat:
> So I did sit and eat.

The primary meaning of "meat" here is food, as in the phrase "meat and drink"; but it also carries the secondary meaning, now dominant, of "flesh."

sense be "known," where we quickly lose whatever knowledge we acquire, what can have value and meaning? The answer is the poem itself, which leads us from wherever we are to the blood of Christ, which it transforms into wine. It is the poem that makes love a "liquor most divine."

"The Sinner" builds on "The Agonie" not only in its return to the trope of measurement, but in its effort to "know Sinne," this time by looking within:

The Sinner

Lord, how I am all ague, when I seek
What I have treasur'd in my memorie!
    Since, if my soul make even with the week,
Each seventh note by right is due to thee.
I finde there quarries of pil'd vanities,
    But shreds of holinesse, that dare not venture
    To shew their face, since crosse to thy decrees:
There the circumference earth is, heav'n the centre.
In so much dregs the quintessence is small:
    The spirit and good extract of my heart
    Comes to about the many hundred part.
Yet Lord restore thine image, heare my call:
    And though my hard heart scarce to thee can grone,
    Remember that thou once didst write in stone.

After experience of the other poems one will readily see much that is wrong here, especially the speaker's assumption that sin can be talked about in simply quantitative terms. He begins with the ludicrous idea that the correct proportion of good to bad in our lives is as Sunday is to the rest of the week, namely one to six; he goes on to show, still in quantitative images, how far he is from meeting even this standard— "the many hundred part." But at the end he shifts ground, and sees that what is wrong is the state of his heart itself, its quality of "hardness"—implied perhaps in the earlier "quarries"—not something quantitative after all. It is the nature of his heart that matters, not the proportion of good acts to bad; sin is not a matter of accounting but of identity.

The poem actually performs what it says, that his heart "scarce to thee can grone," for the images it uses are intellectual, even metaphysical in character, not heartfelt. The speaker can argue and measure, can use his wit to make poetry, even in the complex form of the sonnet, but this is all a far cry from "Alas, my God, I know not what" or "Let me not love thee, if I love thee not." Yet there is after all a "grone" here of a kind, at the end, in the very acknowledgment of the hardness of his heart; the result is that the poem does after all "scarce . . . grone."

But hardness of the heart has implications that go the other way, too, as it did in "The Altar," for hardness is what makes it like a stone, and hence material for an altar, or suitable for the inscription of the law. Its hardness is thus a paradoxical ground for hope, for it enables us to imagine action upon it of this sort. The image of the heart as hard as a stone, which could sound like a cliché, is in this context dense and evocative, in part because it represents a movement from a less adequate way of talking, in part because it is used in such a way as to capture conflict and tension.

The speaker here is entrapped by a mode of thought, the quantitative conception of knowledge, that the speaker in the preceding poem rejected, just as the speaker in "The Reprisall" is more, not less, competitive with Christ than the speaker in "The Thanksgiving." In both cases there is a kind of spiritual backsliding or regression. In the sort of knowledge that really matters there is no law of progress, no law indeed of retention, but a perpetual slipperiness, as we lose our hold on what we once knew and commit afresh old errors.

I am reminded here of Samuel Johnson's *Rambler* essays. When working on them some years ago, I noticed that he commonly began with a platitude or cliché, the kind of thing we normally say to ourselves in a rather empty way about mortality, say, or human fallibility; he would then move in the direction of complication, including what the original formulation left out, until he arrived, by rewriting, not at such a commonplace but at a position, defined in the essay as a whole, that affirmed both sides of an elemental tension and did so in a way that recognized the writer's own limits of mind and understanding. These essays were thus written in a process of continual self-correction. Writing the essays was for Johnson a form of contemplation that took his mind from one condition, embedded in unsatisfactory language, both vacuous and comfortable, to another, in which language worked a different way, by comprising contradiction; and at the same time from one gesture, the affirmance of easy truth, to another, close to prayer. Herbert's poems are similar in their self-consciousness of language and the mind, and in their perpetual movement. But they are vastly more difficult and troubling, for in Herbert—as in our own thinking lives—the movement need not be progressive but can be in any direction at all.

"Good Friday" continues the two images of measurement and writing. It begins with an evocation of "The Thanksgiving" and (for us) of "The Windows":

Good Friday

O My chief good,
　　How shall I measure out thy bloud?
How shall I count what thee befell,
　　And each grief tell?

　　Shall I thy woes
Number according to thy foes?
Or, since one starre show'd thy first breath,
　　Shall all thy death?

　　Or shall each leaf,
Which falls in Autumne, score a grief?
Or can not leaves, but fruit, be signe
　　Of the true vine?

　　Then let each houre
Of my whole life one grief devoure;
That thy distresse through all may runne,
　　And be my sunne.

　　Or rather let
My severall sinnes their sorrows get;
That as each beast his cure doth know,
　　Each sinne may so.

The speaker, asking once more how he can possibly respond to the sacrifice, first considers quantitative solutions: measuring Christ's "bloud" by his "griefs," his "woes" by his "foes," his death by the stars, or "each grief" by a leaf that falls in autumn or by grapes on a vine. But none of these will do: all this is only counting after all, the work of the mind, not the heart, and it does not engage the self:

　　Then let each houre
Of my whole life one grief devoure;

That thy distresse through all may runne,
And be my sunne.

But that image too fails, partly because it is still quantitative, partly because it omits what "The Sinner" brought to our attention, namely that the speaker does not need to borrow grief at all since he has enough of his own. In fact the whole enterprise of grieving for Christ's suffering may be mistaken: What should cause his grief is his sense of his own sins, which should their own "sorrows get."

As with "The Sinner," the poem works by rewriting its images in the direction of greater knowledge: not knowledge as measurement, but knowledge as recognition of our own internal nature and the truth of our circumstances. This shift is reflected not only in the final transformation from outer to inner, but in changes in the quantitative images themselves, as he moves, for example, from counting by "foes" to thinking of the stars, or from the image of leaves falling in autumn to grapes on a vine. Throughout, the mind is ready to move from the simply quantitative to an image meaningful in itself.

Poetry for Herbert is a way of thinking things through by rewriting, usually but not always in a right direction and never arriving at a firm and stable position that knows no doubt. Here the movement is from a kind of confident assertion of a relation to Christ—he will try to count his "woes"—to a kind of despair, in which no connection to God can be imagined. The wish is simply that he should know his own sinfulness, not descriptively or analytically, but by experiencing their consequences, his "sorrows," which may lead to their "cure."

But the poem has a second half, in another key. Originally, in *W*, a separate poem entitled "The Passion," it speaks out of the condition defined in the first part by expanding the image of God as "writing" in a "heart":

S ince bloud is fittest, Lord, to write
Thy sorrows in, and bloudie fight;
My heart hath store, write there, where in
One box doth lie both ink and sinne:

That when sinne spies so many foes,
Thy whips, thy nails, thy wounds, thy woes,
All come to lodge there, sinne may say,
No room for me, and flie away.

Sinne being gone, oh fill the place,
And keep possession with thy grace;
Lest sinne take courage and return,
And all the writings blot or burn.

The image here does not entirely work, in the sense that one cannot wholly imagine it out: how does "the writing" drive out sin? The idea must be a carryover from "The Sinner," that God will write his story on the heart as once he wrote his laws upon a stone. This writing is connected with what Herbert himself is doing: writing and rewriting towards a kind of knowledge that is imaginative, narrative, and experiential in kind, and that cannot be reduced to the quantitative or intellectual; yet a knowledge that disappears as soon as gained, and must be worked towards over and over again. The effect of being "written upon," that is, could be that one could "write," as Herbert shows us how to do this. But then we are told that this is not enough: the heart must be preserved by Christ's continual presence there, as its possessor and defender, and by the instruments of his torture, whips and nails, now being converted into weapons against sin. The movement of the whole poem, in both its parts, is from a kind of self-assertion, to despair, to prayer. The speaker cannot count Christ's woes; but he can say "oh, fill the place."

The next poem, a well-known sonnet, builds upon this image of Christ taking "possession" of a "place":

Redemption

Having been tenant long to a rich Lord,
Not thriving, I resolved to be bold,
And make a suit unto him, to afford
A new small-rented lease, and cancell th' old.
In heaven at his manour I him sought:
They told me there, that he was lately gone
About some land, which he had dearly bought
Long since on earth, to take possession.
I straight return'd, and knowing his great birth,
Sought him accordingly in great resorts;
In cities, theatres, gardens, parks, and courts:

> At length I heard a ragged noise and mirth
> Of theeves and murderers: there I him espied,
> Who straight, *Your suit is granted,* said, & died.

The speaker defines his situation in the language of lease, tenancy, and possession. "Not thriving," he seeks a new arrangement—what we would call restructuring his debt—and looks for his Lord, first in heaven, then in the places on earth he thinks appropriate: "cities, theatres, gardens, parks, and courts." But he finds him only among "theeves and murderers." This narrative belongs to a genre in which one person searches for another—a brother, say, or a friend—who has gone to the city on business, or to make his fortune, or just run away, and failed. One searches for him everywhere, and finds him at last among the lowest of the low, utterly degraded.

Of course, as the audience we read this story differently from the way the speaker seems to mean it, knowing as we do that it is the story of the crucifixion, and that "heaven" is not just another place. This poem is in form a dramatic monologue, with a speaker to be perceived as different from—and knowing less than—both writer and reader. But with all his ignorance, and indeed perhaps as part of it, this speaker has a simplicity and naturalness that has its own appeal; and as for his language, in what better language could one talk about redemption than that of "redemption" itself? His talk about a lease is, after all, just another version of the language of "covenant," which lies deep in both the Old and New Testaments, and in the language of Protestantism as well. "Not thriving" does have an economic meaning, but not only that: in a most general way it says that all is not well with him. And consider what he actually does: he searches out his Lord, first in heaven, then on earth; he does not stop when he fails to find him in expected places, but steadfastly perseveres until he comes upon him, perhaps by accident, in a "ragged noise and mirth."

The speaker is brought in the end to a piece of the truth, but only a piece, and we feel our superiority to him. Yet there is a sense in which the very sense of superiority that the poem stimulates in us is wrong, for what greater knowledge, really, have we? Who are we to patronize his earnestness and simplicity? And notice how the language of lease and covenant is undone here: the way this Lord "takes possession" of the land he had "dearly bought" is by dying among thieves and murderers, an image that completely unravels both the language of property and the narrative of social decline and restoration. The story is ultimately not one of leases, or covenants, or social expectations, but one of world transformation, as the language in which the story is told cannot bear the pressure of the events as we, at least, see them.

Could this ending be read another way, as the narrator seems to do: not as the glorious and redeeming crucifixion at all, but as the ultimate in social decline, a real and ignominious and final death? On this reading, "your suit is granted" would be an empty gesture, for what power has the dying man to do anything? There is nothing in writing, no reliable witnesses; it is an act with no legal effect; and we are explicitly told that he "died." It is after all we as readers who impose upon it the Christian reading outlined above.

This possibility is present throughout, as is the analogous possibility in "The Sacrifice," that what Christ experiences is a final and wholly human death. But in both cases, even on the bleakest of readings, there remains this much: in one poem the willingness to sacrifice, in the other the willingness, at such a moment of pain, and however ineffectively, to "grant a suit." And the simple determination of the narrator also remains, whether that is imagined as a search for God or as the practical action of *homo economicus*. The predominant reading does have a shadow, undermining or reversing it, but incompletely so, for on any understanding one is still in the imagined presence of extraordinary human life.

The bleakness of the shadow has another role to play, this one reinforcing the Christian story, for it is a familiar doctrinal point that Christ really does die, and descend to hell, before rising. He experiences to the full, and beyond it, our experience of suffering and death, and this in a most humiliating form. It is against a death so fully felt and imagined that Easter is to act. In an expression of this the altar cloths and candles and other devotional objects are often removed from a church on Good Friday, stripping it to look as much as possible like a warehouse, say, or an abandoned building, as if the totalitarians had come to power at last and destroyed all churches. For these poems to suggest a real and final death thus cuts both ways, against the Christian story and for it.

In "Sepulchre" the speaker is not distanced from writer and reader as he was in "Redemption," but instead speaks, at the beginning at least, in a way we can only admire, out of human sympathy for another:

Sepulchre

O blessed bodie! Whither art thou thrown?
No lodging for thee, but a cold hard stone?

So many hearts on earth, and yet not one
                         Receive thee?
Sure there is room within our hearts good store;
For they can lodge transgressions by the score:
Thousands of toyes dwell there, yet out of doore
                         They leave thee.

But that which shews them large, shews them unfit.
What ever sinne did this pure rock commit,
Which holds thee now? Who hath indited it
                         Of murder?
Where our hard hearts have took up stones to brain thee,
And missing this, most falsly did arraigne thee;
Onely these stones in quiet entertain thee,
                         And order.

And as of old the Law by heav'nly art
Was writ in stone; so thou, which also art
The letter of the word, find'st no fit heart
                         To hold thee.
Yet do we still persist as we began,
And so should perish, but that nothing can,
Though it be cold, hard, foul, from loving man
                         Withhold thee.

The speaker begins full of sympathy, moved to grieve for Christ and expressing his lament that He has not been received by a human heart, but lodges in a "cold hard stone." The idea is that if we were any good this would not be true: Christ would live in our hearts, which are obviously more suitable habitations for him. But as the speaker develops this thought, rewriting it, his terms undergo a reversal: the hearts of human beings, though large, are "unfit," while the rock is "pure." Our hearts are hard as stones, and themselves use stones to "brain thee"; these real stones, by contrast, "in quiet entertain thee."

In this way the speaker's attention is drawn from Christ's suffering to his own unfitness to receive him; this in turn undoes the possibility of connection that he imagined at the beginning of the poem, performed in his gesture of sympathy, much as a similar imagined connection is undone in "Good Friday." Even in sympathy and imagination, then, we are disconnected from God, except that "nothing can, / Though it be cold, hard, foul, from loving man / Withhold thee." But even this last sentence is ambiguous: "loving man" may be the activity from which Christ cannot be withheld; or "loving" may modify man, and thus define the kind of person from whom he cannot be withheld—and who would qualify?

The meaning of the poem and its bite lie in the way in which the very decency and sympathy of the initial impulse are undone and devalued. Here, as in "The Thanksgiving" and "Good Friday," it is the speaker's best self, not his worst one, that fails him. But it would be wrong to see the poem as working on only one side of this tension, for it necessarily speaks on behalf of these warm and generous impulses as well as against them, just as "The Thanksgiving" speaks on behalf of the music that the speaker promises to make, even though it is inadequate to the occasion of Christ's suffering. As in "Vertue," the life of this poem lies in its affirmance of contradictories, in its resolute insistence on facing the cost of what it claims.

Easter

R ise heart; thy Lord is risen. Sing his praise
　　　　　　　　Without delayes,
Who takes thee by the hand, that thou likewise
　　　　　　　　With him mayst rise:
That, as his death calcined thee to dust,
His life may make thee gold, and much more, just.

Awake, my lute, and struggle for thy part
　　　　　　　　With all thy art.
The crosse taught all wood to resound his name,
　　　　　　　　Who bore the same.
His stretched sinews taught all strings, what key
Is best to celebrate this most high day.

Consort both heart and lute, and twist a song
　　　　　　　　Pleasant and long:
Or, since all musick is but three parts vied
　　　　　　　　And multiplied,
O let thy blessed Spirit bear a part,
And make up our defects with his sweet art.

I Got me flowers to straw thy way;
I got me boughs off many a tree:

But thou wast up by break of day,
And brought'st thy sweets along with thee.

The Sunne arising in the East,
Though he give light, & th' East perfume;
If they should offer to contest
With thy arising, they presume.

Can there be any day but this,
Though many sunnes to shine endeavour?
We count three hundred, but we misse:
There is but one, and that one ever.[7]

Like two other poems named for major Christian feast days—"Good Friday," and, later on, "Christmas"—this poem has a double structure. It consists of two parts, each of which could stand alone as a separate poem, but when they are placed together, as here, we see a relation between them—the first anticipates the second, the second answers the first. In this instance the first poem is a kind of invocation of the Muse, who will in the second sing the "song" that the first has called for.

As so often in Herbert, the speaker addresses his "heart," thus making visible from the outset the sense of dividedness of self that animates his work throughout: the speaker is not a complete self, but a part of a self addressing another part. He is the poet, the maker and speaker; the heart is the center of life and feeling and experience, the material of which an altar, a poem, a life is made. The heart is not the primary speaking part of the self, but it does have its own utterances: it is the heart that "grones," as we learned in "The Sinner," and here it is the heart that "sings." The speaker first calls upon his heart to rise—"Rise heart, thy Lord is risen"—as if it could simply rise, as Christ has risen, and with him. But it is more complicated than that: we quickly learn that the heart is called upon to rise not from death but from sleep, and it is to awake to a task: "Sing his praise." The apparently bold implication of the opening gesture, "Rise heart," is thus diluted to a hope, and to Christ's own wish, "that thou likewise with him mayst rise."

---

7. Notes:

1. *Just* includes "justified," as in "justified by faith alone."
2. *The same* means "the crosse."
3. *Three hundred* is of course roughly the number of days in a year.

But rise to what condition? "His life may make thee gold, and much more, just." This sounds less like a statement of hope than an argument, a reason for awaking, and it is cast in terms that seem dead and conclusory: gold is not an item of major value in any of these poems, and the speaker himself sees it as a misstep, moving on to "just," which not only means the opposite of unjust but also invokes, somewhat flatly, the Protestant principle of justification by faith. The poem has lost the freshness and life and confidence of the opening call—"Rise heart, thy Lord is risen"—though this is partly retrieved in the following stanzas.[8]

As the first stanza called upon the heart to rise, the second calls upon the lute to awake, and the third upon them both together to "twist a song / Pleasant and long," which is of course just what this poem is: an identification of elements, heart and lute, and their twisting together to make a song. But an odd note is struck when the speaker mentions the cross and the lute, the sinews and strings, as if each were similar to the other—the one teaching the other how to sound—for one pair is associated with song and Easter, the other with pain and the crucifixion. And he presents them in a way that makes prominent their radical differences in kind: What can the lute and string really have to do with the cross and the body? By the very grotesqueness of the image, and against the speaker's assertion, we are made to feel that the central experience of the cross is outside language and music alike.

Having put heart in one stanza, lute in a second, and joined them in a third, the speaker, perhaps reminded by his own treble structure, suddenly realizes that his effort is incomplete, for it is in the nature of music to have three voices: "thy blessed Spirit" is necessary to complete the consort, to supply the third element suggested by the image of braiding or twisting. But how are we to read this? The way he calls upon the "Spirit" here seems almost accidental or by the way—oh, we need a third voice, don't we?—rather than driven by the recognition of inherent inadequacy or need. The speaker here is like the artist of the imagination in "The Thanksgiving," captivated by the beauty of his own work, or like the speaker in "Redemption," stumbling upon the Passion and not wholly aware of the meaning of his own experience. On the other hand, to root the call in the very nature of music, in the

---

8. Compare the phrase, "who takes thee by the hand," with "Love" (III): "Love took my hand, and smiling did reply."

need the ear feels for something more, is reminiscent of the poems that reveal language to be a source of meaning external to the self, such as "Heaven" and "Paradise": it is a sign of grace at work in the world. The beauty and ease with which the speaker moves to this recognition, incomplete as it is, affirms his sense of grace at work.

The main feeling of this stanza, the intoxication with its own music, thus has a double signification: intoxication with art, and hence with self; and, in the other direction, openness to the miracle, so gently enacted here, by which the need for the "Spirit" insinuates itself into the consciousness. This double characteristic of art is perhaps the deepest tension in Herbert's verse: he is always aware that to write a poem is to assert the self, one's own will, and necessarily in a prideful way— the better the poem, the greater the pride—yet the fact that it can be done, that the language can be cast in these forms of truth and beauty, is the most consistently enacted ground of hope in a world of radical uncertainty. The poem inherently asserts itself as good in both senses of the term.

The "song" that makes up the second part of "Easter" is beautiful but painful. The voice of pastoral simplicity and naïveté, like that in a folk song, here expresses the kind of emotional exposure and trust we associate with a child: "I got me flowers to straw thy way." But there is nothing this speaker can do, no gift or gesture he can make, that is in any way significant or acceptable. Neither flower nor bough is of any consequence, for "thou . . . brought'st thy sweets along with thee." Just as the speaker in "The Reprisall" came to realize that he could not contest with Christ's suffering, so this speaker realizes that he cannot greet it with an adequate gift. Even the "Sunne" of the heavens—as opposed to that other "Sunne," the Son of God—cannot compete with, cannot stand against this fact. Nothing can; against it, all of our experience pales into insignificance: "There is but one, and that one ever." There is nothing one can do except to lose oneself in the event, and in the song.

But this is a song at once of praise and lament, for, like "Vertue," this poem necessarily asserts the value of what is here erased: of heart, and morning, and gold, and lute, and music, of the simple gift of a simple self. And against the sense of loss and insignificance alike is the poetry itself, asserting itself as a kind of music. One cannot contest, or bring gifts: but one can write a poem.

This series of poems, from "The Sacrifice" to "Easter," connect with each other in very much the way the poems connect across the book as a whole. At a general level there is a movement from a sense of inadequacy and hopelessness to one of acceptance and trust and the acknowledgement of love: here from the Passion to Easter, in the book as a whole from "The Sacrifice" to "Love" (III), or from the lust that obsesses the speaker of "The Church-porch," to love itself. "The Church" begins with Christ's voice on the cross, speaking to those who "passe by," and ends with the voice of Love, speaking to the "I" who has made these poems, welcoming him with smiling reassurance. But it is not only in the direction of the movement, but in its nature, that this series is representative: one poem, as we have seen, will answer another, picking up an image or phrase and developing it afresh, or responding to one dominant feeling by asserting another, and so it will be throughout. Often the movement of the poetry is toward greater knowledge or clarification, but sometimes it is not: the speaker of one poem will forget or occlude what a prior speaker learned. The connection among the poems is much less an order that marches in one direction in a straight line than a sequence like that of dreams, which refer to and build upon and erase one another in oblique and surprising ways, as the colors of oil on water shift, fluidly and as it were by their own motion.

It is in just such a way that Herbert moves from "Easter" to its successor, "Easter-wings."

Easter-wings

Lord, who createdst man in wealth and store,
Though foolishly he lost the same,
Decaying more and more,
Till he became
Most poore:
With thee
O let me rise
As larks, harmoniously,
And sing this day thy victories:
Then shall the fall further the flight in me.

My tender age in sorrow did beginne:
And still with sicknesses and shame
Thou didst so punish sinne,

> That I became
> Most thinne.
> With   thee
> Let me combine
> And feel this day thy victorie:
> For, if I imp my wing on thine,
> Affliction shall advance the flight in me.[9]

This is another poem with a double structure, but of a somewhat different kind: the second stanza does not so much answer the first, or respond to its call, as rewrite it in a different mode, to a different end. The first stanza has as its initial subject all of humanity, telling the story of the Fall of man and enacting it by the shrinking of the lines, until man is indeed "most poore." If this movement worked to its natural conclusion it would end in nothing at all, a blank line; this is the possibility from which the speaker prays to be saved, enacting his hope by the increased length of the lines: "O let me rise / As larks, harmoniously, / And sing this day thy victories." The shape of the whole is both that of the wings—of the lark, of Christ—seen on the page, and, as the poem is read in time, a kind of swoop and rise, in which the force of the fall increases the force of the ascent: "Then shall the fall further the flight in me." This sense of swoop and rise is reinforced

---

9. Notes:

1. Normally, following the 1633 edition, editors represent the stanzas as shrinking symmetrically on both sides, thus taking on the shape of an hour glass. In *W*, the manuscript Herbert saw and corrected, the right-hand margin remains straight, all the indentation taking place on the left. In *B*, perhaps reflecting Herbert's later choice, perhaps the view of the copier, the right-hand margin is slightly indented, more in the first than second stanza. Both manuscripts put the stanzas on facing pages and thus give a dramatic sense of flight sideways, as though a bird is crossing the sky; 1633 is by comparison static, and it emphasizes the vertical dimension. I have chosen here to follow *W*.

2. *Imp* is a technical term from falconry, meaning to engraft feathers on the wing of the bird. Compare *Richard II*, 2.1. 292–93, "If then we shall shake off our slavish yoke, / Imp out our country's broken wing."

3. *Wing* can sometimes mean feather, as in the phrase "birds of the same wing."

4. In both *W* and *B* the stanzas appear on facing pages and are separately headed with the title. Perhaps they are to be thought of as two paired poems, rather than two stanzas of a single poem. (On paired poems in general, see pages 153–69, below.)

by the rhymes: all strong *O* and *A* in the first half, *I* and *E* in the second, the first sound distinctly lower in pitch, the others higher.[10] It becomes a statement of the medieval doctrine of the *felix culpa*, the fortunate fall, without which there could not have been the wonderful display of love and grace in the life of Christ.

The second stanza is different both in subject and feeling: where the first told of the career of generic "man," who "foolishly lost" the "wealth and store" with which he began, this one speaks of the individual life of the speaker, "I," which began not in bliss but in "sorrow." Why in sorrow? The unstated possibilities are either that this is just how things are, without any moral significance at all—the brute fact of the universe— or that this sorrow is the consequence of the original sin described in the first stanza; it is not Adam's alone, we participate in it from birth. This doctrine, as stated, seems unjust—it depends upon the inheritability of sin, and where is the fairness in that?—and it is felt that way here. What did the speaker do to deserve his beginning in sorrow? The wasting away in this stanza is not the consequence of a natural process of decay, as it was in the first, but by the end is the affirmative result of the punishment of "sinne" (not "foolishness"). But by the end it is unclear whether the sin so punished is still Adam's or by now the speaker's own.

The rising portion of the stanza is different too: the hope is not to "rise" but to "combine," not to "sing" but to "feel" the victory, and the imagined success is that—at best—not "the fall" but "affliction" shall "advance the flight in me." The possibility that this may happen is reinforced by the structure of the verse, including the rhyme patterns, but undercut strongly in another way, for it is all expressly conditional, and what is worse, conditional upon an action defined by a word so obscure as to make it nearly impossible to imagine: "If I imp my wing on thine." The dictionaries tell us that "imping" is a process of fastening a feather to the wing of a falcon; but even that does not much help, for how does one imp a wing to a wing? Only if one wing is so small as to be like a feather to the other? The hopeful possibilities are further eroded by the more usual implications of "imp," which of course means

---

10. See generally John Frederick Nims, *Western Wind: An Introduction to Poetry*, 2d ed. (New York: Random House, 1983), 161–63. Nims proposes this exercise to demonstrate the relative pitches of the vowels: "*Whisper* the words 'June,' 'Joan,' 'John,' 'Jan,' 'Jen,' 'Gin,' 'Jane,' 'Jean' in that order. Can you feel how the vowel sounds move progressively up the scale? Now *whisper* them in reversed order. Can you feel them move down the scale?" (Page 180).

a small devilish creature, and by the partial loss of alliteration, which made the ending of the first stanza seem so strong: "Then shall the fall further the flight in me" becomes "Then shall affliction advance the flight in me." After "affliction" and "advance" we expect another word beginning with *a*, but get "flight." And "affliction" is a poor substitute for "fall," since it does not give rise to the sense of swoop and rise.

The poem moves, as Herbert's often do, from initiating a possible action in response to the God he imagines—here, as often, making a song or poem—to a recognition of its impossibility, or worthlessness, after all. The movement is in the direction of difficulty or bleakness, toward the affirmation that suffering is inflicted by this God on the children of Adam, inescapably, with only the most qualified hope that this Fall too may prove to be fortunate. The poem moves by rewriting, as it is itself a rewriting of "Easter," rendering the wonderful moment of conclusion of that poem far more problematic and uncertain, and launching the reader on a far more difficult process than the opening sequence of poems may suggest.

Before going further with the poems themselves, it may be good to return for a moment to a problem raised earlier, when I suggested that the poems that follow "The Sacrifice" are all attempts, all imperfect, to respond to that event, and that as such they speak for us as readers, who likewise must ask how we respond to "The Sacrifice." But is this to confuse two things, the poem entitled "The Sacrifice," to which indeed it asks that we respond, and the underlying events of which it speaks, real or imagined, to which we need not respond at all if we choose not to do so? The poem is real, of course, and asks to be responded to; and as the succeeding poems answer it, they do indeed mark out possibilities with which to compare our own. But why need we respond to the historical fact of the crucifixion of Jesus, if indeed it is a fact, and especially why need we respond to it as if it were the death of the Son of God and not merely the execution of a religious fanatic?

I think this distinction between the poem and what it assumes to be true in the world is not possible, at least in so easy a form, because we cannot engage with a story or a poem—or an argument either, for that matter—without accepting, for the moment at least, the premises on which it works, and as the writer builds upon those premises we find ourselves more and more implicated in them. I am reminded here of what it is like to read a legal case about the law of slavery in the

United States, say from Alabama in 1833: of course I reject many of the premises upon which the case proceeds, but nonetheless as a lawyer reading it I find myself thinking of lines of criticism, of argument and analysis, that work within the discourse on its own terms. This happens even with opinions of the United States Supreme Court: for example, in thinking as a lawyer about the 1842 opinion of Justice Story in *Prigg v. Pennsylvania,* a case that upheld the right of a slave owner to forcibly kidnap her runaway slave on free soil, I have found it difficult, if not impossible, not to find myself speaking of the "legitimate rights"—as opposed to the arguably illegitimate claim made there—of slave owners to their slaves. For under the Constitution as it then existed there were indeed such legitimate rights.[11] To live in the language is to affirm its terms and presuppositions.

Something similar happens I think when one reads "The Sacrifice" and the sequence of poems built upon it: they make sense in terms of each other, but only if the language they speak is accepted as a language one can imagine actually using. One cannot read these poems without thinking of the Passion, the death on Good Friday, the Resurrection at Easter, as if they were real, and without seeing that they give rise to real difficulties of interpretation and understanding, difficulties on which thought and argument is possible. One is then in the position of seeing that sensible things can be said in the language and imagery of Christianity; one has in fact used that language to make sense. One has begun to learn the language of Christianity, and like every language it has its own reality. Of course you can turn from this to your usual ways of talking, just as you can turn from Arabic to English: but you remain one to whom things said in Arabic or Christianity—or the language of slavery—once made sense, engaging both your mind and your feelings. So then where are you? In a position in which some of your innocence is lost: saying that this way of talking makes sense here, in this context, not there, in that one. This is true of all languages, but in the case of theological languages we often resist admitting it, either because we are believers who want to insist upon the universality of our language— this is always true, this always makes sense—or because we are unbelievers who do not want to admit that we have submitted our minds, ever or in any way, to a language of theology.

---

11. For more on this case, see my *Justice as Translation: An Essay in Cultural and Legal Criticism* (Chicago: University of Chicago Press, 1990), chap. 5.

As Herbert is read today—and the same would be true of Milton, of course, or any other religious writer of his time—he speaks to an audience differently situated from his own contemporaries, for whom the language of Christianity was the totalizing and dominant discourse. This is true of none or few of us. But, whether we like to admit it or not, he gives us an experience of theological language that cannot simply be erased. Having read Herbert I am in the position of having said, and meant it, that great things can be done in this language, and I don't mean great things for others: my own mind, my own heart, have been given experiences they would not otherwise have had. In reading Herbert this language makes sense; in the world in which we awake, after doing so, for most of us, it does not. The reader of Herbert is in this way placed in a situation like that of many practicing Christians, who likewise feel that what they say in church, or on religious occasions, or in their prayers, makes perfect sense; that the way they talk at the office, with their colleagues, or in a business relation, likewise makes perfect sense; but that there is an impossible discontinuity between those two situations. A capacity to tolerate such contradictions is required, I think, for the reader of Herbert; it may be one of the great merits of his verse, indeed, that it can help us develop it.

"Holy Baptisme" to "Antiphon"

The first sequence of poems, through "Easter" and "Easter-wings," seems to work as a promise cast in familiar theological terms: that the sacrifice on the cross, and the suffering and loss it entails, will become the triumph of Easter. This movement mirrors what will be the general direction of "The Church" as a whole, from "The Sacrifice" to "Love" (III). But against this dominant narrative line is run the insistent question, What can this mean to us, or rather to me, I who cannot grieve adequately, or sympathize, I who never stop asserting my own needs and imagination, I who am in fact erased by the fact of Easter? "We count three hundred, but we misse; / There is but one, and that day ever." "Easter-wings" makes this note even more prominent and disturbing, as we have seen, and the poems that follow make a new beginning. As the title of the first two poems, "Holy Baptisme," suggests, we here pick up a different narrative line, not the story of Christ, but the career of the individual person, beginning with the first sacrament.

North door of the church at Leighton Bromswold

Holy Baptisme (I)

As he that sees a dark and shadie grove,
Stayes not, but looks beyond it on the skie;
So when I view my sinnes, mine eyes remove
More backward still, and to that water flie,
Which is above the heav'ns, whose spring and vent
Is in my deare Redeemers pierced side.
O blessed streams! either ye do prevent
And stop our sinnes from growing thick and wide,
Or else give tears to drown them, as they grow.
In you Redemption measures all my time,
And spreads the plaister equall to the crime.
You taught the Book of Life my name, that so

What ever future sinnes should me miscall,
Your first acquaintance might discredit all.

This poem is built on a decidedly awkward set of metaphors: as one who sees "a dark and shadie grove" rests not his eyes upon it but looks beyond it "on the skie," so, the speaker says, when I view my sins I look back beyond them to that "water . . . which is above the heav'ns"; this water springs from my "Redeemers pierced side," and makes "streams" that either "prevent . . . our sins from growing thick and wide"—exactly how, it is most unclear—or else "give tears to drown them." This is odd for another reason, which is that if sins indeed grow, like plants, water should help them. Finally, we are told, "Redemption measures all my time, / And spreads the plaister equall to the crime," reducing the action of grace to a kind of Band-Aid.

This is I think an impossible poem—the first of which we can say that—and it comes as a real shock after the extraordinarily accomplished quality of the series leading up to "Easter-wings." But it is impossible in ways that the reader, trained by what we have read so far, is able to perceive, and much of its meaning resides in that very fact, in the way it tests and rewards the developing capacity of the reader to understand Herbert's poetic language. One clue lies in the wildly incongruous set of images—this is poetry gone wrong by any measure—another in the couplet where we see the speaker imagining himself "miscalled" by sins: he imagines himself as innocent, and baptism as a protection against false charges, rather than, as readers of Herbert know he should see himself, as all too full of sin and guilt. This poem is a kind of distorted failure to make sense; it thus enacts, in the structure of "The Church" itself, the kind of "fall" of which "Easter-wings" spoke, a collapse to a position from which life must begin again. As readers too we start again in the midst of distortion and confusion, but this time with the training in reading that the earlier poems have given us. We know, for example, to read this poem as a dramatic monologue, to see the speaker not as "Herbert" but as a part of him, and to see the whole thing as presenting us with a problem, not a solution. The poem speaks of being "miscalled": this in fact identifies its own activity, for it is itself a series of "miscallings," though this profusion of the inappropriate occurs within the tight formal structure of the sonnet, enacting a kind of coherence that the sequence of images seems to erode.

The next poem, also entitled "Holy Baptisme," performs the central trope in Herbert's poetry, namely rewriting, for it is another attempt at the same subject, with the same title:

Holy Baptisme (II)

S ince, Lord, to thee
A narrow way and little gate
Is all the passage, on my infancie
Thou didst lay hold, and antedate
My faith in me.

O let me still
Write thee great God, and me a childe:
Let me be soft and supple to thy will,
Small to my self, to others milde,
Behither ill.

Although by stealth
My flesh get on, yet let her sister
My soul bid nothing, but preserve her wealth:
The growth of flesh is but a blister;
Childhood is health.

The speaker here asks that he be allowed to remain in—or to return to—that state of childhood at which baptism did "antedate my faith in me," that is, when it either preceded the faith he later found as an adult, or, more grimly, supplied for the moment his permanent defect of faith. "Let me be soft and supple to thy will, / Small to myself, to others milde." The conceit continues with the idea that although "my flesh get on" by stealth, "her sister, my soul" asks nothing but the preservation of "her wealth," that is, her condition of "infancie." "The growth of flesh is but a blister; / Childhood is health."

This poem is certainly less twisted than the first, but it is still odd: one cannot remain an infant, nor would it be good to do so; and the very idea of "blister" derives from the physical body the speaker here rejects, undermining his use of the word "health." This is not a healthy speaker. Yet the poem does capture something of the miracle of baptism, that one's own sure-to-be-defective faith is for the moment rendered unnecessary, in a gesture of love for a child. But while baptism is indeed a recognition of our natural limits, its shadow side is that we outgrow its protection, which is withdrawn from us as adults; then our nature no longer excuses but condemns us, and we are ready to be addressed in the wholly different form of the Sacrifice.

One can read these two poems as the expression of a mind trying to work its way out of its own imperfect formulations and feelings, and doing so incompletely, both within each poem and across them both. This is a movement that is repeated over and over again throughout "The Church": a series of poems will work towards a kind of clarification or resolution, as the opening series did, only to be followed by a poem whose speaker seems to know nothing of what we have just painfully worked towards. We begin all over again, sometimes, as here, at a far lower point than the preceding series itself began. Such, for Herbert, is the nature of human thought and experience: not moving by increments towards a goal, but slipping and sliding, forgetting what was known, and beginning again, sometimes in greater confusion.

"Nature," which follows the baptism poems, in a small way concludes the process begun in them:

Nature

Full of rebellion, I would die,
　Or fight, or travell, or denie
That thou hast ought to do with me.
　　　　　　　O tame my heart;
　　　　　It is thy highest art
To captivate strong holds to thee.

If thou shalt let this venome lurk,
And in suggestions fume and work,
My soul will turn to bubbles straight,
　　　　　　　And thence by kinde
　　　　　Vanish into a winde,
Making thy workmanship deceit.

O smooth my rugged heart, and there
Engrave thy rev'rend Law and fear;
Or make a new one, since the old
　　　　　　　Is saplesse grown,
　　　　　And a much fitter stone
To hide my dust, then thee to hold.

This poem makes explicit the feelings of anger and fear that might well lead someone to say, as the speaker in the second "Baptisme" did, that he wished he were a child again. Being an adult, for this speaker at least, means being full of rebellious feelings, from which he needs redemption, if not by returning to "infancie," by direct action now. The three poems just discussed thus work as a progressive uncovering of what is at first hidden from the speaker: in the first, the speaker seems to deny his own sinfulness, casting his fear in terms of being "miscalled"; in the second, he can admit enough of his sense of defect to wish, impossibly, that he could escape by becoming a child again; now, in the third—rightly entitled "Nature," for that is the source of the problem—he can see and say much more clearly that the problem is within, that what he needs is not protection against false charges but amendment of the self, the replacement of the "stone" his heart has become with another, this one engraved with "thy rev'rend Law." But even here he does not quite see that what is required is not a substitution, but a transformation of one thing into another.

In moving from one point to another these three poems make a pattern of their own, in this case one of increasing but incomplete enlightenment. They can be read as engaging us in error and its correction, and in this way as offering us a kind of education. How much is Herbert in control of this process? If "Holy Baptisme" (I) represents as confused a state of mind as I suggest, especially following the great clarifications of "Easter" and "Easter-wings," are we to think that Herbert deliberately wrote this poem "badly," and placed it there as a way of catching us in a confusion he could then clarify? If so, we could read this poem as we do the opening chapter, say, of Jane Austen's *Emma,* meant to define a confused and distorted point of view into which, and out of which, it will be the artist's task to lead us. Jane Austen is in control all the way, even if unconsciously so, as we discover when we learn how to correct our misreadings, not only of Emma herself but of many others in the book.

But this is not the sense one has of Herbert. Rather, the confusions into which he leads us are his own. How are we to regard this fact? From one point of view, there is less conscious control than there is in Austen, say, or Shakespeare, and in this sense less art; from another, as with the essays of Samuel Johnson referred to earlier, this work has the tremendous appeal of authenticity, offering direct engagement with the struggles of another mind. I think Herbert does not see at the outset exactly what is wrong, say, with "The Church-porch" or "Holy Baptisme" (I), so much as feel that something is, without quite knowing what; he then works his way out of it, by stages and with frequent relapses, in the process discovering what he shows us. As he works, we come to see the movements as made by art after all; not by a master hand, in control from the beginning, but by a master heart, struggling with itself towards clarification.

The fact that no one voice has ultimate authority, that the best voice of all is a groan, or a prayer, or a song of the heart in no words, or in simple ones, locates us as readers in a world analogous to his, in which the supposed stabilities of self and language are dissolved. The question this experience raises is how to live on such conditions as these, and this it is the object of his verse to answer, first for Herbert himself, then for his audience. He speaks out of disintegration, moving towards wholeness of mind against both the habits of his culture and the force of his languages. That there are poems that do not resolve, but leave us and him in as bad a state as he began, or in a worse one still, and that even the clarifications that follow are incomplete, is not an indictment of his art but an essential ingredient of it. Likewise one's sense that the conflicts and dissolutions and erasures he experiences are real for him does not diminish but enhances their value. Ultimately, the test of a design within a poem, or across a set of poems, is not whether the author had it in mind when he began, or even recognized it as he wrote, but whether it is there. It is the meaning of the work to us with which we are finally concerned, after all. This is the other side of Blake's vision of art, which holds the artist responsible for every detail of what he has done.[12]

In the second stanza of "Nature" the speaker makes an argument appealing to God's self-interest as creator: if he is not "captivated," the speaker says, his soul will disappear into a wind, "making thy workmanship deceit." This is the kind of false argument a child will sometimes use to a parent, based on the supposed self-interest of the other; what it really expresses is that he is unable to appeal to love, often because he is so full of angry or other unpleasant feelings that he thinks himself inherently unlovable. Here the speaker brings himself to see some of

---

12. "As Poetry admits not a Letter that is Insignificant, so Painting admits not a Grain of Sand or a Blade of Grass Insignificant—much less an Insignificant Blur or Mark." William Blake, *A Vision of the Last Judgment*, in *Selected Poetry and Prose of William Blake*, ed. Northrop Frye (New York: Modern Library, 1953), 394.

this, thus beginning to recognize the reality of sin, conceived of not as misconduct or wrongdoing, but as a state of the heart. Its destructive origins lie not outside in the world, but within. He has thus established the theme of the poem that follows.

Sinne (I)

L ord, with what care hast thou begirt us round!
Parents first season us: then schoolmasters
   Deliver us to laws; they send us bound
To rules of reason, holy messengers,
Pulpits and Sundayes, sorrow dogging sinne,
   Afflictions sorted, anguish of all sizes,
   Fine nets and stratagems to catch us in,
Bibles laid open, millions of surprises,
Blessings beforehand, tyes of gratefulnesse,
   The sound of glorie ringing in our eares:
   Without, our shame; within, our consciences;
Angels and grace, eternall hopes and fears.
   Yet all these fences and their whole aray
   One cunning bosome-sinne blows quite away.

This poem has the form—we shall see it again in Herbert—of a listing of items. The way it works on the reader is this: as the items are listed we become absorbed in trying to apprehend them, and, since they do not all seem to fit together, we are occupied in judging their appropriateness until our mind is overflowing; the closing couplet then takes us by surprise and sweeps our mind of these things, just as sin sweeps away their effects in the world.

The list is wonderful, especially the great and simple line: "The sound of glorie ringing in our eares," which is made great and simple, as readers of "Jordan" will recognize, by the intellectual and moral complexity of the rest of the poem.[13] And there are real puzzles or shocks too, as when we are told that among the good things that protect us are: "sorrow dogging sinne, / Afflictions sorted, anguish of all sizes." These, listed almost as items for sale in a milliner's shop, are among

---

13. This phrase also has the incidental effect that it will make us hear slightly differently the closing lines of "The Windows": "but speech alone / Doth vanish like a flaring thing, / And in the eare, not conscience ring."

the "millions of surprises" the poem promises us. Behind this is another and more ominous sense, that sin is what we naturally like and that we have to be prevented from committing it by constraints. The child needs to be taught goodness in an overbearing and somewhat adversarial way, which of course defines goodness itself not as something that springs from the heart, like love, but as compliance with a structure of commands, perhaps in the form of teachings like those in "The Church-porch." No wonder the "cunning bosome-sinne" blows it quite away, and not an altogether bad thing either.

"Affliction" (I), coming next, develops the idea of "Sinne" that "afflictions sorted, anguish of all sizes" are, or can be, blessings. That poem, as you will remember from the discussion at pages 25–30, tells the story of the speaker's enticement into service—"at first thou gav'st me milk and sweetnesses; / I had my wish and way"—and subsequent betrayal into pain and sickness and bereavement. "Thus thinne and lean without a fence or friend, / I was blown through with ev'ry storm and winde." But the effect of the afflictions of which he complains is to transform his radical self-centeredness into a genuine wish to serve: "I . . . wish I were a tree; / For sure then I should grow / To fruit or shade: at least some bird would trust / Her houshold to me, and I should be just." The poem is written from the point of view of the sentient self, the part of us that shapes our lives—as the close of "The Church-porch" in fact invited us to do—by "joy" and "pain." But this ineradicable instinct, an essential part of our nature, is here marked as ignorance and sin. As in "The Thanksgiving," the breakdown of the assertive and feeling self, against its will, is an act of grace; the best utterance of which we are capable is the cry from the heart:

> Ah my deare God! though I am clean forgot,
> Let me not love thee, if I love thee not.

The next two poems, "Repentance" and "Faith," work shifts and modulations of attitude of just the sort we are learning to expect, in which the speaker, trying to do the right thing, involves himself in increased confusion. In "Repentance," for example, the speaker recoils from the point at which "Affliction" ends, especially from the idea that pain and suffering can work as blessings:

> L ord, I confesse my sinne is great;
>   Great is my sinne. Oh! gently treat

> With thy quick flow'r, thy momentarie bloom;
>> Whose life still pressing
>> Is one undressing,
> A steadie aiming at a tombe.

While the speaker can begin with exactly the statement that the speaker in "Holy Baptisme" (II) could not make—"Lord, I confesse my sinne is great; / Great is my sinne"—the gesture itself is highly stagy, as though this dramatic assertion of piety will itself carry the day. Equally important, what he asks for is to be gently treated, which is inconsistent with what was learned in "Affliction." In fact the poem as a whole to a large degree consists of pleadings for mercy: "Cut me not off for my most foul transgression;" "Sweeten at length this bitter bowl;" and so forth. The correction, such as it is, comes in the final stanza, in which the speaker works himself towards the point he reached in "Affliction," but this time does not quite make it:

> But thou wilt sinne and grief destroy;
> That so the broken bones may joy,
> And tune together in a well-set song,
>> Full of his praises,
>> Who dead men raises.
> Fractures well cur'd make us more strong.

Here the speaker sees that the very punishment he has wanted to avoid is, or can be, ultimately beneficial: "Fractures well cur'd make us more strong." But to put it that way undermines his claim, for what he says is not true in the first place, and even if it were who would break a bone to strengthen it? And, more frightening still, who can promise that our fractures will in fact be "well cur'd"? There is an implicit conditional here, as we have seen elsewhere, which works as a threat, all the more serious because unstated.

"Faith" works in the other direction, beginning in a kind of self-centeredness out of which the speaker will try to write himself. Here, for example, are the terms in which he praises faith early on:

> Hungrie I was, and had no meat:
> I did conceit a most delicious feast;
> I had it straight, and did as truly eat,

As ever did a welcome guest.
. . . .

I owed thousands and much more:
I did beleeve that I did nothing owe,
And liv'd accordingly; my creditor
  Beleeves so too, and lets me go.

For this speaker faith is a kind of magic, which can make food appear
on a table, or debts disappear. It is a power of the imagination or the
fancy: he has only to pretend that something is so, and it becomes so.
What adds force and poignancy to the poem is that what is at the
material or social level crazy—that meals can be produced, debts cheer-
fully dissolved by an act of the imagination—is at the spiritual level for
Herbert nothing less than true: the simplest meal, the Eucharist, is a
truly sacred event, our debts are indeed forgiven us, faith can move
mountains. The very craziness of these claims, as imagined by this
speaker, is a way of defining something very different indeed, their
miraculous nature, as that is perceived by us, the readers: "Crazy, but
true!" Yet the craziness of the speaker remains, for he talks as though
these miraculous transformations were all his doing, and perhaps we
cannot help feeling, "If crazy, how possibly true?"

These stanzas supply the material that is rewritten in what follows.
"Faith makes me any thing," he first says, but then goes on to reframe
it, "or all / That I beleeve is in the sacred storie." Faith is not a
universal magic, then, but works only in accordance with something
outside the speaker, namely "the sacred storie"—the same story that in
"The Windows" was "annealed in glasse," and in the preacher too.
This is a movement in the direction of discipline, for faith is now seen
not as an instrument of fancy but as a force that works from the outside:
"Where sinne placeth me in Adams fall, / Faith sets me higher in his
glorie."

A second shift of imagination presents faith as a great leveler of human
conditions:

A peasant may beleeve as much
As a great Clerk, and reach the highest stature.
Thus dost thou make proud knowledge bend & crouch,
  While grace fills up uneven nature.

It is a miracle of faith that it can cut through all the distinctions we normally make in creating and managing our social worlds. But these verses, uttered as if they were reassuring, actually state a threatening truth, that all the speaker's skill and education, including in poetry, may in the end count for nothing, compared to simple belief. And faith is not after all a magical power of the speaker, but the work of God, and now receives its proper name: "grace." This is wonderful but also disturbing, for it strips us of capacity and distinction. Knowledge and the status it brings—no small matters to the Orator of the University of Cambridge—are rendered trivial.[14]

The movement towards truth in this poem is a movement towards bleakness of vision as well: the speaker recognizes the fear that he has partly suppressed, and comes to see that all virtue, all good action, has its origins outside of us and that therefore we can do nothing ourselves to address that fear. "Faith" is not an instrument of our power, as he thought, but another word for "grace," which is God's action, not to be appropriated by us. In retrospect the crazy opening stanzas read differently: we can now see not only that they are, as I said above, crazy but true, but that it is a measure of the miracle described that grace is extended even to such a one as this speaker, who is at this precise moment captured by his self-aggrandizing imagination. "I did beleeve that I did nothing owe, / And liv'd accordingly." That phrase can now be read with a kind of dread, the reader aware of its significance in a way that the speaker—like an actor in a Greek tragedy—is not.

A poem like this asks to be read not as the coherent utterance of a stable mind, but as an internal drama, the very subject of which is the fluctuating state of the speaker's being, as this is defined or reflected in his various actions with language. It is a form of simultaneous expression and criticism, and its criticism reaches beyond its own particular utterances to any human speech: for every act with language is a definition of self and context alike, including one's various audiences, and can be judged as such. The poem teaches its reader the process of partial self-correction it enacts, for to read it all one must reconstruct the feelings that drive it, including those that are being resisted or denied, and their evolution through the self-transforming rewritings. No firm and stable end is ever reached, in part because the very act of writing or saying anything, including a poem like this one, entails an assertion of the self

---

14. For more on the dangers of our claims to knowledge see "Vanitie" and "The Pearl."

and the imagination, of which the fantasies of the speaker at the beginning of "Faith" are only an extreme example. What can we hope for, then?

Prayer (I)

Prayer the Churches banquet, Angels age,
　Gods breath in man returning to his birth,
　　The soul in paraphrase, heart in pilgrimage,
The Christian plummet sounding heav'n and earth;
Engine against th' Almightie, sinners towre,
　Reversed thunder, Christ-side-piercing spear,
　　The six-daies world transposing in an houre,
A kinde of tune, which all things heare and fear;
Softnesse, and peace, and joy, and love, and blisse,
　Exalted Manna, gladnesse of the best,
　　Heaven in ordinarie, man well drest,
The milkie way, the bird of Paradise,
　Church-bels beyond the starres heard, the souls bloud,
　　The land of spices; something understood.

This is another listing poem, both recalling and matching "Sinne," as a kind of twin. As in that poem the items, here splendid, pile up in the mind of the reader, who is bewildered or overwhelmed in the attempt to sort them out, until the closing gesture, here even more abrupt than there, which redefines them all—this time not by sweeping them away, for the closing phrase is not opposed to what has gone before, but by asserting that all the imagination can do at its best, as here performed, is to achieve, not full knowledge, but "something understood." This simple phrase—like *"My God, My King"* in "Jordan," like "Softnesse, and peace, and joy, and love, and blisse" in "Prayer" itself—derives both its force and its simplicity from the context in which it appears. It thus enacts the familiar tension in Herbert's verse between the knowledge that the imagination is limited, self-centered, and flawed, and the knowledge that it is all we have with which to face the world.

As "Sinne" included the "surprise" of treating "afflictions sorted, anguish of all sizes" as good things, this poem has the surprise of the second stanza, in which prayer is itself seen as a form of self-assertion against the Almighty, indeed as a form of hostile action. This is a theme we have seen before, especially in "The Reprisall," and will see again, especially in "Artillerie." Prayer—even prayer—will always be unjust in

two ways: in that we always deserve worse than we ask; and that the
act of prayer is itself an act, like that of the speaker in "Repentance"
or "Faith," in which we assert self-will and self-nature. And despite its
spare and humble conclusion, this poem is just such an act too. The
display of wonderful images excites admiration not only for prayer, and
God, but for the poet, who finds such amazing resources with which
to define the indefinable. And in the central portion, where prayer is
seen as our weapon against God, the speaker verges on a kind of Faustian
defiance, asserting the value of the human mind and will against the
one whom he can here only imagine as a God of power, not love. Only
then does he speak of "softnesse, and peace, and joy, and love, and
blisse," in a gesture of harmony and reconciliation that derives much of
its meaning from the momentary rebellion that precedes it.

"The Holy Communion," the next poem in the sequence, is a double
poem, like "Good Friday" and "Easter," in which one part answers
another. In this case the first part achieves a clarification that the second
undoes; but it can work the other way as well. This kind of structure
is itself a trope, or mode of expression, that enacts the antiphonal quality
of Herbert's verse more generally: voice answers voice, one version of
a poem answers another, in a perpetual rewriting of the same impulses,
fears, and hopes. It follows "Prayer" and precedes "Antiphon," making
up a small sequence of three poems about the liturgy itself: first prayer,
then the Eucharist, then song.

The speaker in "The Holy Communion" describes what happens in
the Eucharist first by saying that it is "not in rich furniture, or fine
array" that "thou . . . dost now thy self convey," but physically:

> But by the way of nourishment and strength
>   Thou creep'st into my breast;
>   Making thy way my rest,
>   And thy small quantities my length;
> Which spread their forces into every part,
>   Meeting sinnes force and art.

It is through the elements of bread and wine, actually ingested, that
God is present to us, not in architecture, ritual, or vestments: Otherwise,
"thou should'st without me still have been, / Leaving within me sinne."
This sense of physicality recalls the closing lines of "The Agonie":
"Love is that liquour sweet and most divine, / Which my God feels

as bloud; but I, as wine." But there the emphasis was oral, on the response of the mouth to blood or to wine, here it is more fully corporeal, as the verse, in its spreading on the page, imitates the spread of wine's warmth through the body. But the speaker next recognizes that the wine cannot ever reach the soul: what works on it is grace, which is not physical after all. "Onely thy grace, which with these elements comes, / Knoweth the ready way." In both stages the emphasis is on what happens outside language, not in words but beyond them, in the body or the soul; throughout, the actor is not the speaker but God. These are positions to which Herbert must struggle again and again.

In the second part of the poem, written in folk-song or hymn-tune rhythms, like the second part of "Easter," he imagines what things were like before the Fall, when "sinne turn'd flesh to stone": surely Adam, who "did not know / To sinne, or sinne to smother" might then have gone to heaven from Paradise, "As from one room t'another." This in turn gives him his language for describing what the Eucharist does:

> Thou hast restor'd us to this ease
>   By this thy heav'nly bloud;
> Which I can go to, when I please,
>   And leave th' earth to their food.

This rewriting moves the speaker not forward but backward, to the language and mood of self-centeredness out of which it has been Herbert's usual effort to write himself. For to think of the effect of the Holy Communion—which is itself another version of the Sacrifice with which the book of poems begins—as contributing to his "ease" is not the point at which Herbert normally hopes to conclude, even when "ease" is read in the seventeenth-century sense of the term, meaning release from pain—as in "eased the smart"—rather than with our own cluster of associations, such as "easy" and "take your ease." This point is emphasized by the rhyme with "when I please," which itself makes the human will a central value and perhaps as well by the conclusion—"and leave th' earth to their food"—which is not only lame and awkward in rhythm but closes with a word that in this context can only sound ugly. The movement across the two poems here is from a state of relative wisdom and acceptance to self-centeredness and distortion; not of a willful or abnormal kind, however, quite the reverse of that—to a condition so natural that we cannot hope to escape it.

Reading this poetry works on the reader—on this reader at least—as a very slow education of the heart. Certainly it is a mistake to find the meaning of a poem in the religious doctrine it assumes or asserts, as though it existed to prove propositions; the meaning is rather in our experience of the process by which the mind of the poet tries to come to terms with itself, with its language, and with its audiences, divine and human. And this experience is naturally a slow one. I think I am not the only person for whom in reading Herbert time itself seems to change its pace and quality, almost as though one had entered another dimension. This is not surprising, for these poems work not only upon the quick and assertive mind, but upon the heart and imagination, where change takes place slowly if at all.

"Antiphon" (I) concludes, as I read it, not only the short sequence beginning with "Prayer," but the whole series from "Easter-wings":

Antiphon (I)

Cho.   Let all the world in ev'ry corner sing,
               My God and King.

Vers. The heav'ns are not too high,
      His praise may thither flie:
      The earth is not too low,
      His praises there may grow.

Cho. Let all the world in ev'ry corner sing,
               My God and King.

Vers. The church with psalms must shout,
      No doore can keep them out:
      But above all, the heart
      Must bear the longest part.

Cho. Let all the world in ev'ry corner sing,
               My God and King.

This is a kind of closure—it would work as a recessional hymn—in part because it represents a move from verse to music, from words to what lies beyond words. It anticipates the echoings of "Heaven," with which "The Church" itself will end. Its refrain is a gesture of finality, for us recalling the "*My God, My King*" of "Jordan" (I), with the poems that precede it providing the context that makes this sort of simplicity possible and meaningful. The serenity of this utterance is qualified as well by the gentle admonishment, "the heart / Must bear the longest part," a large qualification indeed, for what is said is that the heart must do more than heaven, than earth, than the church. As in "Easter-wings" the focus is on us, small as we are. But it reminds us of something else as well, as we saw in "Easter" too, that the heart cannot only "grone" but sing.

Herbert's Way of Writing

I suggested at the beginning of this book that we might conceive of the work we do as readers of poetry as "learning the language" of another. By this I do not mean merely the special meaning that a writer gives to particular words, though that is part of it: think of the associations Herbert has given "heart" and "stone" in what we have already read, for example. Nor is it only a matter of grammar and syntax, though that too can be part of it. As Cristanne Miller shows, for example, much of the meaning of Emily Dickinson's poetry comes from its grammatical oddities: tenseless verbs that give a sense of timeless truth; self-evidently missing terms, some of which can be recovered, others of which stand as absent spaces to be filled with a range of possibilities; extraordinary repetition, compression, and disjunction; novel punctuation; nouns used as verbs, verbs as nouns; pronouns without antecedents; and so forth.[15] Herbert's work too could be analyzed in such terms; in some of these respects, indeed, he may have been a precursor of Emily Dickinson herself.

By "language" I mean to include more even than these things: voice and gesture, form and tone, in fact all the resources of meaning that the poet employs, including the collapse of language into a "grone" or silence itself. (Recall the end of "The Thanksgiving": "Then for thy passion—I will do for that— / Alas, my God, I know not what.") The

---

15. Cristanne Miller, *Emily Dickinson: A Poet's Grammar* (Cambridge, Mass.: Harvard University Press, 1987). See also Alice Fulton, "Her Moment of Brocade: The Reconstruction of Emily Dickinson," *Parnassus*, 15, (1989): 9–44, which reads poem number 340 in particular as a structure of elaborately defined counterpossibilities.

The similarity between these two poets is worth developing, for Herbert was one of Dickinson's favorite poets and can be seen I think to have influenced her, including in this. For a brief comparison see Miller, *Emily Dickinson*, 160–61. For further discussion of Dickinson and Herbert, see pages 187–88 below.

Fountain in the cloister at Westminster, between the school and the abbey

question we can ask now, having read almost thirty of Herbert's poems, including the two long opening sequences, is what expectations we can properly form about the language of this poetry and the way it works. What are the gestures and voices, the terms and relations, out of which it is made? What is it like to attune oneself to these things?

To begin with—as our reading of "Vertue" showed us and all the other poems confirm—we should now know that it would be a great mistake to accept the image of Herbert as a poet of simple piety, performing his pure devotions. His is a mind, like Shakespeare's, that can hardly say anything at all without instantly affirming its opposite. Far from the cozy and gently pious poetry that at least one tradition attributes to him, Herbert's work is about as tough as it is possible to be: tough on his language and inheritance, tough on himself. The very promises of faith themselves are seen as bleak and empty at the same time that they are affirmed as miraculous and redemptive. It is not that he poses disbelief against belief—nothing that easy—but rather that he believes, and shows us what that means.

This is a poetry rooted not in calm confidence, then, but in conflict and uncertainty and struggle, and our sense of its instability is sharpened when we realize that the speaker in these poems is not simply Herbert himself, but a range of voices asserting themselves, answering each other, often in conflict, with Herbert on all sides. The self from which these poems come is not one but many; innumerable really, for each poem is made of its own voices, and one has the sense that a new poem, if it were found, would present a new set of voices and variations.

The poems are written with an acute sense of their own impossibility in another respect as well, for what poem, what verbal formulation, could possibly express or capture the nature of the infinite and eternal, of the inexpressible, or of a person's relation with it? Devotional poetry in the usual sense is false and sentimental, for to write truly of one's God is in the nature of things impossible. More than this: the effort of all poetry, even Herbert's poetry, is always in part misguided, for it directs attention to what happens in words, in language, when what really matters happens in the heart—the heart that in Herbert never speaks, except in "grones" or songs, but is often spoken to—in a place beyond words. Still worse: it is the nature of poetry itself to stimulate in its author a kind of misplaced pride in his work. What would be best would be the simplest gesture, in words or in life: "*My God, My King*" or a simple effort to "copie out onely that." Yet words are necessary to the very definition of simplicity, and language is necessary to the meaning of silence itself; we cannot evade them. Imperfect as both are, doctrine and life require each other.

We naturally lead our lives by seeking the pleasant and avoiding the painful, but even these most essential categories of thought—affirmed at the close of "The Church-porch"—are flawed. As Herbert makes so apparent in "Affliction," what is painful may be good, what we seek as good may do us harm, and we can never know for certain which is which. It is out of such a sense of confusion and uncertainty—as to himself, his language, his motives, his God—that Herbert writes his poems. As the voices within them answer each other, so the poems answer each other, never conclusively, but always with a kind of essential ambivalence reaching in the end the very act of making a poem itself. For if it is thought of as a coherent expression of a coherent self, speaking to or about the infinite and omnipotent, the act of making a poem is utterly impossible; yet in another sense the poem is all that is possible, for all other forms of speech—the sermon, say, as we hear this voice in Herbert's verse—are far less true than this.

The value of this poetry, to Herbert and to us, may be put this way: that in these poems Herbert defines, or constitutes, himself—his several selves—and does so in relation to his God, who also has several selves: not so much the three persons of the Trinity—Father, Son, and Holy

Spirit—but different personalities. In particular, as we shall later see in greater detail, Herbert vacillates between imagining a God of Power and a God of Love. He thus creates in his verse both himself and his God, and defines a series of relations between them. This may be at first surprising, for our language of "belief in God" assumes both that "belief" is the same and that "God" is the same, at least for people in the same tradition. But this is not true: each person defines belief, God, and self in his or her own way. This is in fact the point of theological discourse, to create and make real for the reader, as a possibility in life, a certain sense of the deity and of the kind of relation with it one calls belief. Think of the difference between the God of Calvin for example and the God of Luther—or the God of Martin Luther King; like these people, Herbert offers us his own God, and his own imagined and achieved relation with Him.

The active sense of their own intellectual and ethical impossibility means that these poems take as their subject the very processes of expression and definition, of constitution of self and other, that they enact. Every phrase, every gesture, defines the self and the deity in one way or another, well or badly—at best imperfectly—and thus becomes the object of critical contemplation. These poems are not so much about experience recollected in tranquillity, as Wordsworth says his are, as they are themselves a form of experience, for him as well as for us, and this experience is its true subject. What does it mean, for example, to start off asking how one can adequately grieve for Christ's suffering, or to start thinking in quantitative terms about Love, or Sinne, or Grief? The poetry is itself a way of responding to the impossible conditions of life; despite what is said in the "Jordan" poems—but in keeping with what is performed there—the poetry is in this sense primary.

The well-known critic Harold Bloom had this to say, in an informal interview, about the uniqueness of Shakespeare:

> The principal insight I've had in teaching and writing about Shakespeare is that there isn't anyone before Shakespeare who actually gives you a representation of characters or human figures speaking out loud, whether to themselves or to others or both, and then brooding out loud, whether to themselves or to others or both, on what they themselves have said. And then, in the course of pondering, undergoing a serious or vital change—becoming a different kind of character or personality, and even a different kind of mind. We take that utterly for granted in representation. But it doesn't exist before Shakespeare.

It doesn't happen in the Bible. It doesn't happen in Homer or Dante. It doesn't even happen in Euripides. It's pretty clear that Shakespeare's true precursor—where he took the hint from—is Chaucer. But Chaucer only does it in fits and starts, and in small degree. Shakespeare does it all the time. It's his common stock. The ability to do that, and to persuade one that this is a natural mode of representation, is purely Shakespearean. We are now so contained by it that we can't see its originality anymore. But the originality of it is bewildering.[16]

What Bloom says here about Shakespeare is even more true of Herbert: as the poems are spun out of the poet's various minds and selves they instantly become the object of contemplation, of perpetual ethical and moral criticism.[17] It is not that the speaker speaks first, then reflects

---

16. *Harper's Magazine,* August 1991, 29–30. This is a fine statement, but I think it is wrong about Euripides. In the central speech in *Alcestis,* for example, Admetus starts off one way, play-acting his grief, and ends up another, full of real grief and a recognition of his circumstances. *Alcestis,* 935–61. The subject of the play as a whole is his transformation from a stick-figure caricature, whose feelings and conduct are dictated by what he thinks a situation calls for, into a person with real emotions, memory, and a capacity for fidelity and friendship. This happens here, in this speech, where talking becomes a mode of reflection and self-transformation.

17. For a brief example, think of "Gratefulnesse," which begins this way:

> Thou that hast giv'n so much to me,
> Give one thing more, a gratefull heart.
> See how thy beggar works on thee
>   By art.

The speaker starts with a two-line prayer; then stops and speaks to the same audience, God, about what he has just been doing. This analysis of his own conduct continues for the next six stanzas, and is followed by a transformed version of his initial prayer, for a grateful heart:

> Not thankfull, when it pleaseth me;
> As if thy blessings had spare dayes:
> But such a heart, whose pulse may be
>   Thy praise.

The speaker begins with a simple prayer; but he quickly distances himself from it, as if it were the work of a skillful rhetorician or courtier, trying to manipulate his audience; he then speaks critically about his own social practice and the context in which it occurs, including a recognition that God must have foreseen our persistent importunities and be ready to tolerate them; at the end of this process he becomes capable of just the sort of direct and open-hearted prayer that at the beginning he

and changes, but that as he speaks he shifts his ground, his attitude, and is transformed, in a poetry astonishingly modern.[18]

Herbert's poems do not make up a sustained argument or a mosaic of different pieces, but a set of fresh attempts of the mind to come to terms with itself, its language, and its world. None of them is final, none reaches a firm conclusion, though a side of Herbert wants desperately to do that. What he is simultaneously learning and teaching his reader is that the very attempt to write a poem of such a kind would itself be mistaken, for whatever point he attains instantly disappears. We live on terms of radical evanescence, in which the only thing possible is the perpetual recommitment of the self to the kind of life and thought these poems themselves reflect: there is growth and movement, but not from one stable position to another; rather in the quality of trust and hope, a shift in the life of the heart from which the words come. The life of this poetry is not in the poems as artifacts, but in the process of poetry-making that produced them, in the process of poetry-reading they require.

There is here a point of similarity with Robert Frost, for whom the poem is also a constant struggle, always remaining to be done again; in his case, as we saw, the struggle is in large part with tendencies to sentimentality and falseness, as these have their origin both in the language the speaker uses and in the speaker's own impulses and needs. In his brief essay, "A Constant Symbol," Frost wrote that a poem is "a figure of the will braving alien entanglements"; for Herbert perhaps

---

could not manage or sustain. His capacity for self-consciousness is at once a bar to authentic speech, for this is what makes him pause in self-doubt at the beginning of the poem, and the means by which he achieves it at the end. The movement of the whole is toward integration: at the beginning the self-conscious aspect of the mind is separated from the gesture of prayer, by the end it is united with it.

18. Does this mean that Herbert's poetry is available to us as it may not have been to earlier readers? In a sense the suggestion is silly: What Herbert and Shakespeare knew must have been known to others, and it is surely a mistake to think that there is progress in the arts. In another sense it is not silly but obviously true: one world provides a context, against which the poems have their meaning, that is necessarily different from any other. It is a mark of a work of genius that it can speak to different generations; not saying the same thing each time, for that would be impossible, but by speaking to its various audiences variously. Think for example of the *Iliad*, still fresh after almost three thousand years, speaking to Simone Weil about the organized violence of fascism and war, as she reveals in what may be the best short piece on that poem ever written, "L'*Iliade*, ou le poème de la force." See *The Simone Weil Reader*, ed. George Panichas (Mt. Kisco, N.Y.: McKay, 1977), 153–83.

more than Frost those alien entanglements are, sometimes at least, the source of wisdom and correction. But for both of them poetry is an activity, a way of starting over again on the same basic problems of life, and it is in the activity itself, not in any summary of positions or propositions, that its meaning can be found.

This is an activity of the reader as well as the poet, for to read Herbert's poetry at all we must become judges of intellectual and ethical character: alert, just as the poet is, to the false, the vain, and the foolish, and to the authentic and true as well. The poetry insists that we do this, and teaches us how to do it, for like a puzzle it refuses to come clear until we have focused on its voices and gestures, asking these questions of them. When we do this we do not find the poet moving firmly towards greater clarification, but rising and falling, twisting in uncertainty. Partly this arises from Herbert's increasing sense of the unreliability of all of his languages: whatever may be the case with his sermons and other public utterances, where he has a social role that justifies certain voices and forms of expression, in his poems, far more private, he seems to find no adequate language, or none, at least, that can simply be copied or adopted. Added to this he has an equally acute and increasing sense of the unreliability of his various speaking selves. He repeatedly finds himself in error and confusion, and threatens to take his reader with him; it is against this pressure indeed that we are forced to become active in the way described above.

When I speak of confusion, distortion, error, and the like, I may be thought to see these as simple matters, as to which Herbert's eyes are for the moment unaccountably clouded, though presumably at the end to become clear. Nothing could be further from what I mean: the truth towards which he struggles, and from which he slips away, is not statable in language, certainly not in doctrinal terms; it is an increased appreciation of the conditions of instability and uncertainty on which he lives and writes (and we do too). Truth in this sense lies not in any one statement or voice, but in gaps and tensions among them, in the process by which one at once speaks and questions what one says. The best that can be done is the poetry itself, full of self-doubt, and animated as it is by a kind of perpetual restlessness.

Chapter 4

Developments

One of the convictions out of which this book is written is that Herbert's poems acquire meaning from their relations and interactions with each other, as one poem answers, or builds upon, or recalls another. Each poem in this way teaches us more of the language in which all are written.

In this chapter I shall continue to work through the poems in the order in which Herbert presents them, occasionally skipping one or two of the less significant ones, but my emphasis will be less on the way sequence itself works as a source of meaning than on three other ways in which Herbert connects his poems: by a kind of syncopation, breaking the series into answering pairs; by a dominant image, repeated through a particular series; and by a substantive ethical theme.

Poems in Answering Pairs

Herbert is a poet who thinks responsively, as we have already seen not only in "Antiphon" but in the answering voices of "The Collar" and even of "Vertue." Or think of "Easter," "Good Friday," and "Easter-wings," where the poem is made of two distinct parts, one responding to another. Sometimes Herbert expresses this habit of mind in another way, by writing pairs of poems on the same theme or with the same title, as we saw in the "Holy Baptisme" poems, where the second rewrote the first. In both of his manuscripts it is common for such poems to appear on facing pages.[1]

---

1. This feature is especially prominent in *W*, where "The Thanksgiving" is paired with "The Second Thanksgiving" (later renamed "The Reprisall"), "The Passion" (later renamed "Good Friday," part 2) with "The Passion" (later renamed "Redemption"), "Easter" (part 1) with "Easter" (part 2) apparently as separate poems, "Easter-wings" (stanza 1) with "Easter-wings" (stanza 2) apparently as separate poems, "Holy Baptisme" (I) with "Holy Baptisme" (II), "Love" (I) with "Love" (II), "The

Herbert's church at Bemerton, and beyond it the rectory

In the series of poems following "Antiphon" Herbert does this several times, as it were marking this way of writing for special attention. I will not pause on the opening pair, both entitled "Love," except to mark the general character of the movement that connects them. The first begins by praising "immortal love," said to have "sprung from that beautie which can never fade." It is contrasted with "mortall love," but this inferior kind of love is soon associated with "wit" and "in-

---

Christian Temper" (I) with "The Christian Temper" (II), and so on. But as he proceeds, this doubling is gradually reduced, marking it as a feature of the early stages of "The Church."

Compare the related practice of locating different poems of the same name—"Affliction," "Justice," "Employment," "Praise," "Jordan," and so forth—throughout "The Church" as a whole. This is a way of drawing lines of connection across the entire text. For example, the first pair in this section, two poems called "Love," are mirrored by a third, "Love" (III), the last of all.

vention," terms that for Herbert cannot be wholly bad, and also with "beautie," which is then, impossibly, on both sides of the contrast. And as in "Jordan," the poem—a sonnet, and thus invoking love poetry of a classic kind—is full of exactly the sort of invention and wit, and beauty too, that it disparages.

By the end the speaker is reduced to a condition of such confusion that any love at all counts as good, including the most humble and physical, the most ordinary and "mortall":

> Who sings thy praise? onely a skarf or glove
> Doth warm our hands, and make them write of love.

This seems to be a kind of collapse, but I think it is rather a moment of redemption, the recognition of something real in the world, though modest, that deserves the name of love.[2] The true collapse comes rather in the second "Love," which reaffirms the doctrinally correct distinction that was so touchingly blurred in "Love" (I), between mortal and immortal love, but does this in a rather mechanical way, with little sense of emotional engagement or risk. In the end the speaker is unable to write himself out of the language with which he begins.

These two poems answer each other in something of a paradigmatic way: the first moves away from the voice that declaims on the folly and vice of man, in what I have called Herbert's sermon style, towards a recognition of the humble yet miraculous way that love actually works in the world, as a gift that warms the hands and calls forth thanks. The second slips back into the position out of which the first emerged. No progress in the rewriting, then, but its opposite.

The Temper (I)

How should I praise thee, Lord! how should my rymes
Gladly engrave thy love in steel,
If what my soul doth feel sometimes,
My soul might ever feel!

---

2. As often in Herbert, the poem has another reading, shadowing the first. Here the last two lines could be read as a continuation of the voice of contempt, saying in effect that praise of "mortall love" degenerates to such trivial things as scarves and gloves.

Although there were some fourtie heav'ns, or more,
  Sometimes I peere above them all;
  Sometimes I hardly reach a score,
    Sometimes to hell I fall.

O rack me not to such a vast extent;
  Those distances belong to thee:
  The world's too little for thy tent,
    A grave too big for me.

Wilt thou meet arms with man, that thou dost stretch
  A crumme of dust from heav'n to hell?
  Will great God measure with a wretch?
    Shall he thy stature spell?

O let me, when thy roof my soul hath hid,
  O let me roost and nestle there:
  Then of a sinner thou art rid,
    And I of hope and fear.

Yet take thy way; for sure thy way is best:
  Stretch or contract me, thy poore debter:
  This is but tuning of my breast,
    To make the musick better.

Whether I flie with angels, fall with dust,
  Thy hands made both, and I am there:
  Thy power and love, my love and trust
    Make one place ev'ry where.

This poem consists of series of imaginings and reimaginings that work, as we are by now not surprised to see, a transformation in the speaker, this time a benign one. First he uses the image of the universe to describe his swings, from forty heavens to hell itself; then shifts to a prayer, as an afflicted person, for relief from the intolerable pains of this, thinking still in spatial or quantitative terms—"too big for me." Then another shift, to an angry demand: Why are you doing this to me? Will you "meet arms with man?"—meaning both "Are you essentially hostile to us?" and, because an honorable warrior picks on someone his own size, "Have you no dignity?" ("Will great God measure with a wretch?") Then still another shift, to a different kind of prayer: not relieve me, but protect me; he imagines his audience as a kind of roof or shed, under which he can "roost and nestle," which in turn suggests a brooding mother bird. He asks in effect to be held: no longer is God seen as the universe or a warrior, but as a loving parent, perhaps even as mother.

Once this imagined connection is made he can return to what troubled him with a different attitude altogether, one of trust and acceptance: "Yet take thy way; for sure thy way is best." "This is but tuning of my breast, / To make the musick better" is an image somewhat reminiscent of the "fractures well cur'd make us more strong" of "Repentance," but very different in feeling: here the speaker is not broken but stretched, and the result is not that he shall be returned to a soundness of body he already enjoyed, but that he will make better music. He will be "tempered," then, both as metal is by heating and cooling, and as a musical instrument is, by being tuned. In this way the image affirms the very act of poetry in which he is engaged. The final stanza is an expression of trust achieved, even more wholehearted than the end of "Easter":

> Whether I flie with angels, fall with dust,
> Thy hands made both, and I am there:
> Thy power and love, my love and trust
> Make one place ev'ry where.

Thus far does the speaker come from the despairing and confused point from which he begins. The very grandiosity of his original imagined elation entails a sense of lowness and smallness, the feeling out of which he begins; he then expresses anger, his sense of which was perhaps the initial bar; this in turn allows him to express the need to be nurtured, the recognition of which leads to trust.

But even here at the end there is a claim of power and importance: the grammar makes "thy power and love" and "my love and trust" equal actors in transforming the universe. And earlier, in the stanza in which he expresses the desire to "roost and nestle," he says that the condition of trust he desires, one of infancy really, will erase not only fear but hope, hardly a desirable end. This poem thus calls for a double response, as in every case in which a speaker asks erasure of the ego: this is what we should aspire to, the loss of self in a merger with the divine that will enable one to say, "Thy will be done"; but it is at the same time what we cannot aspire to, and should not, for every action presupposes the independence and value of the actor, including the poetic act, including the act of trust itself.

"The Temper" (I) does not stand alone. No sooner is this moment of love and trust attained than it is lost, in the opening lines of "The Temper" (II):

> It cannot be. Where is that mightie joy,
> Which just now took up all my heart?

From this point the poem becomes a prayer, riddled with confused metaphors in a way that recalls "Holy Baptisme" (I). The speaker first pleads with God not to use his "dart"; then asks him to fix his "chair of grace" in one spot, "that all my powers / May also fix their reverence":

> For when thou dost depart from hence,
> They grow unruly, and sit in thy bowers.

The speaker concludes by asking that God "Scatter" these powers, "or binde them all to bend to thee":

> Let not thy higher Court remove,
> But keep a standing Majestie in me.

In this rewriting he comes to see that what produced the loss of "mightie joy," leaving him so disorganized, was simply the departure of God. What the speaker thought at the close of "The Temper" (I) to be the joint work of "thy power and love, my love and trust," and hence permanent, he now feels to be simply the choice of God to be present; and what then seemed fixed and universal—"one place ev'ry where"— he now sees as evanescent. His powers are in confusion, a fact that is expressed both in the general incoherence of his metaphors and in the particular metric unruliness of the line, "They grow unruly, and sit in thy bowers."

This is an instance of the "racking" and "stretching" of which the first poem spoke, but this time the speaker cannot write himself out of his sense of loss and confusion, but remains in that condition, a rather awkward poet, shifting his images in an incoherent way. But in this very fact there is a kind of value, for it does express, and quite directly, the sense of dependence and helplessness which for Herbert, or part of him, is our human condition. The speaker can now see more truly than he could before how and why the stretching and racking take place: not so much to do something to him, or for him, but as a simple and accidental result of the absence of God. He no longer attributes to God an intention with respect to him, nor claims to know what that intention is, but rests upon what he has resisted seeing—his utter dependence and the impossibility of comprehension—which, once seen, is so simple as hardly to need utterance; indeed, the right kind of utterance for it is perhaps this very nonpoetic awkwardness. The difficulty here, as elsewhere, is in coming to see what is right before us, namely that we cannot see. "Now I am here, what thou wilt do with me / None of my books will show."

In a way, then, this is an antipoem, written against the coherence, beauty, and hope of the first. He asks at the end not an increase in his powers, nor a shift in his feelings, but simply that God who is absent become present, and become present within him—in this partly imagining himself as the woman, who is entered, rather than as the man, who imposes himself on his world, all in a powerful transformation of the side of him that seeks intellectual and social control, in his verse and elsewhere.[3]

This is the context in which "Jordan" (I) appears (page 48, above), written as it is against complexity and cliché, and in favor of simplicity both of insight and of expression. "*My God, My King*" is an elaboration of the point to which the speaker in "The Temper" (II) has managed to work himself, as well as an explicit echo of the refrain in "Antiphon." But in both cases, of course, the antipoetic quality of the poem exists in paradoxical relation to the existence of the poem itself. And both "Jordan" and "The Temper" are anticipated by "Love" (I) in the simultaneous emphasis both on what happens outside language—"onely a skarf or glove / Doth warm our hands"—and what happens only within it: "and make them write of love."

Although both by their titles also invoke connections elsewhere, the next poem, "Employment" (I), is properly a pair with "Jordan" (I), for it responds explicitly to it.

---

3. Compare the opening lines of "Whitsunday":

> Listen sweet Dove unto my song,
> And spread thy golden wings in me;
> Hatching my tender heart so long,
> Till it get wing, and flie away with thee.

Employment (I)

If as a flowre doth spread and die,
  Thou wouldst extend me to some good,
Before I were by frosts extremitie
              Nipt in the bud;

The sweetnesse and the praise were thine;
  But the extension and the room,
Which in thy garland I should fill, were mine
              At thy great doom.

For as thou dost impart thy grace,
  The greater shall our glorie be.
The measure of our joyes is in this place,
              The stuffe with thee.

Let me not languish then, and spend
  A life as barren to thy praise,
As is the dust, to which that life doth tend,
              But with delaies.

All things are busie; onely I
  Neither bring hony with the bees,
Nor flowres to make that, nor the husbandrie
              To water these.

I am no link of thy great chain,
  But all my companie is a weed.
Lord place me in thy consort; give one strain
              To my poore reed.[4]

The state of mind and feeling from which this important poem issues, its imagined prehistory as it were, is a sense of fruitlessness and incapacity. This is the natural consequence of "The Temper" (II): on the conditions there made vivid, in which human beings are incapable of any relevant action, in which every good thing depends entirely upon grace, what of value can we possibly do or say? "Jordan" in a way makes this point

---

4. Note: *Barren to thy praise* means both empty of thy praise and not responsive to it.

even clearer, and brings it home to the poet himself, for what poem can compete with "*My God, My King,*" if properly meant? Only the funny kind of poem "Jordan" itself is, one that leads us to the limits not only of that poem itself, but of poetry in general.

But see the way the prayer is imagined at the opening of "Employment": not that "I" should be able to do something, but that "thou" should act upon me, so that I should be able to be, or do, something good, in as natural a way as a flower. Here this action is thought of as a kind of extension of the self—recalling "The Temper" (I)—but this time the extension is not a racking or stretching, but a modest opening out in bloom. No sooner has the speaker cast his thought in this rather selfless way, however, than the self intrudes and claims something: not the "sweetnesse and the praise," but the extension itself, and the place in "thy garland" that this flower will have. This is itself a reaction to his awareness that to think, as he is doing, of what he wants as "spreading" or "extending" is already to imagine the self as aggrandizing; so he disclaims that, or tries to, by saying that what will be his is the space alone: all its content, both physical and moral—its "sweetnesse" and "praise"—are "thine."

The next stanza continues this way of imagining things: "The measure of our joyes is in this place, / The stuffe with thee." Here the speaker sees himself as a kind of contentless definer of space, as he was in the garland too: he defines the space that God fills up. But what kind of action or life is possible for such a one? The speaker cannot imagine the life he wants, but he can express the want itself: "Let me not languish then, and spend / A life as barren to thy praise, / As is the dust." Thus far, the speaker has asked for a kind of life effective of "some good"—itself as good a human impulse as one could imagine— yet has found it impossible to imagine one, consistent with his sense of what a human being is. Even the modest image of a flower blooming becomes, in human imaginings, a field for the self-aggrandizing ego to make its claims, and when these are resisted, what is left?

> All things are busie; onely I
> Neither bring hony with the bees,
> Nor flowres to make that, nor the husbandrie
> To water these.

This is a rewriting not so much of the first stanza itself but of the feelings out of which the first stanza came, which are now exposed with a kind of clarity they lacked before. He can now express, in a somewhat self-dramatizing way, the sense of despair to which the first stanza is a response. He started, that is, with a perception or feeling that he could not fully allow himself to have; he thus began his speaking in a double attempt, to express this feeling in occluded form, and to manage it; and when the management fails, the feeling, before intolerable, emerges with simplicity.

> I am no link of thy great chain,
> But all my companie is a weed.
> Lord place me in thy consort; give one strain
> To my poore reed.

At the end, out of the clarity of this feeling—I am no flower but a weed—he is able to reimagine his prayer: not to spread as a flower, nor to take up space in a garland, but to be an instrument of music, in a consort. The "weed" is now transformed into a "reed"—a song-pipe that makes music.

This poem, like "The Windows," is about the process of transformation by grace, and it enacts it in its imagery: from bloom to dying bloom to weed, a kind of deterioration into death; but then the stalk of the weed becomes a pipe, through which music can be made, a reed. This music is not made by itself, but by the breath of another, as the light that shines in the window, or in the preacher, comes from outside them: it is "thy life," not theirs, that transforms them. Music is a way the speaker can fill up space without claiming it for himself, but sharing it with the rest of the consort.

The movement here is very much like that of Keats's poem, "To Autumn," which likewise progresses through the dissolution of organic life (think of the figure of Autumn watching the cider press's "last oozings hours by hours") into the clarity and song of autumn: "Hedge crickets sing; and now with treble soft / The red-breast whistles from a garden-croft." From the tangible and organic and dying to the audible and musical and permanent: from death to art. Here is a way to think of the self doing something valuable that does not seek to fill space, or even to define it; and which is not self-aggrandizing, for the art is ultimately another's, and it is that other who is entitled to the "sweet-nesse and the praise." This is a way of trying to imagine and locate "me" or "I" in a way that does not involve false claims, false prides, but does allow at least for the act and art of music, of poetry. It becomes at once Herbert's justification of his art, in response to "Jordan," and an invocation of his muse. The heart of his own experience and of his art alike is the process of transformation, for which he here prays— "give one strain / To my poore reed"—and which, at the same time, he enacts, in the transformations achieved by the poem itself.

That this poem is itself music, and of a kind typical in Herbert, has on this reading particular importance. Think for example of the way the stanzas are structured: a line of eight syllables (four iambic feet) another line of the same, not rhyming; a line of ten syllables (five feet), rhyming with the first; and a line of four syllables (two feet), rhyming with the second. Two musical systems are placed in counterpoint here, metrical and rhyming; they begin and close together, but in between they run against one another, in a kind of syncopation. The effect of the short last line, here as in "Vertue," is to emphasize it greatly, and especially the climax of it all, when the flower and weed are converted into a reed.

In the twin poems entitled "The Holy Scriptures," which follow immediately, Herbert switches from writing to reading, from his own art, that is, of producing beautiful music, to the sacred text, uttering eternal truth.

The Holy Scriptures (I)

Oh Book! infinite sweetnesse! let my heart
Suck ev'ry letter, and a hony gain,
    Precious for any grief in any part;
To cleare the breast, to mollifie all pain.
Thou art all health, health thriving till it make
    A full eternitie: thou art a masse
    Of strange delights, where we may wish & take.
Ladies, look here; this is the thankfull glasse,
That mends the lookers eyes: this is the well
    That washes what it shows. Who can indeare
    Thy praise too much? thou art heav'ns Lidger here,
Working against the states of death and hell.
    Thou art joyes handsell: heav'n lies flat in thee,
    Subject to ev'ry mounters bended knee.

The speaker here praises the Holy Scriptures, which are to the Protestant the primary source of revelation and truth. This is unexceptionable, but the terms in which he does so are not. The Scriptures are full of "infinite sweetnesse," we are told. We know that "sweet" is a complex term in Herbert, always running the risk of sentimentality, and here it takes the form of imagined regression to infancy: what the speaker wants to do is "suck" the sweetness. Then he imagines Scripture as a kind of snake-oil that will cure all "grief," all "pain": it is a "masse / Of strange delights, where we may wish & take," a phrase recalling the dangerous language of "Affliction"—"I had my wish and way." Then the speaker adopts the voice of a barker or street vendor: "Ladies, look here," he says, this is the mirror that makes you more beautiful, the well that cleans what it reflects. "Who can indeare / Thy praise too much?" he asks. The answer is of course, no one; but the issue here is not the quantity of praise, as he seems to think, but its quality, and the praise he utters is distorted and mistaken from the beginning. One is reminded of "Faith," where the speaker praises faith as a kind of magic, which produces feasts, erases debts, and so on. His rhetorical question is more real than he realizes.

The increasing sense of confusion is manifested here by the awkward shift of images, expressed in obscure language: thou art heaven's "Lidger," that is, "resident ambassador"; or joy's "handsel," that is, "gift" (and particularly a gift that promises still more to follow, or an omen of good fortune). The speaker's grandiosity returns with a vengeance in the imaginings of the closing couplet, where he envisages heaven lying "flat" to him—instead, presumably, of being impossibly high above him—and "subject to ev'ry mounters bended knee." Here the ego is made supreme over heaven itself—this is then the miracle of the Scriptures!—and in a way that has sexually aggressive and male connotations (in the image of "mounting"), which are the direct reverse of the sexual implications of his earlier prayer that God "keep a standing Majestie in me."

This poem locates us in confusion. What we now know to expect is that the next poem will respond, probably in a corrective way, and that is just what we get.

The Holy Scriptures (II)

Oh that I knew how all thy lights combine,
    And the configurations of their glorie!
        Seeing not onely how each verse doth shine,
But all the constellations of the storie.

This verse marks that, and both do make a motion
    Unto a third, that ten leaves off doth lie:
        Then as dispersed herbs do watch a potion,
These three make up some Christians destinie:
Such are thy secrets, which my life makes good,
    And comments on thee: for in ev'ry thing
        Thy words do finde me out, & parallels bring,
And in another make me understood.
    Starres are poore books, & oftentimes do misse:
    This book of starres lights to eternall blisse.

How different this is: instead of launching into praise—praise that cannot help being self-praise—this speaker begins by acknowledging that he does not understand, cannot understand, that which he has just been praising. When he turns from the imagined effects of the Scriptures to their nature, he has to acknowledge that he cannot really read them. He does have a sense of the way in which they work, not directly as exposition, but as art: "This verse marks that, and both do make a motion / Unto a third, that ten leaves off doth lie." They not only "shine" themselves but make a "constellation" that is beyond his grasp. Then the speaker reverts to a consideration of their effects, once more cast in magical terms: "as dispersed herbs do watch a potion"—itself a difficult phrase, implying perhaps the reading of tea leaves, or the making of magic liquors—"These three make up some Christians destinie." But in what sense "make up"? In a kind of astrologer's way, as if you could read your future in the obscure text? So the speaker at first implies (though this would itself be blasphemous) but then shifts ground again: the image now is that his own life makes a text that at once confirms and comments upon the original. It is not that the text determines his life, or the other way round, but that they act on each other: experience illuminates the text, the text experience—a position familiar to readers of "The Windows," where "doctrine and life, colours and light . . . combine and mingle." Here there are two actors engaged in interaction: "my life makes good, / And comments on thee"; and "in ev'ry thing / Thy words do find me out, & parallels bring." It is the text not as a magic heal-all that is celebrated here, nor as plain and authoritative directive, but the text as a complication or puzzle that engages the reader: as the occasion and material for life.

The poem speaks here, of course, not only of the sacred text, but of itself as a text, and of Herbert's poetry more generally, defining the kind of life to which it aspires: not only in each verse, but in the constellation of verses, and involving not only complications at the level of the text, but those that arise from the interaction of the reader with the text. For it is true of his own art, as well as of the Scripture, that "This verse marks that, and both do make a motion / Unto a third, that ten leaves off doth lie," all with a kind of complexity that makes it impossible for us to tell "all the constellations of the storie." This drastically redefines the comment in "Jordan" about "catching the sense at two removes," as though that were a bad thing—it is now seen as an aspect of truth and beauty. The meaning of the Scriptures and the poem alike lie not merely in the part, but in the whole; and the whole includes what lies without the text, as well as within it.

One more point about "The Holy Scriptures" (II): when the speaker says, "And in another make me understood," I think he defines in a single phrase a desire or need that drives much of Herbert's own life, and especially his poetry. I am not sure what "another" refers to— another world? another person? another moment?—but the need and desire is plainly stated: to be "understood." This may sound simple; but when one is a complex and shifting mix of feelings and perceptions, it is almost impossible even to conceive how it might happen. Taken as a whole his poems can I think be read as a display of the self, in its many speakers and responders, of a kind that enables Herbert to say, as he did in "Affliction," "Here I am," and to do so with the hope of being understood.

The final turn is this: as it is the Scriptures that make him understood, when his life is seen in the terms they provide, so it may be the aim or effect of Herbert's own poetry, properly read, to make his readers more fully understood as well: our lives too are texts, which can obtain some of their meaning from these texts of his composition, as his own life does from those they celebrate. What the Scriptures teach the speaker here is not so much to write poems, though that too, but to think of his life as if it were a text; when he does this, it acquires new possibilities for meaning and intelligibility—it becomes imaginable that it should be "understood"—and the same may be true for Herbert's readers as well. This poem shows, in response to "The Windows," how poetry can be a kind of preaching, as far removed from the sermon voice as possible, but still a kind of writing and speaking for the spiritual benefit of his audience.

Following the two poems on the Holy Scriptures comes another pair,

"Whitsunday" and "Grace," which turn attention from the sacred text to the Holy Spirit. The first calls upon the Holy Spirit—"Listen sweet Dove unto my song, / And spread thy golden wings in me." But the speaker quickly recognizes that this won't happen, and the body of the poem tells the history of the world in such a way as to explain why this is so: once you were with us—at Pentecost especially—but now "Thou shutt'st the doore, and keep'st within." When he repeats his prayer at the end, we know it will not work. The poem thus moves from a gesture of hope and trust to an explanation of its failure. Yet at the end he cannot bear to say what he knows, what he has in fact told us, about his situation and his God, namely that He will not listen to his song—that even poetry has no effect—but has withdrawn, leaving the speaker with no meaningful resources of his own.

There is still another dimension to this, a theological one, for the position to which the speaker comes at the end, and cannot recognize, is itself a denial of the Holy Spirit, in honor of whom the poem is supposedly written and whose role is to be the presence of God in the fallen world after the Son has returned to heaven. Although the speaker begins by addressing the Spirit, there is a sense in which he shows that he does not believe in its existence, but can imagine only the Father, withdrawing in anger at our sin, and the Son, here with us for a moment, but now gone. As a matter of Christian psychology, then, this is a speaker who calls upon God but has in fact separated himself from him. On this reading "Whitsunday" is a precursor to "Love" (III), in which the speaker finally recognizes something of the continuing presence and power of love in the world, and that it reaches even him.

"Grace" is an overt acknowledgment of the impotence to which "Whitsunday" leads its speaker, expressed here in a repeated call for grace to "drop from above." The speaker imagines himself as even more passive than he was as the host to the incubating Holy Spirit above: unmoving, waiting for something to drop. This is a position towards which he has been working in his other poems, here most bleakly stated. It looks like despair; but against it is the hope and confidence expressed in the existence of poem itself and its tone—in its sometimes amused, sometimes almost teasing quality, in its aspect of serenity: "The dew doth ev'ry morning fall; / And shall the dew out-strip thy Dove?"[5]

---

5. What if anything is it possible for human beings to do on the conditions described in "Grace"? The next poem "Praise," addresses this question, this way:

The series closes with another pair of poems, "Mattens" and "Even-song," between which a third, "Sinne," was inserted in the final manu-script. The first of these is full of hope, from the beginning to the end.

> I Cannot ope mine eyes,
>   But thou art ready there to catch
> My morning-soul and sacrifice:
> Then we must needs for that day make a match.
>
> . . . .
>
> Teach me thy love to know;
> That this new light, which now I see,
> May both the work and workman show:
> Then by a sunne-beam I will climbe to thee.

"Even-song" looks back with regret and sorrow on the day that "Mat-tens" inaugurated: "What have I brought thee home / For this thy love?" The two poems thus together enact in small the Christian career, beginning in hope and ending in the experience of failure, a fact that is explained by the insertion between these two poems of the new poem, "Sinne." But this is not all. "Even-song" continues:

"To write a verse or two is all the praise, / That I can raise." But by the end he has given up even this.

> O raise me then! Poore bees, that work all day,
>   Sting my delay,
> Who have a work, as well as they,
>   And much, much more.

It is now no longer the speaker who is doing the raising, but God; the speaker's only act is to ask for it. He no longer sees himself as doing enough under the circumstances, using the image of bees in a way that invokes the conclusion of "Employment." The speaker has imagined his way out of his complaint into a partial sense of his own responsibility.

"Affliction" (II) begins with an explicit attempt to argue God into a certain position: "Kill me not ev'ry day, / Thou Lord of life; since thy one death for me / Is more then all my deaths can be." The speaker asserts, that is, that his comparative insignificance is a reason to spare him further pain and death. This is the expression of a clever mind forced by its feelings into impossibly ingenious and self-interested argument. But by the end the speaker sees, or almost sees, the comparison working in a different way, to erase the significance of his afflictions not to God but to him, and then to enable him to see God's own suffering as an act of love: "The crosse took up in one, / By way of imprest, all my future mone."

Yet still thou goest on,
And now with darknesse closest wearie eyes,
Saying to man, *It doth suffice:*
Henceforth repose; your work is done.

The speaker can imagine, that is, not only the inadequacies of human life, but the love and forgiveness of God which erases them. The morning begins with a sense of hope and optimism; with a need for "teaching," felt in the expectation that it will be effective; and with the somewhat zany image—reminiscent of Emily Dickinson—that "by a sunne-beam I will climb to thee." The day concludes with a bleak awareness of limits and waste and incapacity, yet also with the affirmation of the voice that says, "*It doth suffice.*" The speaker no longer sees himself as climbing, but in an image recalling the "nestling" of "The Temper," as "resting" in God, concluding thus: "And in this love, more then in bed, I rest."

In this series Herbert has shown us many ways in which poem can respond to poem: by rewriting away from a point of collapse—in fact a moment of authenticity—into a confused or doctrinal voice, as in the "Love" poems; by a rewriting that undermines a point of momentary bliss, uncovering its mistaken assumptions, as in "The Temper"; by a rewriting that affirms, in a richer way, what the first poem denies, as "Employment" answers "Jordan," claiming the right to its own existence; by a constructive rewriting, straightening out evident distortions and moving the speaker and the reader in the direction of the knowledge that consists in the recognition of ignorance, as in "The Holy Scriptures"; and by a rewriting that transforms a simple and natural hope into a complex and tempered one, as in "Mattens" and "Even-song." One point of this variation is that it tells the reader that you can never know which way things will go; in a sequence in which one poem evidently responds to another, the movement may be from relative distortion to relative clarity, or the other way round. In any event, both voices are real, and must be reckoned with, a task the poems place squarely on the reader.

The Church and the Body

This sequence is followed by another that works in a different way, building on a single set of images that are based on the physical structure of the church—which is of course the dominant metaphor of *The Temple* as a whole. The poems are entitled: "Church-monuments," "Church-musick," "Church-lock and key," "The Church-floore," and, already familiar to us, "The Windows." While each of them is complex, and would repay close attention, I shall here focus on a single line of thought, about the soul and body, that runs through them.

The first of these poems—said by Yvor Winters to be Herbert's best—is an elegant and dramatic work by a speaker engaged in an elaborate literary exercise. He is about to engage his soul in devotion, but hopes that while he is praying his body will observe its surroundings and learn from them.

> While that my soul repairs to her devotion,
> Here I intombe my flesh, that it betimes
> May take acquaintance of this heap of dust;
> To which the blast of deaths incessant motion,
> Fed with the exhalation of our crimes,
> Drives all at last.

The idea, the speaker goes on, is that the church will be a "school" which will teach "my bodie" to find its true nature, "comparing dust with dust, and earth with earth." Learn here "thy stemme / And true descent," he says, that "thou mayst fit thy self against thy fall." The explicit subject of the poem is mortality, more obviously than any we have read. Another subject, less obvious but real, is the voice of the speaker, accomplished and sure, and the kind of sophisticated yet conventional work it produces. Self-certainty or self-assurance of this kind, however skillful and poised and in some sense desirable, is for Herbert a condition out of which he has to work himself, either in a particular poem or, as here where that does not happen, in moving from poem to poem. This voice is the aesthetic and poetic correlative of the great world of state and power and social prestige into which Herbert was born and educated, and it has a deep appeal to him; yet it is as far from the speaking of the heart as it is imaginable to be. Here the speaker thinks of himself as separated both from his body and his soul, as though he were not in need of the education he offers to his body and as though he were also, at least momentarily, distinct from his soul at its devotions. This kind of separation of the self into parts is the opposite of the integrated authenticity for which Herbert continually struggles.

In "Church-musick," which follows next, the speaker begins the process of transformation by imagining himself bodiless, moving with the music in the spaces of the church:

Sweetest of sweets, I thank you: when displeasure
        Did through my bodie wound my minde,
You took me thence, and in your house of pleasure
        A daintie lodging me assign'd.

Now I in you without a bodie move,
        Rising and falling with your wings:
We both together sweetly live and love,
        Yet say sometimes, *God help poore Kings.*

Comfort, I'le die; for if you poste from me,
        Sure I shall do so, and much more:
But if I travell in your companie,
        You know the way to heavens doore.

This is a beautiful elaboration of the image of the separation of soul from body as well as a lovely expression of Herbert's own devotion to music, expressed in rather erotic terms. The last two lines of the second stanza build on the standard love-song form, "Come live with me and be my love," expressing the lover's familiar disdain of the world (also seen in such lyrics as John Donne's "The Sunne Rising"); and the sweetness of the second stanza is a long way from the "lust" that obsessed the speaker of "The Church-porch." The poem concludes in hope, addressing the music itself: "You know the way to heavens doore." But nonetheless, despite—and perhaps in part because of—its beauty, it is a fantasy of escape. This is made plain to us by the beginning of "Church-lock and key," the next poem, which speaks out of a very different kind of experience indeed:

I know it is my sinne, which locks thine eares,
        And bindes thy hands,
Out-crying my requests, drowning my tears;
Or else the chilnesse of my faint demands.

The condition out of which this poem emerges is the speaker's attempt and failure to reach his God, the disappointment of the hope, just expressed, that he would reach "heavens doore." The speaker is in this way recalled from his imagined escape to the reality he tried to leave behind, much as Keats, say, is recalled to the world after his experience of the nightingale's song, and it is felt as a shock. Yet this poem too concludes with an image of hope, though of a different kind, which continues, in a striking and novel form, the musical theme of the last:

> Yet heare, O God, onely for his blouds sake
> Which pleads for me:
> For though sinnes plead too, yet like stones they make
> His blouds sweet current much more loud to be.

This hope is grounded not in church music, or any of the speaker's own capacities, but in Christ's sacrifice, imagined as music of a very different kind indeed. The speaker's sins, recognized at the beginning of the poem only by their disruptive and burdensome effects, are now brought into active consciousness: they are imagined as stones in a stream that make it sing and burble, in this case the stream of Christ's blood. This is an instance of Herbert's familiar insistence on the literal or physical, here to the point of real grotesqueness. It recalls the end of "The Agonie": "Love is that liquour sweet and most divine, / Which my God feels as bloude; but I, as wine." There the opposition was between the disgusting blood and the sense-pleasing wine; here between the violence of the visual image—the stream of blood—and the sweetness of the aural image, the sound of the brook singing over the stones. Both gestures enact the process by which the ugly can be transformed into the beautiful and good.

In "The Church-floore," which follows next, the speaker imagines the parts of the building as a series of virtues: patience, humility, confidence, and charity, which together make a building that "Sinne" cannot stain—for "all is cleansed when the marble weeps"—and "Death" cannot dirty, for "while he thinks to spoil the room, he sweeps." It concludes with an explicit invocation of the central image of "The Altar," namely the analogy between the architecture of the sacred structure and the human heart:

> Blest be the *Architect*, whose art
> Could build so strong in a weak heart.

Instead of the soul separated from the body, at its devotions or soaring with the music, this speaker imagines the soul embodied, as a heart, and given an architecture as real as that of a church. It is in the music of blood and stones, in the arrangement of stones in a church, that we live. Of course it is not only the church and the heart that are created by architecture, but the poem, which creates in language the possibility of balance and order and firmness that it describes.

This is the context in which "The Windows" appears, page 39 above, and this time it should read somewhat differently. We can now see, for example, that the way that this poem imagines the window and the preacher as mutual analogies is supported by what has preceded it, especially by the analogy between church and heart. And the imagined location of the speaker in the church—recalling the end of "The Church-porch"—makes it easier to hear the echoing words vanishing in the church "like a flaring thing," and to contrast to them the permanence of the windows. More deeply, this sequence of poems affirms in its central image the importance of the physical: the physical church, and, by implication, the physical body. The windows become an image of incarnation, the transformation of the physical world by the entry into it of the divine spirit or light. In this way the poem works as a refutation of the conventional views articulated by the speaker in "Church-monuments," which may indeed represent the "speech alone" this speaker now rejects. For there the speaker proposed that his body receive teaching, instruction in its own mortality, and its ultimate worthlessness; but the kind of teaching the rest of these poems offer is quite different, not of the mortality of the body, but of the radical defectiveness of the soul; and, notwithstanding that, of the miraculous presence and acceptance of God, including in the body.

This concentrated set of poems about the physical church is marked for its importance not only by the title of the whole book of poems, *The Temple,* and of the long section of which it is a part, "The Church," but by its reiteration of the concerns of the opening poem, "The Altar." The church is a prototype of a transformation by grace and art: the stones become a building, and a work of beauty; the building becomes a place for reflection and education, seen in the movement from "Church-monuments" to "The Windows"; its edification is thus not only in stone, but in the human being as well, both soul and body. I said earlier that the transformation is by art and grace, and both are required: the physical stones are shaped by physical hands, just as the poem is made in actual language, yet the miracle of its meaning comes from elsewhere. All of this works as a claim for the value of Herbert's poetry itself; it is "thy servant," after all, who "reares" the "broken Altar."

This sequence has an order that suggests a structure for the whole book of poems, which began, first of all, with a poem at the church porch. The implication is that one goes from outside the church to within it, and then follows a progress to an inner sanctum, all in a kind of pilgrim's journey to holiness, perhaps in imitation of the stations of the cross. But this does not quite work: the holiest place in a church is the altar, and we have already been there; what is more, the movements that this series of poems suggest are more similar to those of an idling tourist than those of a soul in pilgrimage. ("Mark you the floore?" begins the speaker in "The Church-floore," speaking like a museum guide.) Like other suggested orderings of the poems in the church—from "Good Friday" to "Easter," from "Holy Baptisme" to "The Holy Communion"—the movement inwards is suggested only, incomplete and placed in tension with other patterns of development. Part of the meaning of these poems is their imperfect suggestion of orderings that never quite materialize.

The Things of This World

As we saw in "Affliction" (I), and to a lesser extent in "The Thanksgiving," Herbert is bound in a way he cannot successfully deny to the things of this world: success and power, pleasure and learning, "sweetnesses" and flowers, to all the things that human beings want. Opposed to these things in him is a sermon voice that declares their worthlessness, but this too is unsatisfactory. It is not so much that the sermon voice says what is untrue as that it speaks a language of doctrine that asserts its own adequacy, when Herbert perhaps above all others knows how inadequate any language is. More than that: despite its doctrinal and moral apparent correctness, the sermon language is self-assertive and self-aggrandizing too, and in this sense sinful; and, as "Vertue" taught us, its image of the world is deeply imperfect. For Herbert, then, the appeal of worldly things and the kind of moralizing that is its most available corrective are both awry; this defines the situation out of which much of his poetry is written, especially the series—following the poems just discussed on the image of the church and body—that runs from "Content" to "The Starre," all of which deal in one way or another with the appeal of the things of this world.

In "Content" the speaker is engaged in a kind of internal argument, the object of which is to persuade himself into patience or contentedness, notwithstanding his various disappointments and deprivations:

South wall of the church at Bemerton, showing original flint construction

Peace mutt'ring thoughts, and do not grudge to keep
    Within the walls of your own breast:
Who cannot on his own bed sweetly sleep,
    Can on anothers hardly rest.

This argument is intellectual, rational, and doctrinal in kind, highly reminiscent of "The Church-porch," and, as the reader will by now expect, the effort does not work. This stanza offers itself as a conclusive argument, motivated perhaps by the speaker's desire to reason himself into the feelings he wants to have but ruefully knows he doesn't; but it is obviously fallacious, for what if my bed is of nails and his of feathers? The poem proves to be full of contradiction and self-erosion, as commonplace is piled on commonplace in an impossible way. For example, the speaker soon asks his "thoughts" to mark how "the fire in flints doth quiet lie," using an image that at once affirms the value of fire and asks us to accept coldness and hardness as the condition of life. "Give me the pliant minde," he says, who can adapt to all things; the reward is that "this soul doth span the world, and hang content / From either pole unto the centre." In other words, the reward of self-denial is self-aggrandizement. Don't think to value fame, he says, especially literary fame, for this is dependent entirely upon the acceptance of others: "And as their wit is, their digestion, / Thy nourisht fame is weak or strong." Here again the speaker necessarily affirms the value of what he asks his "thoughts" to disregard: fame is what counts; the only thing wrong with it is its vulnerability.

The poem concludes with a commonplace that in this context is impossible: "He that by seeking hath himself once found, / Hath ever found a happie fortune." The speaker celebrates the value of finding "himself," but that self has been defined throughout as divided, dependent on others, constituted by ambition, and the like; what is more, the force of the last word, "fortune," is to affirm the very values against which the speaker is supposedly arguing. The whole argument appeals to exactly the kind of egotism he is supposedly trying to wash away. There is no transformation to another voice or perspective, no humiliation or limitation of the assertive and sermonizing voice. As we now know to expect, this poem thus defines a problem, an intellectual and spiritual condition, to which the others in the sequence that follows will be addressed.

"Content" is followed by "The Quidditie" (page 56 above), which in this context reads rather differently from the way it did standing alone. We can now see the speaker's otherwise puzzling valuation of the things of this world—"hawk," "banquet," "renown," "good sword," "gay suit"—as a continuation of the voice that is speaking in "Content"; but here he claims that, despite appearances, they have less value, for him at least, than his verse—"which while I use / I am with thee." This can no longer be read as a mature or ultimate statement of position, as we were earlier tempted to do, but is instead a kind of preliminary groping, a dim intuition, and marked as such by the regression in tone to "*most take all.*"

"Humilitie" continues to distance the speaker from the things of this world, but in a new way, for it starts a new mode of poetry in Herbert, the conscious creation of myth. The story is this: the several "Vertues" ordered various "beasts and fowl," which represent passions or natural forces, to make gifts of submission. As these gifts were presented they were distributed by Humility, apparently matching each natural force to a particular virtue in order to strengthen the latter and purify the former. For example the lion's paw was given to Mansuetude (gentleness) and "on Justice was bestow'd the Foxes brain, / Kill'd in the way by chance." But when the crow brought the peacock's plume, the virtues quarrelled over it to such a degree that they were likely to be disenthroned by the beasts. Indeed, "if the Fox had liv'd to rule their side, / They had depos'd each one."

> Humilitie, who held the plume, at this
> Did weep so fast, that the tears trickling down
> Spoil'd all the train: then saying, *Here it is*
> *For which ye wrangle,* made them turn their frown
> Against the beasts: so joyntly bandying,
>   They drive them soon away;
> And then amerc'd them, double gifts to bring
>   At the next Session-day.[6]

This is a direct rejection of the things of this world—the "banquet," "hawk," and "renown" of "The Quidditie," and the self-expansion of "Content"—a movement in the direction indeed of humility.

This poem expresses a vision of life in which the virtues are not unified, nor themselves very virtuous: they wrangle and are diverted by the peacock's plume (which is indeed lovely); they need the items brought by the beasts; their rule is uncertain, dependent upon the "chance" that cost the fox his life; and at the end they act rather like beasts themselves. The poem is full of ambivalence too, for Humility, the hero of the piece, is also in a sense its villain, destroying this item of genuine beauty; and the virtues here, like God in some other poems, rule by power. This is not a simple allegory, affirming in story what could be stated as doctrine.

Both here and in later poems of this type Herbert so fully succeeds in creating his mythical world that it has the kind of vitality and force that we associate with the real. This is significant especially for the modern reader, since Herbert also uses, all the time, the images and narratives of Christianity, and of the Old Testament as well. These are of course assumed to have a kind of literal or actual truth that the myths of "Humilitie" and other similar poems lack; but I think that an oblique

---

6. Note: *Amerc'd* means "imposed as a fine or penalty."

effect of his explicit myth-making is to redefine the status and character of the Christian story. If the obviously invented myth has such force and vitality and meaning, if it works notwithstanding its obvious lack of literal referent, what does that suggest about the Christian story? That its significance too lies in the force and vitality which it acquires as it is recreated in the poem, the life of myth, not history? This is an issue to which we shall return.

The speaker in "Frailtie," which follows next, begins by making explicit what has so far been only implicit, the radically problematic character of the appeal of things of this world, which, it turns out, cannot be so easily rejected after all:

Frailtie

Lord, in my silence how do I despise
                    What upon trust
Is styled *honour, riches,* or *fair eyes;*
                    But is *fair dust!*
         I surname them *guilded clay,*
             Deare earth, fine grasse or *hay;*
In all, I think my foot doth ever tread
                    Upon their head.

But when I view abroad both Regiments;
                    The worlds, and thine:
Thine clad with simplenesse, and sad events;
                    The other fine,
         Full of glorie and gay weeds,
             Brave language, braver deeds:
That which was dust before, doth quickly rise,
                    And prick mine eyes.

O brook not this, lest if what even now
                    My foot did tread,
Affront those joyes, wherewith thou didst endow,
                    And long since wed
         My poore soul, ev'n sick of love:
             It may a Babel prove

> Commodious to conquer heav'n and thee
> Planted in me.[7]

This speaker consciously knows what the speaker in "Content" could only perform, that while he should wholeheartedly despise "honour, riches, or fair eyes" and call them dust, in fact this is for him impossible. Even when he despises them he has to honor them: "deare earthe, fine grasse." And when he looks upon the things of the world and the things of God and finds the one "clad with simplenesse, and sad events" the other "fine, / Full of glorie and gay weeds, / Brave language, braver deeds" the force of the second threatens to overwhelm him. He cannot escape from the appeal of the peacock's plume, of the "hawk or banquet or renown," or the egotism of "Content."

But now the speaker knows this about himself and is able to ask, from the place this knowledge defines, for help: "O brook not this." The movement from "Content" to "Frailtie" is from a performed self-contradiction of a kind that makes coherent speech impossible, undoing the very possibility of a self, towards an explicit recognition of this very contradiction. In one way this amounts to rather little progress, for nothing is solved, but in another it represents a great advance, for now the speaker has something to say that makes sense and that defines the character of his existence in such a way as to create a sense of possibility: the possibility of being, as the speaker in "The Quidditie" put it, "with thee"—not as the confident speaker of "Church-monuments" tries to do, but as one who begins to know his own radical egotism and incapacity for true speech. He has placed his very language in question, acknowledging that he cannot extricate himself from its force and appeal. "Commodious to conquer heav'n" recapitulates his problem perfectly: "Commodious" is normally a term of approbation or approval, but here it has the opposite significance.[8] The impulses captured in his language are themselves the root of sin.

---

7. Notes:

1. *It may a Babel prove* refers to "this," which in turn refers to his admiration for the world's Regiment.

2. *Commodious* means "capable" or "serviceable."

8. In a letter to his stepfather Herbert says of the position of University Orator, which he hoped to get, that "the commodiousness is beyond the Revenue." *Works of George Herbert,* 369.

"Constancie" answers "Frailtie" by presenting an apparently idealized alternative to such weakness:

W̱ho is the honest man?
He that doth still and strongly good
pursue,
To God, his neighbour, and himself most true:
Whom neither force nor fawning can
Unpinne, or wrench from giving all their due.

The poem proceeds in this remorseless rhythm to describe the person who "never melts or thaws," a monstrous possibility. The poem concludes:

This is the Mark-man, safe and sure,
Who still is right, and prayes to be so still.

Emerson called this a "noble poem," and in a sense it is;[9] in another sense it is terrifying, for its hero, the man free from error, is inhuman. He is a person who knows he is right and acts accordingly. In fact, as is also the case with Milton's *Paradise Lost,* the speaker's language of insistent and unexamined conclusion—"honest," "good," "true"—is expressive of the force of will that drives him. The great lesson of "Frailtie," and of the other poems too, is that we can not know that we are right; what we can know is that every act of self-assertion has its roots in the self. Such an ideal as "Constancie" is unattainable, and if it were attainable it would be awful, a fact that is enacted for us in the end-stopped lines and heavy rhythms: the poem marches along like its hero, full of force but without any of the uncertainties or conflicts that typically give life and value to Herbert's verse.

In this context the first line of "Affliction" (III) is an extraordinary and welcome shock: "My heart did heave, and there came forth, *O God*!" This is not the sophisticated and poetic mind of "Church-monuments," or the self-sermonizing voice of "Content," and certainly not the voice of the successful moral agent in "Constancie," but the

---

9. Ralph Waldo Emerson, *Journals and Miscellaneous Notebooks* (Cambridge, Mass.: Harvard University Press, 1969) 7: 45.

cry of a person speaking out of suffering and distress. After the in-humanity of "Constancie" it comes as an enormous relief. More than that: to this speaker God is not a remote figure of power, to be supplicated, but a presence both in the world and in him:

> M y heart did heave, and there came forth, *O God!*
> By that I knew that thou wast in the grief,
> To guide and govern it to my relief.

Here the speaker achieves a momentary, and witty, way of recognizing the central fact represented in "The Sacrifice," namely God's participation in human suffering, including now his own. He begins with a com-plaint—"O God!"—but converts it instantly into a ground of faith, proof of God's love for him. He thus imagines a God who suffers for humanity not once, but repeatedly, and whose love is present in his own suffering, a fact that alone makes it endurable. "Hadst thou not had thy part, / Sure the unruly sigh had broke my heart." The poem concludes:

> They who lament one crosse,
> Thou dying dayly, praise thee to thy losse.[10]

Composed in reaction to the moral perfectionism of "Constancie," this poem takes the speaker an important step along the path to "Love" (III). More than any poem so far, except "The Sacrifice," it imagines God as a loving being in human life. This is as far from the asserted moral self-sufficiency of "Constancie" as one could imagine. "Affliction" answers it by imagining and asserting a different sort of constancy: not the rhythmic self-assertion of the moral man, but a divine presence in all suffering.

This series of poems reaches its culmination in the next:

The Starre

> B right spark, shot from a brighter place,
> Where beams surround my Saviours face,

---

10. That is: those who lament only your death on Good Friday do you an injustice, since you die daily, in us and for us.

Canst thou be any where
So well as there?

Yet, if thou wilt from thence depart,
Take a bad lodging in my heart;
For thou canst make a debter,
And make it better.

First with thy fire-work burn to dust
Folly, and worse then folly, lust:
Then with thy light refine,
And make it shine:

So disengag'd from sinne and sicknesse,
Touch it with thy celestiall quicknesse,
That it may hang and move
After thy love.

Then with our trinitie of light,
Motion, and heat, let's take our flight
Unto the place where thou
Before didst bow.

Get me a standing there, and place
Among the beams, which crown the face
Of him, who dy'd to part
Sinne and my heart:

That so among the rest I may
Glitter, and curle, and winde as they:
That winding is their fashion
Of adoration.

Sure thou wilt joy, by gaining me
To flie home like a laden bee
Unto that hive of beams
And garland-streams.

Perhaps more fully than any we have read, this poem expresses the
possibility of happiness, touched with feelings of longing. Our sense of
the fullness with which it does this is a result, in part at least, of the
way it calls upon the language that the whole series of poems has been

making. The closing image of the bees returning to the hive, for example, invokes the bees of "Employment" (I), and "Praise" (I) too, who were engaged in significant work that the speaker felt as a rebuke. The other part of the image, the hive of "beams," recalls the end of "Mattens"—"then by a sunne-beam I will climbe to thee"—and looks forward to the "hive of sweetnesse" of "Home." The spark, which he asks to take a "bad lodging" in his heart, recalls at once the star imagery of "The Holy Scriptures" (II) and the central image of "Sepulchre," where the speaker lamented the fact that Christ had "no lodging" but a stone, rather than a human heart. It also anticipates "Artillerie," which begins with the image of a spark landing in the lap of the speaker. The language, "glitter, and curle, and winde," anticipates that of "Jordan" (II), where the speaker remembers his verse, "curling with metaphors a plain intention," and rejects ornamentation of that sort; to accept it here implies acceptance of his own verse and verse-making.

Most striking of all, however, is the tone of intimacy and confidence in this poem that allows the speaker to talk to the star, a mediator between him and his God, as to a friend: "let's take our flight." The greatest significance is built into that intimate "us," here casually reduced by an apostrophe to a single letter. The ease and naturalness of address are confirmed by the playfulness of the imagery, and by his confidence that the star will "joy" in bringing him "home." The speaker feels a trust and security that allow his poetic mind to sing and sail, which in other circumstances balks and stalls, and this ease itself is his best expression of felicity.

Evanescence

For Herbert poetry is a kind of thought; not logical or deductive or assertive or reducible to propositions, even to propositions of faith and Scripture, but a form of life, an activity. It is a series of attempts, each partial and evanescent, to work towards clarification, always on the understanding that the illumination, or shift of perception or feeling, will be momentary, and that when it is done the process of life, of writing poetry—of being a poem—will have to begin all over again. God is not to be found in physical temples or "furniture," not even in texts of law or Scripture, but in moments of self-realization and correction, in what I have earlier called the movement towards prayer. The life is in the movement, not the prayer itself; in the dismantling of the structures of feeling and thought with which it begins, and the construction of others; in the breakdown of defenses and the movement toward a bareness of soul; and in the performance of what can come to the soul when such bareness is achieved. This is to be found, more than anything else, in who the speaker is able to become in relation to the "thou" he addresses. This is the life it is the object of Herbert's poetry to achieve, for himself, and to demonstrate for us; this is what he means when his speaker says, in "The Quidditie," that the reason he writes verse is not its splendor, or social value, but because "it is that which while I use I am with thee."

I have said that Herbert's poetry has a quality of evanescence, by which I mean to point to many things: the sense that the seeming permanence of the poem is in fact delusive; that the meaning of the poetry for the writer as well as the reader is not in any position it establishes, not even in the comprehension of contraries, but in the activity itself; that no sooner is a poem written than another must be written, in a process that goes on throughout life; that life is thus at its center the making of poems, whether of a formal or an informal kind—or, to put it the other way round, that Herbert's poetry catches and records, and thus makes the object of conscious thought and improvement, processes of mind and feeling that make up the central stuff of life; that our work with language is always a struggle with its false claims to meaning of a sort it cannot have; that life is lived most intelligently and fully not in the creation of monuments or in the attempt to utter firm and stable truths, but in the bright moment at which the self is put into question and language fails—a moment that can be at once a failure of mind and a kind of epiphany.

Such a sense of things is hard to express in language—it calls in fact for a poet of Herbert's kind and quality, which I am not—and it may help define the quality I suggest to think of two other writers, both American, with whom there are important lines of relation.

I begin with Emerson, who was himself much influenced by Herbert, and who remains influential in our own day. Not that there are not differences: of course there are, and they are in fact as interesting as the similarities. But there is a deep similarity too, which may be more easily visible in Emerson than Herbert. It is easier for us to misread Herbert as simply affirming, with great beauty, what can be said directly and simply in the theological language of his day, than it is to read Emerson, perhaps the greatest language eroder of the American tradition, in such a mistaken way.[11]

I shall take as my text Emerson's early book *Nature,* still read in high school and college courses. It is prose, of course, but Emerson is at least as much a poet here as he is in his formal verse. This book opens with the assured voice of the essayist, speaking accepted truths to an audience whose civilized identity is affirmed with nearly every word: "To go into a solitude, a man needs to retire as much from his chamber as from society." To speak thus of what "a man" needs, as if all men were the same—and all people were men—is to affirm that we are all knowable, and that what is known can be stated as a kind of public truth. We are imagined as cultivated beings, as those who know and live in something called "society"—as opposed, for example, to living with "other people"—and we inhabit not ordinary rooms but "chambers," of which indeed we have enough so that we can claim one as our singular possession. The desire for "solitude" is that of the overbusy man, not of the lonely or marginal person, and is itself a kind of luxury, on a small scale analogous to that of the country home, which derives its meaning from the city with which it is contrasted and from which, in America at least, its economic support usually comes.

The next sentence is: "I am not solitary whilst I read and write, though nobody is with me." Here the escape is redefined: not just from "society" and all that it entails, but from the very sense of the cultivated life that his diction has implicitly invoked, from the books and papers of his study. We here start a journey out from an established point, and it is most unclear where it will lead. "But if a man would be alone, let him look at the stars." The goal is no longer the solitude of the first sentence, implying and affirming as it does its correlative society, but "to be alone," and what "man" of the first sentence would choose that? Notice that the way to achieve this condition is no longer to "retire," as from one room to another, but to "look at the stars": just you and them, just looking. And with what effect? "The rays that come from those heavenly worlds will separate between him and what he touches." The self is now imagined to be entirely stripped of all the

---

11. On Emerson's style see especially Richard Poirier, *The Renewal of Literature: Emersonian Reflections* (New York: Random House, 1987), to which my own reading of Emerson is indebted.

social qualities it was impliedly given at the beginning and conceived of as an entity not in relation to other people, by contact or withdrawal, but in relation to everything in the world that is not itself, that is with what Emerson will soon call "Nature."

This progressive dislocation of the mind continues until on the next page we read the famous sentences: "Standing on the bare ground,—my head bathed by the blithe air, and uplifted into infinite space,—all mean egotism vanishes. I become a transparent eyeball; I am nothing; I see all; the currents of the Universal Being circulate through me; I am part or parcel of God." A kind of impossible and vatic talk, it may seem, a sort of parody of transcendentalism. But it is given much of its meaning by its context, particularly by its juxtaposition with the normal and civilized voice with which he began, for it thus enacts the process of transportation it describes. Consider for example the following sentence, preceding by two or three the one just quoted: "Crossing a bare common, in snow puddles, at twilight, under a clouded sky, without having in my thoughts any occurrence of special good fortune, I have enjoyed a perfect exhilaration." The effect of this juncture of styles is to create a text the very point of which is to attain a kind of simultaneous dislocation both from language and from the world our language defines. Almost as if by magic it resists to the death all summary in propositional form. Emerson thus brings his reader to experience what in his essay "Experience" he later calls the "evanescence and lubricity of all objects."

For another example we might turn to the last pages of that essay, where Emerson begins by saying, "Hankering after an overt or practical effect seems to me an apostasy," as if it were silly or ineffectual to imagine one's thoughts having consequences in the world; yet concludes in nearly direct contradiction: "the true romance which the world exists to realize, will be the transformation of genius into practical power." Here is the point at which the transition is achieved:

> I have not found that much was gained by manipular attempts to realize the world of thought. Many eager persons successively make an experiment in this way, and make themselves ridiculous. They acquire democratic manners, they foam at the mouth, they hate and deny. Worse, I observe that in the history of mankind there is never a solitary example of success,—taking their own tests of success. I say this polemically, or in reply to the inquiry, Why not realize your world? But far be from me the despair which prejudges the law by

a paltry empiricism,—since there never was a right endeavor but it succeeded. Patience and patience, we shall win at the last.

With the enormous differences between these two writers there is this point of great similarity: their sense of the "evanescence and lubricity" of all things, and the consequent sense that the meaning of a poem, or a certain kind of prose, is in part its effect in dislocating the reader from the furniture of language—like the furniture of the chamber—and inducing a kind of bareness of soul. This effect is in turn certain to be momentary: it cannot be achieved again by the same process it was achieved before, but must be recreated afresh by each of us, in our reading and writing alike. More than Emerson, perhaps, Herbert extends the lubricity to include the human personality itself, and the kind of moral drama each enacts with his language is different. Yet these writers share a sense of human life as fundamentally evanescent, perpetually created and creative.

Another American writer of whom I often think in connection with Herbert is Emily Dickinson. I said in connection with the image at the end of "Mattens"—"By a sunne-beame I will climbe to thee"—that I was reminded of her poetry, and much the same thing happens at the end of "The Starre," when Herbert speaks of "a hive of beams / And garland-streams." Compare Dickinson's "Or Butterflies, off Banks of Noon, / Leap, plashless as they swim"; her repeated images of bees; her use of "noon" as a way of talking about heaven; her extravagant images—"Inebriate of air am I." Then think of the synaesthesia at the end of Herbert's "Christmas": "Till ev'n his beams sing, and my musick shine."

Both of these poets take as their subjects their own shifting spiritual condition; their conception of their God and their relation with him; their ability to face their own deaths and that of others; their sense of isolation and disconnectedness; and the question, Of what value can poetry be on conditions such as these? Unlike Frost or Wordsworth, say, who start with an event or situation in the natural world, or Shakespeare, who starts with a social event or moment, both of these poets start with the mysteries of their inner life, which both of them feel cannot be put directly into language. This leads them into the kind of poetry that draws constant attention to the limits of the languages in which it is written. Both poets speak, in Dickinson's phrase, of "internal difference, / Where the Meanings, are."

Here is what Alice Fulton says about Dickinson: "Dickinson is primarily an ontological poet with a unique ability to forge inner landscapes from abstract, rather than concrete language and to express ideas—states of being if you will—without resorting to an objective correlative."[12] This is true of Dickinson and almost as true of Herbert too. Both are difficult poets, and largely for the same reason, that they are both poets of interior life.

But both are social poets too, speaking in Herbert's case especially to God, in Dickinson's to God and nature. Both speak as if the social relations they create were possible and intelligible: "A narrow Fellow in the Grass / Occasionally rides," she writes; "You may have met Him—did you not" "A Bird came down the Walk— / He did not know I saw—". Herbert, as we have seen, creates in every poem a social relation with his God. Yet in both cases these are partly metaphors, displaced usages, ways of talking about what cannot be talked about directly except in a most unsatisfactory language of doctrinal assertion. Finally, the achievement of each is of a similar kind: they do not create a few masterpieces, like Keats's odes say, each of which can stand alone, but instead work out a whole new way of doing poetry. Like Picasso, or Gertrude Stein, it is in their style, in a new way of talking, that we find their greatest gift to us.

These similarities are perhaps not surprising, for Herbert was one of Dickinson's favorite poets. In fact, a transcription of "Mattens" found its way into an early volume of her poems: her editors did not recognize it as Herbert's, but thought it hers.[13] There are of course differences as well: but I hear these voices answering one another across the years and perhaps, as with Frost as well, to attend to one may help us hear the other better.

---

12. Alice Fulton, "Her Moment of Brocade: The Reconstruction of Emily Dickinson," *Parnassus* 15 (1989): 9–44, 22.

13. Cristanne Miller, *Emily Dickinson: A Poet's Grammar* (Cambridge, Mass.: Harvard University Press, 1987), 202 n.10.

The Acceptance of Love

Chapter 5

Imagined Identities and Relations

In a world with infinite time and space, this book would continue just as it has begun, discussing Herbert's poems one at a time in the order in which they appear in "The Church." But this is impossible, and in any event, as I said at the outset, my aim is not to provide a complete or comprehensive reading of Herbert's poems, but to establish a sense of the way his poetry works, one that will carry us into verse as yet unread, making what at first seems strange appear increasingly familiar—or, in some cases, make what at first seems simple and clear appear increasingly complex or mysterious. The hope is that as we learn this poetic language we may hear it speak, not only to those in a remote past among whom we have to imagine ourselves, but directly to us, as we are situated now, or as we have become situated in reading it; by this it may acquire an importance of a new kind.

Instead of working through the poems in the order in which they appear in "The Church," then, I shall here trace out a set of thematic connections that, to my mind at least, are crucial to the meaning of Herbert's verse, focusing particularly on the way he imagines his God and himself and the way these imaginings change across the book as a whole. Is his "Lord," for example, a God of power or of love? Of justice or mercy? And who is he himself, as revealed here: a speaking voice, a brain, a mind, a heart? Capable of what knowledge, what speech? The fact that these identities and relations are all expressed in language calls upon us to ask as well how he imagines language itself, its capacities and successes, its failures and dissolutions.

Before looking at his poetry with these questions in mind, however, it may be helpful to recall that all of us perpetually imagine the world that we inhabit, including the other people who live there too, and that we necessarily imagine ourselves as well. We cannot live as human beings without such imagined identities, relations, and contexts. Thus we imagine our families—father and mother are wise and loving, brother Peter

The River Nadder between Bemerton and Fugglestone

a pest—or our towns and schools: I am from "Midland," which is a center of life, an important place, or perhaps marginal, out of things; I go to "Rose Valley Junior High" and say that this is a good school, or a prison. Politics is an extreme version of this, in which we imagine the major parties, one good and the other bad, and ally ourselves with one, often pinning the hopes of the nation on the election of a particular candidate. Internationally we construct our world as well, arranging things called nations on a map, with the north at the top, say, and North America at the center, and beyond that we imagine the solar system, the galaxy, the universe. And for everything we imagine we construct a history: the "Big Bang" and the consequent expansion of the universe; the "discovery" of America; our family's arrival on the continent and subsequent successes or failures; our own childhood; and all this is told in the form of imagined stories of the past. We cannot help it; we must constantly imagine self and world and other and reveal these imaginings whenever we speak or write. The world we experience is the world we think. Yet usually we see the world not as if it were in any way imagined, but as if it were simply real, natural, just the way things are. Our imaginings are our reality; our stories are true. This is in fact why it is so difficult to focus critical attention upon them: if they disappear, as mere fictions, what have we left? Sometimes the discovery that our more idealistic visions of the world are imagined leads people to argue vociferously that we should abandon them and face the "realities" of power, or economics, or race and class. But these realities are of course also in part imagined, often in a more simple and less satisfactory way than those they replace.

Our imaginings reflect both the culture and the self. Thus we have each of us an array of inherited languages, a set of practices and gestures and stories that construct the world in certain ways and provide us with many of our central terms and motives. But these languages do not work like machines; they are material for our lives, and what we make them mean is at least partly up to us. While you and I attend the same church or synagogue, for example, or the same college, or live in the same city, there is a sense in which these places are very different, and not just because we are exposed to different facets of them. We construct our worlds differently. So too, when we both speak the language of the law—or trout fishing or the church or parenthood—there is a sense in which the language is the same for both of us, yet we use the language differently, to create different experiences, and different meanings too.

What is true of the rest of the world is also true of religious life, perhaps most of all true of "God." In one sense all Roman Catholics, say, have the same God, defined by creed and practice and experience, and join in common prayer to him; yet in another sense, "God" is surely different for different members of that church: for one person he is stern, a source of commandment and threat, for another kind and forgiving, for another not a "he" at all but perhaps a "she," and so on. Out of the materials we are given by our culture, each of us thus imagines his or her God—or the universe without a God—and we are in part responsible for what we create.

A field of religious belief and feeling is thus two inconsistent things at once: a screen on which an individual projects his or her own internal drama; and the source of many of the terms and feelings in which that drama is itself defined, a source indeed of that individual identity itself. Psychologists call the first process transference. In psychoanalysis, for example, the analyst physically disappears from the field of vision to help the patient project upon the absent person his or her own feelings and expectations, which were formed so early in life as to seem a part of nature, and in this way to expose them to examination. The patient will thus imagine the analyst at one point as malevolent, at another as unbelievably trustworthy, as full of love or contempt, and in the process of analysis all these imaginings become the subject of conscious thought and attention.

As for the second process—the way the self is partly made by the culture—one need only reflect on the ways in which one's own ways of imagining the world and oneself have been made by others, who have provided the categories, and the narratives, by which we construct the world: the family, the school, the city, the nation, the species. It is a great mistake to think of most of this as chosen by us: these are simply the terms on which we live. Much the same is true with respect to religious belief, especially in a world like Herbert's England, where no one could have escaped the force of the language and narratives of Christianity. The question is not whether one is a Christian, but what one makes that fact mean. This is what is at stake in one's choice to be a Puritan or Anglican, say, or an Anabaptist or a Roman Catholic.

How about those choices themselves? They can be expressed in terms of theological position or belief, as propositions, but this erases the really interesting question, which is why one would believe—or disbelieve— what the Puritans or Anglicans believed about the Scripture or the doctrine of election or the furnishing of the church. There is no point outside of culture from which such choices could be made, no position of uncommitted neutrality at which one could balance the probabilities, the pros and the cons. If there were such a position, free of culture, how is it imaginable that any choice could be made? Commitments of belief are not arrived at by pure logic or abstraction, but are always actions in a cultural context: acts of affiliation or disowning, of iden- tification or rejection, and not with respect to propositions merely but to communities and languages, whole ways of life that establish meaning and identity. It is accordingly somewhat misleading to speak of belief either as propositional or as chosen. While we do of course have some freedom to choose, that choice is never context-free but is always a response to something we did not choose; and while one's beliefs can be cast in propositional form, they are never simply that. Much of it must be simply discovery, learning who one already is.

All this is a way of leading up to a suggestion, that the central drama of Herbert's verse lies in its ways of imagining God, and the speaker, and the relation between them. Who is this suffering Christ, this Father who allows him to suffer, this mysterious Holy Spirit? Christian theology tells us that God is a source of commandments, for violation of which justice calls for punishment: punishment of a people, as in the Old

Testament; of all human beings, if Adam is seen to sin for us all; and of the individual who, in the church in which Herbert was a member, confessed every day, with the rest of the congregation, that "we have left undone those things which we ought to have done; and have done those things we ought not to have done; and there is no health in us." But what can Herbert make these things mean? And who am "I": sinner, yet forgiven? If a sinner, why forgiven? And who am I as a speaker, constantly asserting myself in my broken languages?

These are the questions that animate Herbert's work at the deepest level. I think, indeed, that they motivate the writing of it, and specifically of it as poetry, since for Herbert questions of this kind cannot be answered at the level of doctrine or theory, however strongly a side of him would like to do it, but require composed and written responses, actual enactments. The question, for us and Herbert alike, is not who God or the poet "is," but who Herbert makes his God in his very way of addressing him, and who he makes himself. And to these questions we cannot expect firm, clear, or consistent answers, for by now we know that Herbert's "I" is not one but many, a cluster of countering strains and gestures and feelings and moments—like, as he says in "Giddiness," a "Dolphin's skinne" shimmering with color. "He is some twentie sev'rall men at least / Each sev'rall houre." "God" too is infinitely various, at least as perceived or constructed by this mind.[1] Thus Herbert

---

1.

Justice (I)

I cannot skill of these thy wayes.
Lord, thou didst make me, yet thou woundest me;
Lord, thou dost wound me, yet thou dost relieve me:
Lord, thou relievest, yet I die by thee:
Lord, thou dost kill me, yet thou dost reprieve me.

But when I mark my life and praise,
Thy justice me most fitly payes:
For, I do praise thee, yet I praise thee not:
My prayers mean thee, yet my prayers stray:
I would do well, yet sinne the hand hath got:
My soul doth love thee, yet it loves delay.
I cannot skill of these my wayes.

Notice that the behavior of God here consists of alternations between one mode of being and another; on the understandings made explicit in "Affliction" (I), this could be both coherent and beneficial. The speaker's behavior by contrast is simply weak and self-contradictory.

cannot rely on any one perception, sentiment, statement, oath, faith, moment, or any other expression or act. On the conditions on which he conceives himself to live, the writing of a sequence of poems, catching an array of possibilities, may be the only imaginable way to address these questions of identity and relation. In this sense the poems are his life.

"God"

Almost every Herbert poem enacts one definition of God or another, as we have already seen. Think of "The Sacrifice," for example, presenting Christ as suffering uniquely, both as God and man; or "The Collar," in which the speaker's God, if it is God, knows just when to call upon him; or "Affliction" (I), in which the pains and miseries inflicted by God are seen as working to the speaker's good; or "The Windows," in which God transforms the soul of the preacher into something as beautiful and radiant as a church window; or "Easter," in which the beauty and power of Christ are so overwhelming that he has no need of anything the speaker might give, thus rendering him useless; or "Easter-wings," in which the punishment of sin descends unjustly from Adam to each of us; or "The Temper," in which God at first seems to stretch and rack the self, as if on purpose, "to make the musick better," but is then seen simply to absent himself; or "Whitsunday," in which the Spirit is first imagined as present, then as gone from the earth. What follows below, then, is not meant as a representative sample of Herbert's ways of imagining God—that would require *The Temple* itself— but as the discussion of a small number of poems that seem to present with particular clarity certain important tendencies of Herbert's mind.

To all Angels and Saints

Oh glorious spirits, who after all your bands
See the smooth face of God without a frown
           Or strict commands;
Where ev'ry one is king, and hath his crown,
If not upon his head, yet in his hands:

Not out of envie or maliciousnesse
Do I forbear to crave your speciall aid:
           I would addresse
My vows to thee most gladly, Blessed Maid,
And Mother of my God, in my distresse.

Thou art the holy mine, whence came the gold,
The great restorative for all decay
                    In young and old;
Thou art the cabinet where the jewell lay:
Chiefly to thee would I my soul unfold:

But now, alas, I dare not; for our King,
Whom we do all joyntly adore and praise,
                    Bids no such thing:
And where his pleasure no injunction layes,
('Tis your own case) ye never move a wing.

All worship is prerogative, and a flower
Of his rich crown, from whom lyes no appeal
                    At the last houre:
Therefore we dare not from his garland steal,
To make a posie for inferiour power.

Although then others court you, if ye know
What's done on earth, we shall not fare the worse,
                    Who do not so;
Since we are ever ready to disburse,
If any one our Masters hand can show.[2]

The speaker here expresses his love for what is both beautiful and holy—
the saints and angels, especially Mary the mother of Jesus—yet at the
same time acknowledges that this love is itself forbidden by "our King,"

---

2. Notes:

1. The speaker begins by imagining the angels and saints in heaven, each crowned,
   but holding her crown in her hands. This is of course a Catholic image of heaven,
   and especially of Mary.
2. *Not out of envie or maliciousnesse:* as usual, such denials have the effect of affirming
   just what they deny, here that the speaker wishes he were such a one as they.
3. *Thou art the holy mine* invokes "Avarice," the immediately preceding poem, which
   is about the digging of gold, and its essential character as dirt.
4. *'Tis your own case:* speaking of Mary's own patience and quiescence until addressed
   with an affirmative command. Presumably this refers to her remaining a virgin,
   waiting for the special purpose God has for her.
5. *We are ever ready to disburse,* etc.: we will happily make payment as soon as
   someone can show us an order signed by our master.
6. Notice that this poem's deeply undermined reverence for "our King" would
   reach the earthly king as well as the heavenly one.

the judge who will decide our fates at the last hour, whom we therefore "dare not" offend. The King's opposition is not grounded in reason or love, as the speaker sees it, but is simply an exercise of power: he "bids no such thing." The speaker's only role is to obey or disobey; what constrains him to the former is not love, but fear. And what the King demands of him is itself terrible: that he stifle his love of the beautiful and sacred.

In a manner reminiscent of the "Jordan" poems, this poem has another layer of meaning, for the poem itself, despite its artifices of evasion, violates the prohibition it articulates. True, the poem is not the overt "vow" or invocation of "speciall aid" that is explicitly forbidden, but it is nonetheless an act of homage. Although it abjures prayer to Mary and the saints, it is in fact just the prayer that it abjures: a "posie for inferiour power."

The speaker here divides God up, as it were, into two personalities: the punitive and unreasoning King, and the angels and saints, whom he sees as lovely, kind, full of understanding and sympathy. This split is certainly justified by the tradition, which represents God in just these two opposing ways, in the Old Testament as well as the New, and perhaps nowhere so clearly as in the incredible story of Christ's crucifixion: the ultimate act of the loving God, sacrificing himself for humanity, yet the ultimate act of the punitive God as well, exacting this price, from his own son, for the sins of humanity. When we ask, or Herbert does, whether it is possible to imagine God more coherently, more satisfactorily, the question is thus both personal and cultural. It matters to him, nothing more so; and it matters to his world as well, which is shaped by this language and its conceptions of God and man. As was true for Milton, the transformation of this way of thinking is an act of public as well as a private meaning.

In this poem there is more than a hint that this double construction of the holy is the speaker's doing, not built into the nature of things. We are told for example, ambiguously, that this mysterious King "bids no such thing." Does this mean "forbid," as the speaker seems to assume, or only a kind of silence? Is it the speaker, then, whom we are to see as constructing this God so punitive and controlling?

Compare the following:

Decay

S weet were the dayes, when thou didst lodge with Lot,
   Struggle with Jacob, sit with Gideon,

Advise with Abraham, when thy power could not
Encounter Moses strong complaints and mone:
    Thy words were then, *Let me alone.*

One might have sought and found thee presently
At some fair oak, or bush, or cave, or well:
Is my God this way? No, they would reply:
He is to Sinai gone, as we heard tell:
    List, ye may heare great Aarons bell.

But now thou dost thy self immure and close
In some one corner of a feeble heart:
Where yet both Sinne and Satan, thy old foes,
Do pinch and straiten thee, and use much art
    To gain thy thirds and little part.

I see the world grows old, when as the heat
Of thy great love, once spread, as in an urn
Doth closet up it self, and still retreat,
Cold Sinne still forcing it, till it return,
    And calling *Justice,* all things burn.

The speaker in this poem looks back with nostalgia on an earlier time, that of the Old Testament, when God was actually present in the world: seen by Moses face to face, heard speaking from the burning bush or the cloud of fire, confronted directly in Jacob's dream, and so on. Now, by contrast, as the world grows old, he is immured in "some one corner of a feeble heart." God's greatness once filled the world with his presence, but has now decayed—hence the title—into the minuscule, withdrawn from the world into merely interior life. What was a mighty figure striding the earth has become a ghost of its former self, pinched and tormented by sin and Satan; it may even be defeated by them in the end.

Then, in the last image, these elements are refigured: the speaker sees the reduction in size either as a concentration of heat, or as a withdrawal only temporary, but in either event the heat will not remain trivial long but will soon return, or expand, and "all things burn," presumably in punishment of sin. The "heat" of thy "great love" is a complex and in this context frightening pun, since for Herbert "heat" and "hate" were nearly homonyms.[3]

---

3. Compare "Love" (II), which begins "Immortal Heat, O let thy greater flame . . ."

What is wrong with all this? Nearly everything; the poem needs to be read as a dramatic monologue, like one of Robert Browning's, say "Up at a Villa—Down in the City," which praises town life, and condemns the country, in terms that no one could accept. Think, to begin with, of the Old Testament world as this speaker represents it: "lodging with Lot"—that word again recalling, as always, "Sepulchre": "No lodging for thee, but a cold hard stone"—is not a reference of unmixed felicity, alluding as it does to the destruction, by fire, of Sodom and Gomorrah and the conversion of Lot's wife into a pillar of salt. The man who lodged with Lot was protected by him from homosexual rape, that is true, but Lot achieved this only by substituting his own daughters as victims to the mob. (Genesis 19.) And God's availability to us, as imagined here, involves in fact a kind of diminution, a reduction in scale to the human: Moses could see him plain. The appeal is after all not so much that of greatness as that of familiarity. Yet—the chain of associations reveals—this familiarity was itself for the most part only apparent. One was never where God actually was, it seems, but at best where he recently had been: "He is to Sinai gone."

The world for which this speaker yearns is represented by him as in fact far more problematic than his feelings of nostalgia suggest, indeed as inconsistent with some of his claims for it. Nonetheless, there is a real appeal here, and it lies in the sense not so much of the power of God as his accessibility, his presence or immanence in the world—in some "fair oak, or bush, or cave, or well"—and this is so even if that presence is perpetually evanescent, that is, not really a perceptible presence at all.

The distortion becomes vastly greater in the second half of the poem, when he describes the situation "now," by which he means, though he does not say so and perhaps does not know it, in the world created by the events of the New Testament. He sees what has happened in terms of a diminution in God's size and power and significance, a reduction in his availability, and his movement from the great exterior world to the unattractive and confined spaces within. But all this could be described very differently: as finding a lodging not with Lot, but in a human heart, where God's presence is not felt less immediately but infinitely more so, and where its effect may be the inward transformation of the self. The movement inwards is not a diminution, in fact, but a miraculous intensification, a transformation of the God of power into the God of love—whom this speaker imagines not that way at all, but as the God of "heat."

The speaker, that is, tells a story but gets it wrong. Like the speaker in "Redemption," he does not understand the meaning of the story he tells, and in that way, more powerfully than in any other, defines the quality of heart and mind that stands in the way of his own transformation. He cannot recognize the act of love for what it is, but thinks only in terms of power and justice.[4]

While the definition of God and speaker is a question addressed throughout the poems—it is central to all of them—there are certain poems where it emerges with special clarity. One of these begins thus:

---

4. "Sion" rewrites "Decay" in a way that makes at least partially explicit what the speaker here misses, namely that the transition from the Old to the New Testament is an increase in love and aspiration and power:

Sion

Lord, with what glorie wast thou serv'd of old,
When Solomons temple stood and flourished!
   Where most things were of purest gold;
   The wood was all embellished
With flowers and carvings, mysticall and rare:
All show'd the builders, crav'd the seeers care.

Yet all this glorie, all this pomp and state
Did not affect thee much, was not thy aim;
   Something there was, that sow'd debate:
   Wherefore thou quitt'st thy ancient claim:
And now thy Architecture meets with sinne;
For all thy frame and fabrick is within.

There thou art struggling with a peevish heart,
Which sometimes crosseth thee, thou sometimes it:
   The fight is hard on either part.
   Great God doth fight, he doth submit.
All Solomons sea of brasse and world of stone
Is not so deare to thee as one good grone.

And truly brasse and stones are heavie things,
Tombes for the dead, not temples fit for thee:
   But grones are quick, and full of wings,
   And all their motions upward be;
And ever as they mount, like larks they sing;
The note is sad, yet musick for a King.

The entry of God into the heart is here seen not as a diminution or a loss, but as an act of grace and power. "Sion" also responds to the desire expressed in "Afflic-

Dialogue

Sweetest Saviour, if my soul
　　Were but worth the having,
Quickly should I then controll
　　Any thought of waving.
But when all my care and pains
Cannot give the name of gains
To thy wretch so full of stains,
What delight or hope remains?

The speaker here begins to imagine a God of love, but feels utterly barred from him by his own worthlessness. Whatever he may be told as a matter of doctrine, it simply does not make sense that God should care for him. No matter what he does—no matter what the "care and pains"—he cannot make himself a "gain" to anyone; his "stains" are too deep to be removed. The love he begins to imagine is thus impossible; the very imagining of it is therefore incoherent, and consequently overcome by another way of thinking, in which he sees himself as isolated and hopeless—a despair that is qualified only by the fact that he is able to express it in the form of a question, implying the possibility, however remote, of a favorable answer.

To this voice another answers in the next stanza, saying in effect that what motivates me is none of your business. It is my choice and that is all you need to know:

What, Child, is the ballance thine,
　　Thine the poise and measure?
If I say, Thou shalt be mine;
　　Finger not my treasure.
What the gains in having thee

---

tion" (I) and elsewhere for an untroubled life: the life we lead at its best is not untroubled, but one of struggle, and pain, and risk; often the best thing we have to offer is not a poem, but a "grone." Here the groan—like the affliction that gives rise to it—is a sign of God's presence in us, a sign that one is becoming, as the whole book of poems promises, a "temple": not of Solomon's kind, made of gold and glory, but a temple built in a human heart. The utterance that is at once a song and a "grone" from a suffering heart—that is, a poem—is the truest possible speech.

Benches at Leighton Bromswold

Do amount to, onely he,
Who for man was sold, can see;
That transferr'd th' accounts to me.

To the first speaker, however, this is not the conclusive argument it
seems to be. He cannot give up his insistence that God's action be
comprehensible, and to be told not to concern himself with the question
does not meet his need. The effect is not a return to his starting point
but a further descent into despair. This time he really gives up:

> But as I can see no merit,
>   Leading to this favour:
> So the way to fit me for it
>   Is beyond my savour.
> As the reason then is thine;
> So the way is none of mine:
> I disclaim the whole designe:
> Sinne disclaims and I resigne.

It makes sense that the speaker should do this. After all, the "Saviour" spoke in terms of gain and loss, accepting the acquisitive metaphors of the speaker's own opening remarks, and in these terms there is indeed no answer. And insofar as the "Saviour" says it is none of your business, speaking in a voice of peremptory command, he is an authoritarian figure—rather like the King in "To all Angels and Saints," who "bids no such thing"—whom it is difficult indeed to see as motivated by love. And, in any event, how can one give up the need to imagine one's world in a coherent or tolerable way? The speaker thus speaks as we all should do when he says that the "reason" makes no sense and that therefore the "way" is "none of mine." He therefore must "disclaim the whole designe"; his own want of merit, his sin, require it (even though there is a near-recognition in the last line that the disclaimer itself is the real sin).

The "Saviour" speaks again, but, significantly this time not so much to the speaker as about him. He has as it were turned away, in his own gesture of hopelessness:

> *That is all, if that I could*
> *Get without repining;*
> *And my clay, my creature, would*
> *Follow my resigning:*
> *That as I did freely part*
> *With my glorie and desert,*
> *Left all joyes to feel all smart— —*
> Ah! no more: thou break'st my heart.

The "Saviour" here says that this, the very act of "resigning" that the speaker feels as a gesture of hopelessness, would in fact be enough—at least if he could get it without the speaker's "repining," i.e., his fret or complaint. The resignation must be a true resignation of the will. If it were, it would promise, or threaten, to be like Christ's own, which is the free exchange of "all joyes" for "all smart." This is a way of imagining the sacrifice of Christ not as the triumph it will ultimately become but as a real assumption of the human condition, perhaps including—as we have also seen it expressed in "The Sacrifice" itself— genuine despair. (God is "in the grief" indeed.) To this act of the "Saviour," seen from the point of view of the suffering actor, the speaker responds with a cry that breaks through what is said and brings it to a halt. This is another version of the breakdown of discourse we have seen before, from "The Thanksgiving" on. But this one is ambiguous. Does the speaker's cry arise from sympathy for the suffering of another, voluntarily undertaken for his sake? Or from his own fear at the prospect of suffering so himself? It may be either feeling that cracks his composure and forces out the ejaculation with which the poem closes: if the latter, in a gesture of despair, if the former, in a momentary recognition of love and a resignation of the self to its claims.

If we see the cry as one of sympathy—and this is the dominant reading, I think—we have a performance of the way in which we might understand the Sacrifice itself as meant to save, as I suggested earlier, by reaching those whose hearts and minds could not be touched by anything less. On this view, the terrible suffering of Christ is not exacted by a punitive God to satisfy his own demands for justice, but is freely given as the only way that he can make himself seen and felt as a God of love, against the speaker's deep-seated sense of himself as worthless and deserving punishment, and against, as well, his vision of God as caught like him by the moral logic of sin, and thus committed to punishment. It is the thickness of our moral and emotional hides, our own insistence upon a language of acquisition and rights and our consequent desire for punishment, that requires this sacrifice. Nothing else could reach us. But I think the poem can be read the other way, too, as ending in a disclaimer of another kind, in the speaker's expression of his own natural incapacity to tolerate the prospect of his own suffering.

A different sense of possibility is achieved by the speaker in "Grieve not the Holy Spirit." He has apparently just read or heard the passage in Ephesians that makes this command, and responds to it thus:

Ephesians 4. 30.
Grieve not the Holy Spirit

And art thou grieved, sweet and sacred Dove,
   When I am sowre,
   And crosse thy love?
Grieved for me? the God of strength and power
  Griev'd for a worm, which when I tread,
  I passe away and leave it dead?

Then weep mine eyes, the God of love doth grieve:
Weep foolish heart,
And weeping live:
For death is drie as dust. Yet if ye part,
End as the night, whose sable hue
Your sinnes expresse; melt into dew.

When sawcie mirth shall knock or call at doore,
Cry out, Get hence,
Or cry no more.
Almightie God doth grieve, he puts on sense:
I sinne not to my grief alone,
But to my Gods too; he doth grone.

Oh take thy lute, and tune it to a strain,
Which may with thee
All day complain.
There can no discord but in ceasing be.
Marbles can weep; and surely strings
More bowels have, then such hard things.

Lord, I adjudge my self to tears and grief,
Ev'n endlesse tears
Without relief.
If a cleare spring for me no time forbears,
But runnes, although I be not drie;
I am no Crystall, what shall I?

Yet if I wail not still, since still to wail
Nature denies;
And flesh would fail,
If my deserts were masters of mine eyes:
Lord, pardon, for thy Sonne makes good
My want of tears with store of bloud.

The speaker begins with a half-credulous, half-incredulous response to his reading of the scriptural injunction—"Grieve not the Holy Spirit"—as he suddenly realizes that this language affirms a possibility he had never contemplated, and now can scarcely believe, namely that the "sweet and sacred Dove" could actually be grieved for him. What does this recognition mean? How can he respond to it? "Then weep mine eyes," he says, because the "God of love"—no longer the God of "strength and power"—"doth grieve": "Weep foolish heart, / And weeping live."

But he goes beyond weeping: he imagines a future, as human beings must, this one with himself as the central, and virtuous, actor, sending mirth from his door. And he shall not only weep, he shall make music— or poems—that shall accompany the weeping, in a kind of harmony. Like the speaker in "The Thanksgiving," he becomes the hero of his own imaginings.

In an affirmance of logic and doctrine he imposes a sentence on himself: "Lord, I adjudge my self to tears and grief." But what kind of grief is this? It is not actually felt as grief, as sorrow or pain, but is asserted as an intellectually or doctrinally necessary conclusion. What has happened to the feelings into which he was startled by the command, "Grieve not the Holy Spirit"? He has regressed from feeling into logic, from a momentary recognition of the possibility of love to a version of his sermon voice.

The speaker goes on to acknowledge that no imagined experience of grief, of weeping, or lute playing can possibly be adequate to the perpetual clear spring of love that his sinning grieves. He is actually worse off than he was before, for he now sees that as a consequence of his nature he cannot maintain the weeping that he has promised (which he now calls "wailing"). At the end he turns away from his effort to imagine himself acting well, away indeed from the poetic impulse itself, to the simple formula, with awkward and thudding rhymes, of the last two lines.

The movement of the whole is thus from the startled recognition, against his sense of what necessity requires, that he is indeed loved, to a kind of imagined life of virtue, with himself as hero, led in response to that recognition; this in turn becomes a kind of dead and despairing intellectualization; and from this, at the end, he manages an imperfect prayer. This is perhaps the best that one can do, and Herbert's poetry shows us that it cannot be done once and for all, but must be done over and over again, perpetually.

The Bag

Away despair! my gracious Lord doth heare.
　　Though windes and waves assault my keel,
　　He doth preserve it: he doth steer,
　　　Ev'n when the boat seems most to reel.

Storms are the triumph of his art:
Well may he close his eyes, but not his heart.

Hast thou not heard, that my Lord JESUS di'd?
    Then let me tell thee a strange storie.
    The God of power, as he did ride
    In his majestick robes of glorie,
    Resolv'd to light; and so one day
He did descend, undressing all the way.

The starres his tire of light and rings obtain'd,
    The cloud his bow, the fire his spear,
    The sky his azure mantle gain'd.
    And when they ask'd, what he would wear;
    He smil'd and said as he did go,
He had new clothes a making here below.

When he was come, as travellers are wont,
    He did repair unto an inne.
    Both then, and after, many a brunt
    He did endure to cancell sinne:
    And having giv'n the rest before,
Here he gave up his life to pay our score.

But as he was returning, there came one
    That ran upon him with a spear.
    He, who came hither all alone,
    Bringing nor man, nor arms, nor fear,
    Receiv'd the blow upon his side,
And straight he turn'd, and to his brethren cry'd,

If ye have any thing to send or write,
    I have no bag, but here is room:
    Unto my Fathers hands and sight,
    Beleeve me, it shall safely come.
    That I shall minde, what you impart,
Look, you may put it very neare my heart.

Or if hereafter any of my friends
    Will use me in this kinde, the doore
    Shall still be open; what he sends
    I will present, and somewhat more,

> Not to his hurt. Sighs will convey
> Any thing to me. Harke, Despair away.[5]

This poem is written in part as a response to its immediate predecessor, "Longing," which is one lengthy cry of despair: "Lord JESU, heare my heart / Which hath been broken now so long, / That ev'ry part / Hath got a tongue!" "The Bag" begins with an answer: "Away despair! my gracious Lord doth heare." The speaker here looks to Jesus, as in "Grieve not . . ." he looked to the Holy Spirit, as a way of dealing with his conflicted and sometimes dreadful imaginings of God the Father. It is Christ to whom Herbert turns, in a way that is both doctrinally correct and psychologically sensible, for his main image of Christ, as we saw in "The Sacrifice" and "The Agonie," is as one who suffers out of love for others.

When the speaker tries to give content to his affirmation he first thinks, in a rather mechanical way, of himself as a ship, Christ as his protector; and, characteristically, this position itself becomes confused or clouded. Are the storms also the work of Christ? And why does he close his eyes? The evident inadequacy, or tailing off, of that effort motivates another, this one cast in terms of a story or myth: Christ descends among us, casting off his splendid clothes and giving them to the cloud, the fire, the sky. In a wonderful gesture we are told that Christ, when questioned about what clothes he would wear, "smil'd and said as he did go, / He had new clothes a making here below." This language catches some of the self-confidence, the happiness and acceptance, of "Love" (III): "Love took my hand, and smiling did

---

5. "The Bag" has a quality of grotesqueness that requires comment, both for itself—what could be more grotesque than the image of the body as post bag, opened for business by the spear wound?—and for Herbert's capacity to present it in such a way as to make it seem perfectly normal. We have seen grotesqueness before: in the comparison between "stretched sinews" and musical "strings" in "Easter"; in the image of sins as stones making Christ's blood burble and sing, in "Church-lock and key"; and in the image of Christ's body being pressed for its blood, in "The Agonie," which is repeated in "The Bunch of Grapes." Compare "Church-rents and schismes," which ends with the image of eyes that might "lick up all the dew" or "Praise" (III), which compares a tear in God's eye to "streamers neare the top / Of some fair church, to show the sore / And bloudie battell which thou once didst trie." In "The Bag" the control of the grotesqueness by the poet expresses Christ's control over the hideousness of his own situation, a display of wit in the face of destruction.

reply, / Who made the eyes but I?" The image in "The Bag" is a highly visual and surrealistic moment: one could imagine a splendid eighteenth-century painting of such a scene.

We have noticed already, in "Humilitie," that Herbert has the capacity to make his imagined world real and vivid to us not only when it consists of voices we can learn to recognize but when it consists of narratives that cannot in the usual sense be true. In "The Bag" Herbert fuses two styles or modes of writing, this kind of myth-making[6] and biblical narrative: he makes his own myth about Christ. There is no textual warrant for most of this story in the Bible, yet it is here affirmed, affirmed just as the narrative of "Humilitie" is affirmed: as expressing imagined truth. Yet the subject of this myth, Christ, is one for whom Herbert's religious language makes claims not of imaginative but literal truth, claims that are the driving force of creed and catechism.

In this poem the central credal event, Christ's sacrifice, is cast in re-

---

6. For another instance, consider "The World." Here Herbert tells a story of a house built by Love, where Fortune came, and claimed to be the builder, saying that "her fine cobwebs did support the frame." But they were swept away by Wisdom. Likewise Pleasure came and made alterations, building "balconies, terraces." But these were removed by "Laws." Then Sin came and, like a sycamore tree working within the walls, tore at the stones and beams; but Grace shored up the fabric and cut the shoots. Then Sin combined with Death and razed the building "to the very floore," at which point "*Love* and *Grace* took *Glorie* by the hand, / And built a braver palace then before."

How does this poem work? In particular, since it is obviously a kind of allegory, why does it not collapse into a form of propositional assertion? I think the answer lies in its reversal of our expectations: as Wisdom could protect the building against the excesses of Fortune, and Laws against those of Pleasure, so we expect other virtues to defend it successfully, as Grace indeed does manage to do against Sin. But to our surprise the narrative is not one of success, after all, but of failure, for Sin comes back with Death and razes the building to the floor. In the context the poem has defined, this is not just a propositional utterance but an experience, the experience of expectation upset, and upset in ways that are threatening indeed, for the mistake we make about the building is the same mistake we make about ourselves—the self as building being a common trope for Herbert—whose end we do not foresee either. The optimistic assertion of the last two lines, which claim that the story is one of success after all, confirms us in our original expectation and is in turn—in a qualified way—confirmed by us: this has the air of rightness after all, a sense reinforced by the order of the stanzas, which require something to come after Death and Sin have done their work. We are then not merely told something by this myth, but involved in the experience of life, death, and resurrection.

Other myth-making poems include "The Pilgrimage" and "Peace."

duced, even commercial, language: "He did endure to cancell sinne."[7]
What is made bright and vivid is another part of the imagined story, the
descent from heaven and Christ's promise on the cross to convey anything
from one of his "friends" to his father, "and somewhat more, / Not to
his hurt." This promise is the ground upon which the speaker says
"Harke, Despair away."

To combine myth-making and biblical material in this way redefines
both. The kind of enhanced reality that the imagination can give to a
wholly fictional story can belong to credal or doctrinal events, as we
also saw in "The Sacrifice" as well; yet the credal events are in this
way also released from their fixation in a literal historical language.
When made a myth of, they become not less true but more so. This
is in turn to place in a different way the entire theological language
within which Herbert has been living and working from the beginning.
It is his own capacity to imagine, to tell anew, to create the truths of
story and poem, that enables him to move at the end into a more
confident relation with what he has been told and experienced. This
gesture will receive its fullest performance in "Love" (III) itself, when
he speaks of God in a mythical or imagined way that does not depend
on the theological iconography that dominates Christian thought. It is
in part the dissolution of the language of theology, its simultaneous
reduction and elevation to the status of myth, that enables him to
appropriate its truths, to make them his own, and to feel them in his
heart.

The modernist perception that language is not a transparent series of
labels for things, but catches up the mind in twists and perversions, in
the tensions and contradictions of a culture and of human life itself, is
one out of which Herbert functioned all the time. Every one of his
poems is an essay in the impossible: an attempt to define a coherent
self, a proper relation with a God both omnipotent and loving, and to
do so in a language true and beautiful. None of these things can be
adequately done, and the poems are simultaneously demonstrations of
the ways in which that is true—they are in this sense a series of failures—
and performances of the ways, nonetheless, that a mind and heart can
live on such conditions; in this they are wonderful successes.

---

7. Compare here "Christmas," the story of the nativity first seen through the eyes
of an ordinary traveler, then made the occasion for the beautiful hymn that concludes
"Till ev'n his beams sing, and my musick shine."

Language

There is for Herbert, then, no pure or objective way of imagining God, or anything else for that matter. Every attempt to imagine is a drama among various sides of the self and a struggle with various languages, with no possibility of a permanent or fixed resolution. Every truth is provisional, and takes its life and meaning from its strained relations with countering truths; or, better, the only possible truth lies in the very strains and collapses of language of the kind that this sort of poem achieves.

One might put it this way: that taken together these poems define a condition that their speakers and Herbert himself share, part of which is that he knows that he must imagine his world and that he cannot do so accurately. One problem is that just as he begins to perceive the miracles of creation and of love, and wishes to praise and give thanks, these very impulses become those of self-aggrandizement, self-assertion, and self-pleasure—especially when they are expressed in the form of art, as is always the case in these poems, for the artist must take pride in his work in order to make it in the first place. Another is that the moments of most full-hearted perception and feeling—I have called them moments of prayer—are indeed momentary and incomplete and must be achieved over and over again, and freshly too, out of the feelings and thoughts in which he finds himself, not in some ritual way. In a real sense, then, as I suggested above, Herbert's poetry is his life itself, for without these records and enactments of achievement there would be nothing but raw experience, upon which he had no perspective; yet it is also true that for Herbert his poetry is both deeply flawed, centered as it is in the claims of the self which he can not and will not give up, and in a sense beside the point, for what really matters is not to be found in words but in the heart.

Language itself, the most fundamental material of thought, proves inherently unreliable. Again and again we see language dissolve under pressure as the speaker's terms lose the distinctions essential to their significance, or as fundamental images reverse their associations: the speaker starts off thinking that he knows what to say and how to say it, and ends with fragments in his hands. Often the breakdown of his language is experienced by the speaker as a bad thing, but seen by the reader as a good one, as we saw in "The Thanksgiving" or "Affliction" (I), where the collapse is the moment of greatest success. But this only adds to the sense that one can have little faith in one's own judgment or knowledge.

This is a poetry of gesture, I have said, but in what gestures can the speaker have confidence? Think of the instances of the sermon voice we have seen, all of which prove impossible; yet equally impossible is it for Herbert (or for us) to give it up. Or of "Repentance," which begins with an assertion of wholehearted confession that cannot be maintained; or of "Grieve not the Holy Spirit," which begins with a moment of fresh life, then retreats to doctrine, only at the end awkwardly making an acknowledgement of another kind; or of "Jordan" (II) which ends with a rule of life—"copie out onely that"—that is itself impossible to follow. Throughout Herbert's work we are first invited to accept certain linguistic formulations and gestures, then educated in their defectiveness or impossibility.

Here is another example:

Time

Meeting with Time, Slack thing, said I,
Thy sithe is dull; whet it for shame.
No marvell Sir, he did replie,
If it at length deserve some blame:
  But where one man would have me grinde it,
  Twentie for one too sharp do finde it.

Perhaps some such of old did passe,
Who above all things lov'd this life;
To whom thy sithe a hatchet was,
Which now is but a pruning-knife.
  Christs coming hath made man thy debter,
  Since by thy cutting he grows better.

And in his blessing thou art blest:
For where thou onely wert before
An executioner at best;
Thou art a gard'ner now, and more,
  An usher to convey our souls
  Beyond the utmost starres and poles.

And this is that makes life so long,
While it detains us from our God.

> Ev'n pleasures here increase the wrong,
> And length of dayes lengthen the rod.
>   Who wants the place, where God doth dwell,
>   Partakes already half of hell.
>
> Of what strange length must that needs be,
> Which ev'n eternitie excludes!
> Thus farre Time heard me patiently:
> Then chafing said, This man deludes:
>   ·What do I here before his doore?
>   He doth not crave lesse time, but more.[8]

Here we have two distinct voices, the speaker's and that of Time. The speaker begins in assurance, both intellectual and social: he can tease Time, or banter with him, about his "dull blade." To this Time's reply, cast in the confident and familiar tones of a working-man, is gentle: most people, he says, find his scythe too sharp.

In response the speaker gives a little sermon, in the terms of which, at the beginning at least, he is wholly confident: Oh yes, he says, maybe that was so once, but it is no longer, after Christ's gift of eternal life. Indeed, he adds in a slightly patronizing way, this transformation is good for you too: no longer are you an executioner, you are now a gardener, "An usher to convey our souls / Beyond the utmost starres and poles." This stanza is doctrinally correct, of course, and in one sense beautifully cast; but there is within it a tone of self-certainty, condescension even, that puts it in question. It is a good example of the way that for Herbert what matters is not the propositional content of an assertion but the spiritual condition of the speaker, and here we know that something is wrong.

---

8. Notes:

1. In the last four lines of the first stanza we hear Time speaking, in a blunt and concise way. The next three and one-half stanzas are all the speaker, down to "Thus farre Time heard me."

2. The *sithe* was once a "hatchet," that is an instrument of destruction. Now it is a "pruning knife," an instrument of husbandry.

3. *Ev'n pleasures here increase the wrong* means "even our best times continue our separation from God."

4. *Wants the place* means "lacks" as well as "desires."

In the next stanza possibilities so far repressed by the speaker now emerge: first he says, "this is that makes life so long," speaking as if he were himself in a state of affliction, regretting the length of life and wishing for death. But in fact the life he is leading affords him much satisfaction, as his robust and good-humored voice makes plain. Life is not "long" for him. Then he says that pleasures are "wrongs": but in what sense? A wrong to us, for they extend our life, which he now claims to be worthless though he obviously loves it? Or wrongs in another more threatening sense, that our pleasures are likely to be themselves wrongs, incurring God's wrath? This leads to dark possibilities, suggested in the phrase "partakes already half of hell," the implication of which is that soon he will have the whole thing. Imaginings and feelings thus reveal themselves in contradiction to his expressed confidence in the future. In particular the "already" suggests that another sort of eternal life may lie before him, one that would make eternity—or timelessness—an altogether different sort of proposition: hell, not heaven.

After this much, Time, chafing, cuts him off, thus performing in the conversation just the function he performs in life. "He doth not crave lesse time, but more." This remark means many things: that what the speaker wants is eternity, which, as Time sees it, is nothing but time to the infinite degree; that he wants more time before he dies, enjoying life fully and fearing, as he dimly does, the possibility of hell; and that he wants more time in another sense as well, more time to continue this garrulous speech. In each of these ways the meaning of the central term from which the poem has proceeded, "time," is complicated to the point of erasure.

Artillerie

A s I one ev'ning sat before my cell,
  Me thoughts a starre did shoot into my lap.
I rose, and shook my clothes, as knowing well,
That from small fires comes oft no small mishap.
    When suddenly I heard one say,
    Do as thou usest, disobey,
    Expell good motions from thy breast,
Which have the face of fire, but end in rest.

I, who had heard of musick in the spheres,
  But not of speech in starres, began to muse:

But turning to my God, whose ministers
The starres and all things are; If I refuse,
    Dread Lord, say I, so oft my good;
    Then I refuse not ev'n with bloud
    To wash away my stubborn thought:
For I will do or suffer what I ought.

But I have also starres and shooters too,
Born where thy servants both artilleries use.
My tears and prayers night and day do wooe,
And work up to thee; yet thou dost refuse.
    Not but I am (I must say still)
    Much more oblig'd to do thy will,
    Then thou to grant mine: but because
Thy promise now hath ev'n set thee thy laws.

Then we are shooters both, and thou dost deigne
To enter combate with us, and contest
With thine own clay. But I would parley fain:
Shunne not my arrows, and behold my breast.
    Yet if thou shunnest, I am thine:
    I must be so, if I am mine.
    There is no articling with thee:
I am but finite, yet thine infinitely.

The reversals and dissolutions of this poem multiply throughout. At the beginning the speaker naturally thinks of the star that shoots into his lap as a source of danger. His reaction derives from knowledge—"as knowing well, / That from small fires comes oft no small mishap"—and a knowledge that is both based on ordinary experience and cast in the slightly heightened form of a proverb or saying (or at least one in the making). But stars do not fall into our laps, and we as readers know that the "starre" in Herbert is often an image of grace and love. The speaker's knowledge is no knowledge after all, and he is explicitly told this. The star represents a "good motion," not a danger; do not expel it. Though it has the "face of fire" it will end in "rest."

The speaker is serene, wise, and self-confident: this startling event does not terrify him, or even confuse him. He can adjust to the reversal of feeling it requires. It merely causes him to "muse," an activity that brings him to accept his new understanding of his situation.[9] The "fire" is thus transformed in meaning; it becomes the opposite of what it had seemed; and the speaker—unlike most of us—sees and accepts this transformation: "I will do or suffer what I ought."

The poem could stop right there but it does not. With remarkable confidence, good humor, and calmness the speaker lets his imagination go, thinking of his own activities of prayer and weeping, and defining them freshly as "starres and shooters too." This provides a context and history for the original event, and suggests, faintly, a ground of complaint: his "tears and prayers"—now transfigured, in a reversal of the movement by which the fire became "good motions," into "starres and shooters"—work up to "thee"; "yet thou dost refuse." This is a complex and somewhat contradictory moment, in which the speaker at once displays an extraordinary capacity to claim an equal status with "thee," and expresses a sense that he is aggrieved. Why aggrieved? Because he has an even more powerful weapon than his prayers, God's promise, which sets "thee thy laws." It is this—not his own merit nor, more tellingly, God's love—upon which he will rely. The speaker's gesture—holding another to his promise—is indeed a kind of hostile act, and this confirms the hostility of the earlier imagery, which we are likely so far to have slid over as ironic or witty. The reversal is reversed, as the relation is redefined in terms of aggression and opposition. The contract he describes is really a form of love, though he cannot see it.[10]

The speaker has no language in which to go beyond what he has said. He says that he would "parley" and to that end asks God to "shunne not his arrows"; but this is hardly a gesture appropriate to negotiation. At the same time he exposes his own breast, an act inconsistent, at the level of metaphor, with "shooting." In the last lines the collapse is complete: "mine" and "thine" merge, as we earlier saw them do in "Clasping of Hands" (page 87, above), and we are told

---

9. Compare "Even-song": "I muse, which shows more love...."

10. To require that someone make a promise is to express mistrust; this is also the effect, though less obviously, of the invocation of a promise: To say "Do it, because you promised" implies a lack of confidence that you will do it because it is right, or out of love or generosity. "Artillerie" picks up this difficulty; it is also present in "Justice" (II) and "The Discharge," both of which express reliance on God's promises.

that "There is no articling with thee": no way to express in language this relation, and in particular no way to invoke the promise as a hold on God, as he has just tried to do.

Compare:

The Holdfast

I Threatned to observe the strict decree
    Of my deare God with all my power & might.
    But I was told by one, it could not be;
Yet I might trust in God to be my light.
Then will I trust, said I, in him alone.
        Nay, ev'n to trust in him, was also his:
    We must confesse that nothing is our own.
Then I confesse that he my succour is:
But to have nought is ours, not to confesse
        That we have nought. I stood amaz'd at this,
        Much troubled, till I heard a friend expresse,
That all things were more ours by being his.
        What Adam had, and forfeited for all,
        Christ keepeth now, who cannot fail or fall.

Here the speaker is engaged in conversation with "one," evidently an authority, who tells him that none of his responses to God is effective or appropriate: he cannot obey God; nor trust in him; nor confess that "nothing is our own." No gesture is of value: his role is to be silent, mute.

The divestiture of meaning and capacity is even more marked than this suggests, for the last two responses, trusting and confessing, are themselves first suggested by the interlocutor, before they are rather sadistically stripped away. It would be understandable to trust *him* no longer, in any event, though the somewhat dimwitted speaker does not quite see that; instead he seizes at a possibility suggested by still another unnamed interlocutor, a "friend," who gives him something to say: "all things [are] more ours by being his." But this formula is itself impossible: it is either meaningless, a kind of verbal trick, or it revives the central egotism of the "mine-thine" distinction. And the closing couplet, emphasized as so often in a sonnet of this type, repeats the problem: to think of the moral and spiritual history of humanity, and its relation to God, in terms of "forfeiting" and "keeping" is to keep alive that same egotism and to reduce questions of character and relation to possession. The speaker is carried into silent passivity; but what then fills the vacuum is doctrine, mere words. The formula is doctrinally true, but otherwise false; it certainly does not give the speaker much to say against the claims of the earlier interlocutor.

But as we saw in "Paradise" and "Heaven" (pages 59–61, above) language can work in the opposite direction from these examples, not as the dissolution of meaning but as the manifestation of grace. The very fact that the echoes work as they do in "Heaven," for example, is a demonstration that there are sources of meaning in the universe external to us, and benign ones. Much the same is true of the fact that words can lose their initial letters and still have meaning, as in "Paradise," or that "The Altar" and "Easter-wings" can fall into the visual shapes they do. In a poem entitled "Our life is hid with Christ in God," Herbert creates a sentence that runs diagonally across it— "My life is hid in him that is my treasure"—thus revealing the Word that is hidden in the world. But, as I suggested earlier, the point can be made even more generally, for these are simply intensified instances of what is true of poetry itself, namely that one's thoughts and expressions can be cast in forms that enrich and transform them. Language is not only a mark of our own incapacities, and of the dissolutions of meaning that surround us, but, as Herbert's poems repeatedly show, a source of redemption.

The Self

It should by now be a truism that all of Herbert's poems are definitions of self, as their various speakers represent or attain various possibilities of life and language. In what follows I shall examine a small number of poems, exemplifying three different modes of self-presentation that Herbert commonly uses: self as deluded; self as confused; and the self reduced to the heart.

Life

I Made a posie, while the day ran by:
    "Here will I smell my remnant out, and tie
                My life within this band."
But Time did becken to the flowers, and they
By noon most cunningly did steal away,
                And wither'd in my hand.

My hand was next to them, and then my heart:
I took, without more thinking, in good part
                    Times gentle admonition:
Who did so sweetly deaths sad taste convey,
Making my minde to smell my fatall day;
                    Yet sugring the suspicion.

Farewell deare flowers, sweetly your time ye spent,
Fit, while ye liv'd, for smell or ornament,
                    And after death for cures.
I follow straight without complaints or grief,
Since if my sent be good, I care not if
                    It be as short as yours.[11]

Read the first time through, this is a sweet piece about the gentleness with which nature, rightly understood, can remind us of our mortality, and do so in such a way as to make it acceptable. The flowers die; they are next to my hand, my heart; I too shall die, like them; but also like them, it matters not if my life be short, so long as my scent be good. The meaning of life lies not in its length but in its quality. This is all very pretty, and comfortable too.

But on rereading, especially in light of "Vertue," real difficulties emerge. First, as was the case with "Vertue," the death of the flower is actually not the same as the speaker's death, for the flower is part of an organic cycle: its seeds will produce new flowers, the new flowers new seeds, and so on indefinitely, while human life is linear and its end final. Still more ominous is the condition stated in the last sentence—"if my sent be good"—which makes us ask, at least on a second reading, What if it is not? The answer to that question is too terrible even to contemplate, like the phrase "partakes already half of hell" in "Time," for it suggests a kind of freedom from death that is worse than death itself. It is quality not quantity that counts, all right, but who are we to assume that our quality is good?

The identification with the flower works in a particular way: this voice, naive and simple, failing to pause at its own conditionals, is

---

11. Notes:

1. I have added the quotation marks in the first stanza in order to indicate the break between direct speech and self-quotation.
2. *Sent* means "scent."

impliedly asserting that its own goodness is as natural as that of the flower and indeed associated with it, for the speaker's first impulse after picking the posy is just to smell it, and to smell it the whole rest of his life. He will keep company with flowers and even try to make himself one: to "tie [his] life within this band." This gesture of feeling and imagination is a slightly stagy poetic act—"Here, this is how I shall live"—of a kind we have seen before, for example in "The Thanksgiving." It is the speaker's dramatic imagination that converts the dying bouquet into a gentle admonition: not really Time's statement at all, then, but the speaker's own. The whole gesture depends upon his imagining himself into a world full of significance, significance directed to him in the form of messages. He could have just thrown the flowers away; instead, he sees them speak to him. The result is that instead of smelling out the rest of his life the speaker is made "to smell my fatall day."

Why is the suspicion said to be "sugar'd"? Simply because the flowers are pretty and smell sweet? Probably so, but there are other possibilities: because they do not really die, as the speaker will; because the flowers died this morning and the speaker will not do so for a long time; or because the death of another being creates a surge of happiness and optimism in the observer. In the last stanza the speaker turns away from contemplating any of these possibilities to speak in another version of the voice that planned to "smell [its] remnant out." He bids a formal farewell to the flowers, as an elegant poet making a performance, slightly posturing, and declaiming upon their value: "Fit, while ye liv'd, for smell or ornament, / And after death for cures." He intends no contrast with himself, but the reader of Herbert will draw one nonetheless, and feel that the speaker here is dangerously blind to his own situation, a judgment confirmed by the speaker's confidence that his scent will be good.

It is the speaker, then, who is sugaring the suspicion here, and he even tells us this is so, in a phrase we might have slid over the first time through: "I took, without more thinking, in good part / Times gentle admonition." It is just what "more thinking" would lead him to that he seeks to evade, and that the poem obliquely insists upon. This thinking would not result in calling the admonition gentle, nor in our finding it easy to take it "in good part."

Despite these warnings in the second stanza—or perhaps because of them—in the third the speaker collapses into a new version of his first voice. He insists upon a vision of the world that is too sweet, too gentle, and engages in a self-satisfied piece of dramatic posturing—a fact that is marked for us, among other things, by the repetition of "if" twice in the same line, which stresses the conditional character of the statement, and by its awkward off rhyme with "grief." The speaker is thus caught up in his capacity to create verbal formulas that make the world tolerable. The poem throws in question, of course, not only such plainly marked sentimentalities as these, but the nature of the poetic imagination more generally. Is this, perhaps, in more complex ways, what every poem does, to insist upon a false version of the world against intolerable truth?

I am reminded here not only of "Vertue" but of Robert Frost's famous poem "The Road Not Taken," which takes as its explicit subject a sentimentalizing and posturing tendency very similar to that of "Life." In Frost's poem, you will remember, the narrator describes a choice of roads, saying that he took the one less worn by travel, "and having perhaps the better claim." But he instantly corrects himself, shaking off that formulation as false and portentous:

> Though as for that, the passing there
> Had worn them really about the same,
> And both that morning equally lay
> In leaves no step had trodden black.

He then imagines a future moment—perhaps at a retirement dinner—when he will say:

> Two roads diverged in a wood, and I—
> I took the one less traveled by,
> And that has made all the difference.

The speaker of Frost's poem has told us that this characterization is false; yet he now expresses afresh his sense of his own susceptibility to it, in an extreme form, marking his disquiet in part by the awkward rhythm and rhyme of the last word. So too in Herbert's poem the speaker both gives us his sentimentalized version of experience and shows it to be false, but in this case the falseness is never recognized. He accepts Time's admonition "without more thinking."

One purpose of the poem, and of others like it, may be to engage the reader in exactly that, "more thinking." But there is no assurance here that even this would lead us to the kind of knowledge that would enable us to be confident in our own utterances. Quite the reverse, in fact: such a confidence would depend upon a view of the self as unitary or coherent, which Herbert perpetually undermines; a view of language as pure and neutral, free from distortion and partiality, and able therefore to carry the weight of plain propositional truth, a view that Herbert destroys. His poetry is about the impossibility of that kind of statement, indeed about the impossibility of that kind of coherence in human life at all.

If the speaker in "Life" is self-deluded, charmed by his own powers of imagination, the speaker of the next is deeply confused:

Conscience

Peace pratler, do not lowre:
  Not a fair look, but thou dost call it foul:
Not a sweet dish, but thou dost call it sowre:
          Musick to thee doth howl.
      By listning to thy chatting fears
      I have both lost mine eyes and eares.

          Pratler, no more, I say:
My thoughts must work, but like a noiselesse sphere;
Harmonious peace must rock them all the day:
          No room for pratlers there.
      If thou persistest, I will tell thee,
      That I have physick to expell thee.

          And the receit shall be
My Saviours bloud: when ever at his board
I do but taste it, straight it cleanseth me,
          And leaves thee not a word;
      No, not a tooth or nail to scratch,
      And at my actions carp, or catch.

          Yet if thou talkest still,
Besides my physick, know there's some for thee:
Some wood and nails to make a staffe or bill
          For those that trouble me:
      The bloudie crosse of my deare Lord
      Is both my physick and my sword.

How is one to read this attack on the "conscience"? As a healthy rebellion against the punitive side of the personality that is preventing Herbert from recognizing love? So it has been read by Helen Vendler, but I think this is wrong.[12]

For me the best way into this poem is to hear it as a dialogue, and to try to imagine the voice to which the speaker is responding. Is the speaker's interlocutor really calling everything that is fair foul, everything sweet sour? Or is that the speaker's own misreading or mishearing? The speaker tells us this much: that what he wants is to be untroubled, to let his "thoughts"—not his heart—work like a "noiselesse sphere"; he thinks that he can get this by his "Saviours bloud," which will so cleanse him that it will leave his "conscience" nothing to say. If you keep it up, he goes on, I'll make a sword of the cross and beat you with it! But in all of this—in his image of himself as thoughts, in his desire to be untroubled, in his version of the effects of Christ's sacrifice, and in his imagined use of the cross—the speaker is represented as distorted, and in ways that are by now familiar. Not a healthy rebellion, then, but an unhealthy one, perhaps most of all in his reading of the Sacrifice. For him Christ's death is not an act of love, or even of suffering at all, but a doctrinal event that shifts the balance of power between himself and his conscience.

Is his conscience in fact punitive, as he asserts? I think it is rather the responding part of the speaker that is punitive here, not only in the aggressive imagery in which he dismantles the cross to make a "staffe or bill," but in his reading of what the conscience says. Consider, for example, the line "Musick to thee doth howl." Can that be the voice of conscience? Of all things, not that; there is no moment in Herbert in which music is seen as anything but good, as beautiful and sacred. The conscience is seen as punitive by the side that opposes it, as Milton's God is by Satan. It is possible even to imagine that the conscience—called by the speaker the prattler—is speaking to the speaker not as he describes at all, but in the wholly different tones, say, of love, in "Love" (III), who "smiling did reply." What this speaker sees is a struggle between a punitive conscience and himself, in which Christ will give him power; what he does not see, or recognize, is the love, and loveliness, of his interlocutor—his savior—and the possibility of his own life.

---

12. Vendler, *Poetry of George Herbert*, 235–38.

From "The Altar" on, Herbert's image of the central self has been the heart. This is conceived of as a part of the self that is different from the speaking voice; it is the part upon which God works, especially by the infliction of griefs or afflictions, as "The Altar" suggests when it says, "A HEART alone / Is such a stone, / As nothing but / Thy pow'r doth cut." It is often contrasted with a stone, as in "Sepulchre"—there to the disadvantage of the heart—or said to be like a stone as at the end of "The Sinner": "Remember that thou once didst write in stone." It is the heart that is the source of "grones," those expressions more suitable and acceptable even than prayers or poems. "My heart did heave, and there came forth, O *God!*" Or, in "Sion":

> And truly brasse and stones are heavie things,
> Tombes for the dead, not temples fit for thee:
>   But grones are quick, and full of wings,
>   And all their motions upward be;
> And ever as they mount, like larks they sing;
> The note is sad, yet musick for a King.

In "Jesu" the heart of the speaker is fragmented; when he comes to pick up the pieces he finds that they have letters on them *J, es, u.* He interprets this as "I ease you" and sees at once that this also spells *Jesu.* In "Longing" the speaker imagines that "ev'ry part" of his broken heart "hath got a tongue" to plead with Christ. "The Church-floore," like "The Altar," draws an analogy between architecture—the temple— and the heart; and no doubt when the holy light shines "within" the preacher in "The Windows" and transforms him, it is his heart within which it shines. In "Gratefulnesse" the speaker asks for a grateful heart; and in "Confession" he imagines a heart smoothed by confession into a kind of hardness that will make it impenetrable to sin. In "Good Friday," "Decay," and "Sion," he imagines God coming to live within his heart and working there. As "Love" (I) and (II), "Jordan" (II), and later "The Forerunners" all tell us, the "heart" is to be distinguished from the mind or "brain," which is responsible for "invention." And "Sighs and Grones" is built of stanzas the last line of which, the "grone," echoes and transforms the first, the "sigh": "O do not use me" becomes "O do not bruise me"; "O do not urge me" becomes "O do not scourge me"; "O do not fill me" becomes "O do not kill me." It is one measure of the closure achieved in "Love" (III) that the speaker there does not divide himself into his heart and something else, but allows himself to be addressed, and to speak, as one person.

Two especially important poems about the heart are "Love Unknown" and "The Offering." The first is a dialogue between the speaker, who has experienced great and puzzling afflictions, and another, who interprets his experience to him. The speaker says he made a gift of his heart to his Lord, but it was first seized upon and washed and wrung in a fount; then it was scalded; then it was pricked with thorns. He is mystified, hurt and wondering. As he says at the beginning of the poem, his "tale is long and sad." The interlocutor gently suggests that the heart was foul and needed washing, hard and needed scalding, dull and needed pricking, and says at the end:

> The Font did onely, what was old, renew:
> The Caldron suppled, what was grown too hard:
> The Thorns did quicken, what was grown too dull:
> All did but strive to mend, what you had marr'd.
> Wherefore be cheer'd, and praise him to the full
> Each day, each houre, each moment of the week,
> Who fain would have you be new, tender, quick.

But the speaker does not recognize what the interlocutor tells him, except in a dull and perfunctory way, nor does he understand the full meaning of what he himself says, for example when he tells the interlocutor "But all my scores were by another paid, / Who took the debt upon him." The concluding interpretation is in one sense correct, but in another false, for the speaker's heart has not, for all we see, in fact been made "new, tender, quick." This is another poem—like "Redemption" and "Decay"—in which the speaker describes a God of love that he himself cannot understand or recognize.

"An Offering" is also a kind of dialogue. This one begins with the interlocutor, to whom the central figure is offering up his heart:

An Offering

Come, bring thy gift. If blessings were as slow
As mens returns, what would become of fools?
What hast thou there? a heart? but is it pure?
Search well and see; for hearts have many holes.

Yet one pure heart is nothing to bestow:
In Christ two natures met to be thy cure.

O that within us hearts had propagation,
Since many gifts do challenge many hearts!
Yet one, if good, may title to a number;
And single things grow fruitfull by deserts.
In publick judgements one may be a nation,
And fence a plague, while others sleep and slumber.

But all I fear is lest thy heart displease,
As neither good, nor one: so oft divisions
Thy lusts have made, and not thy lusts alone;
Thy passions also have their set partitions.
These parcell out thy heart: recover these,
And thou mayst offer many gifts in one.

There is a balsome, or indeed a bloud,
Dropping from heav'n, which doth both cleanse and close
All sorts of wounds; of such strange force it is.
Seek out this All-heal, and seek no repose,
Untill thou finde and use it to thy good:
Then bring thy gift, and let thy hymne be this;

Since my sadnesse
Into gladnesse
Lord thou dost convert,
O accept
What thou hast kept,
As thy due desert.

Had I many,
Had I any,
(For this heart is none)
All were thine
And none of mine:
Surely thine alone.

Yet thy favour
May give savour
To this poore oblation;
And it raise

> To be thy praise,
> And be my salvation.

Here the speaker is not, as usual, a version of the poet's soul, but his interlocutor, the one who speaks to him—as if "Time" began with an address by Time rather than to him. This speaker is bluff, hearty, confident, a friend to man, a version indeed of the wise interlocutor of "Love Unknown."

In the vividness and directness of his speech, his earthy good humor and want of pretense (at least in the first stanza), this speaker is almost Shakespearean; and there is certainly a comic force here that gives the whole poem a tone of confidence and hopefulness. With a friend of such assurance and good will, what can we lack? The person he addresses brings a gift in return for the blessings he has received; this gift is a heart, which is all that one could possibly give; yet, we are told, according to the economy of gift-exchange, his heart is not enough. It is probably full of holes, like most human hearts, and even if it were complete and pure it would be "nothing to bestow." The hearty optimism of the speaker's voice is erased by the simple moral facts.

In stanza 2 the speaker answers himself, wishing first for a propagation of hearts to match the blessings, then claiming that one might be enough: one man may speak for an entire nation, after all. But, as stanza 3 asserts, this is beside the point. As so often in Herbert we come to see that the issue is not quantity but quality: "But all I fear is lest thy heart displease, / As neither good, nor one." Your heart has been divided and split by lusts and passion; if you can put your heart together again, you may offer "many gifts in one." But, like the injunction "copie out onely that," there is no ready way to imagine how this could possibly be done. At this point we are told to turn to the balsam-blood, dropping from heaven, an "All-heal": search this out, without rest; then, when you have used it, come back with your gift, a healed heart. The gruff optimism and strength of the speaking voice is confirmed: there is a way, after all.

Then, as with many of Herbert's most important poems—"Easter," "Good Friday," "Christmas"—we see that the first part of the poem sets up a second half, a song to be sung on the conditions it has established. And what a song it is: the primary actor here is not the speaker but God, who has converted sadness into gladness; the "gift" is not a present transfer of a heart, or anything else, but an assertion: "keep what you have." Indeed the idea of a self that can make a gift, that has something "mine" that can be "thine" is erased; the terms fundamental to the social practice upon which the whole poem turns—the gift—disappears. There is a paring away of the self here that will recall "Affliction" (I). The final stanza defines what is possible: not a gift in return for blessing, from me to thee, but an oblique hope, that "thy favour / May give savour" to—what? A "gift"? No: to an oblation, a gesture of humility, which converts into praise and salvation.

What is imagined here is a transformation of gesture, from a gift in return for a blessing, with all that that implies, to an oblation. This implies a reduction in the sense of the self's capacity and power (though not to the point of despair as in "The Holdfast"), and also an expansion of it, for what becomes possible in the end is a song or poem. The poem justifies its own art.

Chapter 6

Reading George Herbert

My aim in this book has been to record the process by which I have begun to learn to read the poetry of Herbert, with the object both of helping others read their way into this difficult literature and, more generally, of suggesting a way of thinking about what it can mean to learn to read the work of another. For me, as I have said, it is helpful to think of this kind of reading as learning the language of another, by which I mean not only that we come to appreciate more fully the special significance the writer gives to certain terms over the course of his work—"heart," "stone," "sunne"—but also that we become familiar with his voices, transitions, and gestures—such as Herbert's declamations in a sermon voice, his movements from distortion towards prayer, his poems that first set up a song and then sing it, and so forth. As we learn to read one gesture in light of another, one poem in light of another, we should acquire an increasing sense of attunement to the whole performance and feel our expectations engaged, surprised, and disappointed in increasingly coherent and familiar ways.

The present chapter tests that hope in reading, first, four late poems—all of which, like those just read, have to do with the definition of God, of the speaker, and the relation between them—and, second, the sequence of poems with which Herbert brings "The Church" to a close. I give the first four poems extended readings, meant in part as a summary of what we have already done; I present the poems of the final sequence with much less by way of commentary, and with some omissions.

Four Late Poems

The first poem is very well known:

The Pulley

W hen God at first made man,
 Having a glasse of blessings standing by;

Herbert's church at Fuggleston

Let us (said he) poure on him all we can:
Let the worlds riches, which dispersed lie,
    Contract into a span.

So strength first made a way;
Then beautie flow'd, then wisdome, honour, pleasure:
When almost all was out, God made a stay,
Perceiving that alone of all his treasure
    Rest in the bottome lay.

For if I should (said he)
Bestow this jewell also on my creature,
He would adore my gifts in stead of me,
And rest in Nature, not the God of Nature:
    So both should losers be.

Yet let him keep the rest,
But keep them with repining restlesnesse:
Let him be rich and wearie, that at least,
If goodnesse leade him not, yet wearinesse
    May tosse him to my breast.

One way to read this poem is to see it as another of the myth-making poems, like "The Bag," which combine the force of invented story with that of Christian iconography. This is a creation story, like Genesis, but one of Herbert's own invention; it has the life of something new, yet the "God" of whom he talks is not simply his own creation, for that word and character derive much of their meaning from the contemporary language of theology and, of course, from the story of creation in the Bible. As we saw in "The Bag," this combination of modes works upon both, to help us see that the two modes are not so distinct as we might have thought. To start with the explicit myth, such as the story in "Humilitie," it obviously has the truth not of literal historicity but, at its best, of correspondence with our moral circumstances. We don't say, "This is what happened" but "This is what human life is like." We know from the start that this is the way to read what I have called his myths; what the combination of modes suggests is that much the same may be true as well of the canonical events of the Bible, which are also claimed to be historically true.

    These events, that is, have a correspondence truth as well as a supposedly literal one, and their meaning, like that of the myths, depends in the end less on a literal belief in their historicity than on the way in which their narration identifies certain central and problematic facts of human experience and defines a relation among them. To return to the Garden of Eden story, for example, the main issue there is what differentiates humans from other animals: our life of labor, the dangers and difficulties of human childbirth, our capacities for language and reason, and, above all, our sense of moral right and wrong. How could all this possibly have come about? To ask this question in this way is to invite a response in terms of causation and narrative sequence. The story told in response may claim the force of literal historicity, but that will mean little unless it also teaches us something about the nature and meaning of our own circumstances; and if it does this, the question of its historicity recedes in importance. To ask "how all this happened," then, is to ask not only for an explanation that makes our circumstances probable but for a story that makes them more intelligible.

So too with "The Pulley": what it seeks to explain is man's restlessness, his sense of his own incompleteness and imperfection, his constant dissatisfaction and disquiet. How can this have come about, especially from a God of love and power? The answer the poem seems to offer is that this "restlesnesse"—this anxiety and doubt and uncertainty and sense of quest and unfulfillment—is a good thing, not a bad one, despite what it may feel like as we experience it. In this the poem builds on the expectations established by the "Affliction" poems and others like them, in which the speaker, occupied as he necessarily is with questions of "joy" and "grief," cannot recognize what is good, or bad, for him.[1] We already know that what a speaker most complains of may be most in his own interest.

One of our deepest desires is for rest, but to be a good thing, the "rest" must have the right conditions and objects. To "rest" in our own nature, as "God" says here, would be fatal: it would be like resting in the wrong kind of language, in the formulas and clichés with which the speaker of a Herbert poem so often begins and which it is so often the effect of Herbert's poetry to complicate and undo. One way, indeed, to think of Herbert's poetry is that it works again and again as a kind of restlessness itself, a disquiet with its own effusions and feelings and ways of talking. Yet no greater blessing could exist than to end in rest

---

1. The *wisdome, honour, pleasure,* here plainly blessings, closely match the "learning, honour, pleasure" that are rejected by the speaker in "The Pearl."

of the right kind; not in our abilities or virtues or minds, but in his "breast."[2] And the poetry itself, though working by a kind of restless tossing, and though inducing that restlessness in the reader, has as its ultimate object a kind of repose.

In "Josephs Coat," which just precedes "The Pulley," the speaker discovers that his pains now come with unexplained joy, just as earlier his joys came with unexplained pain: "Wounded I sing, tormented I indite, / Thrown down I fall into a bed, and rest." But this is at best an acceptance of variegation for its own sake, seen from the point of view of the one who suffers it: "I live to shew his power, who once did bring / My *joyes* to *weep,* and now my *griefs* to *sing.*" The variation the speaker experiences here has no moral or social significance; it is simply an exercise of power. But in "The Pulley" the experience is ordered in the narrative and imagined as the work of a loving as well as a powerful God; the restlessness is not simply to be endured, and its benefits accepted, as in "Josephs Coat," but to be understood itself as an intended "blessing."

Or so it seems. What happens if we look at "The Pulley" as another poem about the definition of God? First, as befits the form of fable and myth, we see him not as a mysterious being, but as wholly comprehensible, an ordinary workman at his bench, surrounded by tools and equipment in a congenial disarray—the glass is "standing by." He has a kind of creator's pride, wanting his creature to be as fine as possible: "Let us poure on him all we can." Yet at the end he finds "rest" alone in the bottom—as Pandora in a parallel story found "Hope"—and withholds it. Why? "He would adore my gifts in stead of me," we are told, and this is shocking. It may make sense in a theoretical way, for it is in Herbert's world doctrinally correct that man should adore his Maker, but, as a social and ethical matter the desire to be adored seems selfish, vain, and tyrannical: a God of power after all, then, as incomprehensible as the God of "Josephs Coat," and not in any sense we can imagine a God of love.

Yet in saying "both should losers be" this God includes man's welfare,

---

2. To "roost and nestle there," as the speaker said in "The Temper" (I); or, in "Even-song," "in this love, more then in bed, I rest." Or consider "Artillerie," where the one who shot the "starre" into the speaker's lap tells him, "Do as thou useth, disobey, / Expell good motions from thy breast, / Which have the face of fire, but end in rest." All of these are connected, I think, to the famous phrase, "the peace of God, which passeth all understanding" (Philippians 4:7).

not just his own; and the last stanza has a wonderful tone of affectionate acceptance. Here God recognizes and deplores what man will do with his gifts, yet finds a way to respond to these conditions: he says "Let him keep the rest"—everything, that is, except rest itself—but "with repining restlesnesse." Man's goodness is no ground for confidence, but this God does have some hope for him, based on the effects of "wearinesse": as he is worn down by life and affliction he may turn in the end to God's breast. This is the speech of an accepting and loving God, doing what he can with us; and it redefines "wearinesse" and "restlesnesse," not as the afflictions we imagine them to be, but as good things, sufferings inflicted out of a desire to prevent worse suffering. The withholding of the last blessing turns out to be itself a blessing, and to lead in the end to the very rest it denies us. And to shift our focus to the speaker of the poem, we can see that to describe God in this playful and accepting way is itself an act of extraordinary confidence.

In "The Pulley," as in "Vertue," it is said that it would be a mistake to rest in nature: but unlike that poem, here there is really no imagined nature in which to rest—no day, no rose, no spring—and this makes the injunction more bearable; and, on the other side, in place of the bare doctrinal assertion that the sweet and virtuous soul will "chiefly live" when "the whole world turn[s] to coal," we have here an imagined social relation between the creator and his creature, affectionate and accepting. It is marked by the creator's desire to make perfect, by his wish to be adored, and by his regretful recognition of man's own nature, which requires that he withhold the last gift. On our side the relation is marked by our misunderstanding, by certain error, but also by our recognition of those laws of probability or, more properly, possibility—"*may* tosse him to my breast"—that may yet work to pull us up. God is still a God of power, with an element of sadism too, but one who wants in the end to take us to his breast. It is characteristic of Herbert that these two images both remain at the end, contrasting, themselves a source of disquiet or restlessness.

The Priesthood

Blest Order, which in power dost so excell,
 That with th' one hand thou liftest to the sky,
And with the other throwest down to hell
In thy just censures; fain would I draw nigh,
Fain put thee on, exchanging my lay-sword
　　　For that of th' holy Word.

But thou art fire, sacred and hallow'd fire;
And I but earth and clay: should I presume
To wear thy habit, the severe attire
My slender compositions might consume.
I am both foul and brittle; much unfit
        To deal in holy Writ.

Yet have I often seen, by cunning hand
And force of fire, what curious things are made
Of wretched earth. Where once I scorn'd to stand,
That earth is fitted by the fire and trade
Of skilfull artists, for the boards of those
        Who make the bravest shows.

But since those great ones, be they ne're so great,
Come from the earth, from whence those vessels come;
So that at once both feeder, dish, and meat
Have one beginning and one finall summe:
I do not greatly wonder at the sight,
        If earth in earth delight.

But th' holy men of God such vessels are,
As serve him up, who all the world commands:
When God vouchsafeth to become our fare,
Their hands convey him, who conveys their hands.
O what pure things, most pure must those things be,
        Who bring my God to me!

Wherefore I dare not, I, put forth my hand
To hold the Ark, although it seem to shake
Through th' old sinnes and new doctrines of our land.
Onely, since God doth often vessels make
Of lowly matter for high uses meet,
        I throw me at his feet.

There will I lie, untill my Maker seek
For some mean stuffe whereon to show his skill:
Then is my time. The distance of the meek
Doth flatter power. Lest good come short of ill
In praising might, the poore do by submission
        What pride by opposition.[3]

This poem addresses the concern of "The Windows"—"Lord, how can man preach thy eternall word?"—with the difference that here the focus is less on preaching than on the speaker's qualifications for the sacred office of the priesthood more generally. As one theme of "The Windows" is the transformation that is required of the person who is to preach well, so here the life of the poem is itself a kind of transformation, a movement of the speaker from one condition to another.

At the beginning the speaker sees the priesthood as an office of immense supernatural "power," and it is the imagined exercise of that power that appeals to him: lifting "to the sky" and throwing "down to hell." He imagines that this power, which actually is God's own, would belong to him if he were a priest; it is a "sword" that he wishes to have. This stanza thus marks, as so often in Herbert, a distortion of mind and feeling out of which the speaker will partly work himself.

The first step of self-examination is to realize that his initial gesture—his wish for the priesthood—assumed that he was fit for the office, which is not true: "I [am] but earth and clay." The speaker is by his nature barred from the office. ("He is a brittle crazie glass.") Yet, he goes on, earth can be transformed by fire and art into the finest porcelain; the unexpressed implication, and perhaps wish, is that he too might be subject to such a transformation. This is a possibility at once hopeful and frightening, for the transformation he describes—by fire, in a furnace—is a severe one indeed. The speaker accordingly turns away from this possible line of thought to a sententious reflection, that earth is the substance both of the porcelain and of those that own it, which is in turn to suggest that the transformation by fire, whether of clay or man, is in the end no such thing, for each retains its essential character as earth.

He also implicitly recognizes that the priest needs a transformation greater even than the conversion of clay to porcelain, for his task is to

---

3. Notes:

1. *Where once I scorn'd to stand:* this is clay, made by artists into fine porcelain china for display on the tables of the rich—"the boards of those / Who make the bravest shows."

2. *Come from the earth:* the rich and powerful, like the china service, are made of earth, an image invoking God's language in speaking to Adam: "For dust thou art and unto dust thou shalt return" (Genesis 3:19).

3. *The poore do by submission,* etc. It makes sense that poor praise God by submitting, but how do the proud do so "by opposition?" Presumably they fail and thus demonstrate God's power.

"serve him up, who all the world commands." Here he is still seeing the greatness of God in terms of his power, but in the next two lines another possibility is imagined.

> When God vouchsafeth to become our fare,
> Their hands convey him, who conveys their hands.

At the moment of Communion he imagines himself and his God acting in a reciprocal and harmonious relation, like a dance.[4] But no sooner is this possibility stated than the speaker recoils from it:

> O what pure things, most pure must those things be,
> Who bring my God to me!

Now he sees himself disqualified not only by his weakness but by his impurity, a much more serious flaw: "Wherefore I dare not, I, put forth my hand / To hold the Ark." His wish to become a priest has been transformed into an expression that he dare not do so. The reason for this is partly a sense of disparate power; partly a sense of disqualification by impurity; partly a fear of the transformation that would be required of him; but partly, I think, a turning away from the extraordinary intimacy implied in the line: "Their hands convey him, who conveys their hands." At this moment the speaker touches the possibility that the God whose priest he would be is a God of love, not power, and he cannot bear to contemplate it.

Out of all this comes a new gesture, a transformation from the opening wish into something else entirely: "I throw me at his feet." Here he abandons the ambition for power expressed in stanza 1 and converts that impulse into a gesture of humility, in which he accepts his status as mere raw material. No longer an actor with a wish or will, the speaker now says that he will wait. But this transformation too proves imperfect, for, as he turns to imagine the future moment when he will be called by God, he finds himself saying: "Then is my time." This marks the reemergence, after all, of the ambitious self of the first stanza, the one who still sees the issue as one of power, and who, like a Renaissance courtier, speaks of flattery as though it were

---

4. Compare the closing line of "Marie Magdalene": "And yet in washing one, she washed both."

an acceptable and proper art. The proud flatter by opposition—for their opposition is certain to prove fruitless, as Satan's was—the meek by submission. All this is to threaten to redefine the gesture, "I throw me at his feet," as a species of flattery, instrumental in character, rather than as a sincere expression of humility. As is usual in Herbert, there is a transformation here, but it is to say the least incomplete. On my reading, the poem catches at its center the plight of the person who cannot bear to contemplate the possibility that God does not offer power but love.

The Crosse

WHat is this strange and uncouth thing?
    To make me sigh, and seek, and faint, and die,
Untill I had some place, where I might sing,
    And serve thee; and not onely I,
But all my wealth and familie might combine
To set thy honour up, as our designe.

    And then when after much delay,
Much wrastling, many a combate, this deare end,
So much desir'd, is giv'n, to take away
    My power to serve thee; to unbend
All my abilities, my designes confound,
And lay my threatnings bleeding on the ground.

    One ague dwelleth in my bones,
Another in my soul (the memorie
What I would do for thee, if once my grones
    Could be allow'd for harmonie):
I am in all a weak disabled thing,
Save in the sight thereof, where strength doth sting.

    Besides, things sort not to my will,
Ev'n when my will doth studie thy renown:
Thou turnest th' edge of all things on me still,
    Taking me up to throw me down:
So that, ev'n when my hopes seem to be sped,
I am to grief alive, to them as dead.

    To have my aim, and yet to be
Further from it then when I bent my bow;
To make my hopes my torture, and the fee

> Of all my woes another wo,
> Is in the midst of delicates to need,
> And ev'n in Paradise to be a weed.
>
> Ah my deare Father, ease my smart!
> These contrarieties crush me: these crosse actions
> Doe winde a rope about, and cut my heart:
> And yet since these thy contradictions
> Are properly a crosse felt by thy Sonne,
> With but foure words, my words, *Thy will be done.*

This too is a poem of transformation: the complaint with which it begins is transformed into a prayer—"Ah my deare Father, ease my smart!"—and the image of the cross, seen first from the outside as a "strange and uncouth thing" is internalized and becomes the "crosse actions" that "doe winde a rope about, and cut my heart," thus recalling the cutting of the heart described in "The Altar." The focus on the self is transformed into a focus on "thy will."

The poem begins with the complaint that this "strange and uncouth thing" made him "sigh, and seek, and faint, and die" until he had found some place to "serve thee"—by which Herbert evidently refers to his call to the priesthood, and also, as his reference to his wealth and that of his family suggests, his decision to rebuild the church at Leighton Bromswold, which he did in the shape of a cross.[5] His complaint is that just at the moment of success all was taken from him: "to take away / My power to serve thee; to unbend / All my abilities, my designes confound, / And lay my threatnings bleeding on the ground." But this language is unwittingly revealing: "serving thee" is here defined in terms not of God's will but his own power and abilities and designs. The speaker had a plan of achievement and success, emphasized by the extraordinary repetitions of "I" and "me" throughout the poem, and it is of the frustration of his will that he primarily complains. "Besides, things sort not to my will, / Ev'n when my will doth studie thy renown." His effort to serve is an expression of his will, and it is as

---

5. Before his rebuilding the nave was significantly wider than the choir, with aisles on both sides. The transepts were accordingly quite stubby. Herbert narrowed the nave by moving the outer walls in to eliminate the aisles. In so doing he made the nave and choir of a common width and effectively extended the transepts, creating the shape of a cross.

such that he values it. "To have my aim, and yet to be / Further from it then when I bent my bow." This locates value in the achievement of his own will, which is as much his own—and as plainly will—as the aim of an archer toward a target.

What works the conversion, partial as it is, is the image of the cross itself. The speaker uses the word to describe the cutting of his heart: "these crosse-actions / Doe winde a rope about, and cut my heart." (Compare "Affliction" [I]: "Thus doth thy power crosse-bias me.") This reminds him of his first topic, the cross itself, which is the starting point not only of this poem, but of this book of poems, and indeed his life, as he makes plain in "The Sacrifice." He is recalled, for the moment, into seeing that his suffering is not his alone but "felt by thy Sonne." It is this recognition that enables him to say at last "thy will be done."[6]

"The Flower" is one of Herbert's most complex and important poems, and I shall work through each of the stanzas in order.

> How fresh, O Lord, how sweet and clean
> Are thy returns! ev'n as the flowers in spring;

---

6. This act of submission, in which the speaker gives up the claims of will out of which the poem has been written, is beautiful and moving. But the submission is at least slightly qualified by the speaker's claim that these are "my words," when of course they are Christ's, used both in the Lord's Prayer and in his prayer, just before the crucifixion, when he first asks that this cup be taken from him, then says, "nevertheless not my will, but thine, be done" (Luke 22:42).

The brevity of the submission also raises the question whether it is not overpowered by what precedes it, a possibility also suggested with respect to "The Collar," where so much of the energy of the poem lies in the rebellion, so little in the submission: "And I reply'd, *My Lord*." Compare "The Pearl," where the speaker says that he knows the ways of "Learning," "Honour," and "Pleasure," devoting a stanza to each that richly enacts its appeal—"I know the wayes of Pleasure, the sweet strains, / The lullings and the relishes of it"—yet concludes each stanza with the phrase, "Yet I love thee." The very simplicity of this phrase, as of "thy will be done," gives it force and poignancy, as an enactment of obeisance, yet a great deal of poetic and emotional weight remains on the side of what is nominally rejected.

The submission in "The Crosse" seems to me a much more complete resolution, for here the speaker is not simply asserting one thing against another, but undergoing a present transformation of his heart and imagination. He does this in "The Collar" too, in a way, but there the main motive for repentance is fear at his own revealed nature, and the ending is really a return, not an advance. Here he accepts the very frustration of his will and hopes of which he has been complaining.

To which, besides their own demean,
The late-past frosts tributes of pleasure bring.
Grief melts away
Like snow in May,
As if there were no such cold thing.[7]

The speaker here begins, as so often in Herbert, with a spiritual experience for which he has—and in the nature of things can have—no adequate language. He has felt something that he now calls a "return," which itself implies an earlier departure; and as the plural makes plain this is not the first time this has happened, but the most recent in a long sequence. His "Lord" is in this way imagined as a visitor or guest, who leaves and comes back repeatedly. But this image does not do much to capture the feeling of it, and the speaker turns to nature for his primary simile: "Ev'n as the flowers in spring."

This movement from the spiritual to the natural is just the opposite of the movement typical of Robert Frost, who often begins with an imagined natural scene—a walk in the woods, or a talk by a brook, or the mending of a wall—which he describes in such a way as to give it, and his language, new dimensions of meaning. In this sense Frost's poetry is anagogic, leading upward from the particular. As we saw earlier, Herbert's poetry is in this respect more like Dickinson's and works the other way, beginning with a spiritual event; his images, natural and social, are meant to give that experience more precise and vivid meaning; they then become the material, always imperfect, with which he must work, always imperfectly. This may explain why it is harder to remember the poems of Herbert than those of Frost: there is seldom a visualized context, with actors and action—seldom a story of the usual sort; instead, the drama lies in the speaker's struggle with his feelings and his language as he expresses himself in continuously shifting terms.

Here Herbert's opening words are themselves rather empty or conclusory: "fresh and sweet and clean." They must be given meaning by what follows or remain vacant. The image of the "flowers in spring" does give them somewhat greater definition, but it is a somewhat hackneyed image. The speaker does not rest with it, however, but extends it in a complex and surprising way: he imagines "late-past frosts" as

---

7. Note: *Demean* means "demesne" or "domain."

a kind of social actor bringing "tributes of pleasure." This is at once a return to the social imagery implied in "returns" and an invocation, at the level of touch and sensation, of a highly particular experience, when one moment's pleasure or comfort is enhanced by an earlier, and recent deprivation: the frost gives us greater pleasure at the flower, as the cold gives us greater pleasure at warmth. This works both as an act of definition—"fresh and sweet and clean" have been given more specific meaning—and as a shift of attention to what preceeded the present moment, and we know that this is our old friend, affliction. The rhythm and consonance of "late-past frost" gives these words an emphasis that will be explained only later in the poem, when they are defined as "tempests" that "fell all night."

The last three lines of this stanza are a marvel of Herbert's tact: "Grief melts away / Like snow in May" catches the sense of elation and relief and bliss; the speaker is in the feeling, and so are we. Then the correction: "As if there were no such cold thing," which of course reminds us that there is; and we need reminding, because it seems so unimaginable to us, in the grips of one feeling, that another could be real. And the "cold thing" works, as Herbert's images often do, to unite the physical and the spiritual, for it refers at once to "snows" and to "grief."

> Who would have thought my shrivel'd heart
> Could have recover'd greennesse? It was gone
> Quite under ground; as flowers depart
> To see their mother-root, when they have blown;
> Where they together
> All the hard weather,
> Dead to the world, keep house unknown.

The repetitive withdrawals have left the speaker with a "shrivel'd heart." He is now less taken with the freshness of the return than with the surprise that his heart "Could have recover'd greennesse." Where has it been during the period of frost and snow? It had gone quite underground, we are told, as flowers depart "To see their mother-root, when they have blown." This image reverses things: it is now the heart, not the Lord, that is a flower, and it is the heart too, not the Lord, that departed. And as the figure continues, it radically shifts in feeling: "Where they together / All the hard weather . . . keep house unknown." The period of frost and affliction is here defined as one of sociability and warmth, of snugness and comfort. The only hint that something is amiss is in the very last word, "unknown," and this too could be seen as a good thing, especially when we learn, as we shall, what it means to be known by this Lord.

> These are thy wonders, Lord of power,
> Killing and quickning, bringing down to hell
> And up to heaven in an houre;
> Making a chiming of a passing-bell.
> We say amisse,
> This or that is:
> Thy word is all, if we could spell.

Like the speaker in "Josephs Coat," this speaker sees the action of the Lord as a manifestation of power without a moral meaning. The condition of our life is simply one of subjection to alternation and variation of treatment: "killing and quickning," "bringing down to hell / And up to heaven in an houre." "Making a chiming of a passing-bell" can be read, nicely, either as making a sad occasion joyous or as taking joy at misery and loss. The point is that either way the speaker is simply subject to the whim and vagaries of a Lord of power.

We have now been told that "greening" is good and also that life "under ground" is good: which is true? We have been told that the "Lord" is like a flower, and that the speaker is: which is true? We cannot know. Our capacity to orient ourselves in this world has been undone. The last three lines capture the point to which the poem has led us: the speaker cannot confidently characterize his experience in any language; he is wrong if he thinks he can state the conditions of life. His task, in fact, is not to speak at all but to read; even that is impossible, for he cannot "spell," by which is meant that he cannot make sense of his experience. What the poem describes is the experience of seeking a moral meaning in the universe and not finding it.

> O that I once past changing were,
> Fast in thy Paradise, where no flower can wither!
> Many a spring I shoot up fair,
> Offring at heav'n, growing and groning thither:
> Nor doth my flower
> Want a spring-showre,
> My sinnes and I joining together.

The speaker here imagines a paradise beyond change, and himself within it, as a flower that cannot "wither" (or "shrivel"). The dream is to be released from this endless cycle of withdrawal and return: if the speaker cannot specify what is firm and true, at least he knows that this perpetual transition is unendurable. He then retells the story he has already been telling, but now with somewhat different implications: "Many a spring I shoot up fair," like a flower straight from the earth towards heaven. Life—"greennesse"—is here defined as a kind of "growing" that is at the same time a "groning." What of the spring shower? This is the image by which his sins are defined, but it is highly ambivalent: does the shower provide water and thus help him grow? Or is it an assault upon him? Or is it just an integral part of the process?

> But while I grow in a straight line,
> Still upwards bent, as if heav'n were mine own,
> Thy anger comes, and I decline:
> What frost to that? what pole is not the zone,
> Where all things burn,
> When thou dost turn,
> And the least frown of thine is shown?

This stanza continues the thought of the last: while the speaker grows and groans straight up "Thy anger comes, and I decline." This anger too is ambiguous: is it the brute and unintelligible force of a God of power? Or is it morally motivated? One can see a seed of sin, I suppose, in the phrase "as if heav'n were mine own," a confidence that may be thought to rise to the sin of pride. But in fact this flower does just what flowers are supposed to do: it grows straight towards the light. The person for whom the flower is an image is doing the same. And as for the confidence, what human action is possible without it? Despair is a sin, after all, and hope a virtue. It is hard to feel that the anger that falls on this flower is righteous rather than random or sadistic; indeed the hint that it is based on blame has a touch of hypocrisy, for it may be a false justification for destructive action otherwise motivated.

The affliction is now no longer mere withdrawal, it is hostile attention: "What frost to that?" "Greening" has been redefined as exposure of the self to unmotivated or mysterious injury; to live is to suffer an aspiration never to be attained, and this begins to explain, after the fact, why the life underground seems so cozy: it was free of this sort of attention. To be "unknown" in this way is an advantage.

But this knowledge cannot stand against the appeal of "greennesse":

> And now in age I bud again,
> After so many deaths I live and write;
>   I once more smell the dew and rain,
> And relish versing: O my onely light,
>   It cannot be
>   That I am he
> On whom thy tempests fell all night.

The speaker cannot help affirming with the deepest pleasure the fact that he "buds again," and "smell[s] the dew and the rain"—even though we know, and he knows, what this has led to in the past. Hope— perhaps the very hope for which he was brutalized before—springs once more into his heart, the hope essential to life. The cry at the end is like the cry of a child who cannot believe that this has been done to him, the victim of abuse who insists on seeing the parent as good. In this highly qualified sense it is a performance of hope, and of confidence in his audience, against the facts of his experience.

"And relish versing": life for this speaker is poetry, speaking and writing, not merely reading.[8] Writing is an image for living, and it works like the flower: living by emergence, bit by bit. But as readers of Herbert we know, if we know anything, that this very fact is filled with danger and moral uncertainty.

>   These are thy wonders, Lord of love,
> To make us see we are but flowers that glide:
>   Which when we once can finde and prove,
> Thou hast a garden for us, where to bide.
>   Who would be more,
>   Swelling through store,
> Forfeit their Paradise by their pride.

Here the speaker once more redefines the story he has told, claiming now to see that this is the action not of the Lord of power, but the "Lord of love," and that the function of the afflictions he has described

---

8. Compare once more "The Pearl": "I know the wayes of Pleasure, the sweet strains, / The lullings and the relishes of it."

is to teach us something, making us see that we are but "flowers that glide." Presumably now we shall not "forfeit [our] Paradise by [our] pride." But the example of pride he has given, a flower growing straight up "as if heav'n were mine own," is what flowers do by nature, and where is the sin of it? I read this stanza as a return of its own, a partial return to a voice of doctrinal assertion that I have earlier referred to as Herbert's sermon voice. Here it is the voice of one who has been driven by experience into submission.

Look at the central terms of the stanza: "Lord of love," he says; but where have we seen anything that could be called love in what he has told us? Or the image of the "flowers that glide": this image is given none of the richness and complexity of the earlier stanzas. Though itself fresh and lovely it stands for but a single idea, the insignificance of human life; and this idea is itself inconsistent not only with what the speaker has been urging on us from the beginning, but with the act of making a poem itself, for it is meaning that the speaker has been seeking in his life and his poem is a claim of meaning. He adopts at the end a stance that purports to be an act of acceptance, but it is not and cannot be simply that. As the flower grows, the poet writes, and each asserts itself—"would be more"—in a way that this speaker says destroys all hope. We all forfeit our paradise. And compare this "Paradise" with the one dreamed of earlier on, where we would "past changing be." Here the promise is fulfilled, but the state described is not immortality, but a kind of death. Life itself, in the flower or in the poet, is the central value of this poem, and to it this kind of "paradise" is opposed, not only in its deathlike quality, but in the drama the poem enacts: it is life that triggers punishment. This is a cosmology that reminds us of "Vertue," but it is even more bleak and threatening.

What is it that causes this regression or reversal in the speaker? It is, I think, mainly the cry of pain and love at the end of the next to last stanza—"O my onely light, / It cannot be / That I am he / On whom thy tempests fell all night." What the speaker here asserts as impossible is not only possible but a fact, and a simply intolerable one— it has indeed been he upon whom "thy tempests" fell all night. The tempests must therefore be converted into benign lessons for his own good, as the speaker then claims. But there is another possible reason for the change too. The cry itself addresses a concerned and loving audience, someone there to listen; this assumption may be wrong either because the audience is not loving, as I have just suggested, or, perhaps still more threatening, because the audience is not there at all. In this case the speaker's suffering would lack even the meaning of a random exercise of power. It would not be even that intelligible. Finally, there is a third and touching possibility, seen also I think in "The Priesthood," that the speaker here is withdrawing from the sense of momentary confidence implied in his own cry, from the momentary contact with love itself.

Final Transformations

At the end of his book Herbert's poetry moves into a chorus of confidence and hope, much more dense with moments of achieved understanding and acceptance than any other group of poems, and concluding with Herbert's most complete performance of that kind, "Love" (III). There are cracks in his confidence, of course, and qualifications and under-minings of his hopes, but the feeling of the set of poems as a whole is that he has at last attained much of the capacity to accept love towards which he has been working from "The Sacrifice" on.

This movement begins I think with "The Glance." Here he imagines God as a lover, whose "sweet and gracious eye," when it first fell upon the speaker, filled him with a "sugred strange delight" which he felt "be-dew, embalme, and overrunne [his] heart, / And take it in." During all the "bitter storms" that followed, this "sweet originall joy" was at work within his soul and "got the day." This is the voice of one who has felt rescued or redeemed, and his language for expressing it recalls not only "The Altar," which makes the heart so central, but "Good Friday," "De-cay," and "Sion," where the heart was also entered by the sacred spirit. One is reminded as well of the explicit eroticism of "Church-musick"—"Now I in you without a bodie move"—and "The Temper" (II): "keep a standing Majestie in me." The experience is represented here as a phys-ical one—a sensation in this respect like that with which "The Flower" begins—but this one endures. And the experience is a ground for hope as well: if this is what a mere glance does, "What wonders shall we feel, when we shall see / Thy full-ey'd love!"

This image has overtones of peril, of course, for it is a tradition both of the Old Testament and the classical world that a human being cannot look upon a god and live. But the main feeling is one of hope, which is mostly confirmed—not eroded, as so often in Herbert—by the poems that follow: first, Herbert's version of the Twenty-third Psalm, at once ex-pressing and qualifying trust; then "Marie Magdalene," in which the speaker can imagine that the sinner and the Lord are so blended that "in washing one, she washed both"; and then "Aaron," the lovely invocation of possibility for a priest, answering both "The Windows" and "The Priesthood," in which the speaker imagines himself putting on the clothes of holiness, one by one, until he can say: "Come people; Aaron's drest."[9]

Reciprocity returns as a theme in "The Odour," in which the speaker imagines the phrase "My master" to have an "orientall fragrancie," which is increased, as the scent of a pomander is when it is worked in the hands, by "pardon of my imperfection," which would "warm and work it sweeter then before."

9.

Aaron

Holinesse on the head,
Light and perfections on the breast,
Harmonious bells below, raising the dead
To leade them unto life and rest:
Thus are true Aarons drest.

Profanenesse in my head,
Defects and darknesse in my breast,
A noise of passions ringing me for dead
Unto a place where is no rest:
Poore priest thus am I drest.

Onely another head
I have, another heart and breast,
Another musick, making live not dead,
Without whom I could have no rest:
In him I am well drest.

Christ is my onely head,
My alone onely heart and breast,
My onely musick, striking me ev'n dead;
That to the old man I may rest,
And be in him new drest.

So holy in my head,
Perfect and light in my deare breast,
My doctrine tun'd by Christ, (who is not dead,
But lives in me while I do rest)
Come people; Aaron's drest.

The fact that the rhymes and line lengths can be repeated in this way is itself an affirmation of sources of meaning external to the writer, in the language and the world. Notice too that this poem ends with an invitation, the gesture with which "Love" (III) begins: "Love bade me welcome."

The Odour. 2 Cor. 2. 15

How sweetly doth *My Master* sound! *My Master!*
  As Amber-greese leaves a rich sent
    Unto the taster:
  So do these words a sweet content,
An orientall fragrancie, *My Master.*

With these all day I do perfume my minde,
  My minde ev'n thrust into them both:
    That I might finde
  What cordials make this curious broth,
This broth of smells, that feeds and fats my minde.

My Master, shall I speak? O that to thee
  My servant were a little so,
    As flesh may be;
  That these two words might creep & grow
To some degree of spicinesse to thee!

Then should the Pomander, which was before
  A speaking sweet, mend by reflection,
    And tell me more:
  For pardon of my imperfection
Would warm and work it sweeter then before.

For when *My Master,* which alone is sweet,
  And ev'n in my unworthinesse pleasing,
    Shall call and meet,
  My servant, as thee not displeasing,
That call is but the breathing of the sweet.

This breathing would with gains by sweetning me
  (As sweet things traffick when they meet)
    Return to thee.
  And so this new commerce and sweet
Should all my life employ and busie me.[10]

---

10. Notes:

1. The passage from Corinthians referred to in the title is this: "For we are unto God a sweet savour of Christ."

2. *Pomander*: a mixture of aromatic substances packed into a ball and carried as a preservative against infection. Herbert is imagining one of the ingredients to be

Here we have an explicit response to the "Employment" poems, in which he says that what will occupy him is not a task, or a duty, but a kind of perpetual interchange of breath: "My master," "My servant," felt as a kind of dance or song. The movement in the poem is from isolation—the moment in which the speaker is simply intoxicated by the pleasures of the phrase—to reciprocity. What effects the change is a set of multiple recognitions: that the phrase works as a call upon another; that this call implies the reality of its audience; and that there is indeed something sweet in him, the speaker, to which a master might respond. Though it is expressed as a hope not a fact, this poem seems to me to be the fullest imagined harmony between the speaker and his God yet achieved in *The Temple*.

This brings us to a major rewriting of the "Jordan" poems:

The Forerunners

The harbingers are come. See, see their mark;
  White is their colour, and behold my head.
But must they have my brain? must they dispark
Those sparkling notions, which therein were bred?
      Must dulnesse turn me to a clod?
Yet have they left me, *Thou art still my God.*

Good men ye be, to leave me my best room,
  Ev'n all my heart, and what is lodged there:
I passe not, I, what of the rest become,
  So *Thou art still my God,* be out of fear.
      He will be pleased with that dittie;
And if I please him, I write fine and wittie.

Farewell sweet phrases, lovely metaphors.
  But will ye leave me thus? when ye before
Of stews and brothels onely knew the doores,

---

wax, which is warmed and softened by the working of the hands. When this happens it gives off its perfume more strongly.

3. Compare the reiterated phrase "my master" with Emily Dickinson's frequent use of "master," especially in letters no. 187, 233, 248. See *Emily Dickinson: Selected Letters,* ed. T. Johnson (Cambridge, Mass.: Harvard University Press, 1958), 141, 159, 167.

Then did I wash you with my tears, and more,
      Brought you to Church well drest and clad:
My God must have my best, ev'n all I had.

Lovely enchanting language, sugar-cane,
Hony of roses, whither wilt thou flie?
Hath some fond lover tic'd thee to thy bane?
And wilt thou leave the Church, and love a stie?
      Fie, thou wilt soil thy broider'd coat,
And hurt thy self, and him that sings the note.

Let foolish lovers, if they will love dung,
With canvas, not with arras, clothe their shame:
Let follie speak in her own native tongue.
True beautie dwells on high: ours is a flame
      But borrow'd thence to light us thither.
Beautie and beauteous words should go together.

Yet if you go, I passe not; take your way:
For, *Thou art still my God,* is all that ye
Perhaps with more embellishment can say.
Go birds of spring: let winter have his fee;
      Let a bleak palenesse chalk the doore,
So all within be livelier then before.[11]

Here the speaker affirms, as "Jordan" and "The Windows" did, the

---

11. Notes:

1. *Harbingers* are king's messengers, who here go ahead of the court on a journey to arrange housing, which they do peremptorily, by marking with chalk the door of the houses they claim as quarters. The speaker's conceit is that his white hair shows that this has happened to him; though he is grateful that they have left him his "best room," his heart.
2. Notice the distinction between "brain" and "heart," also present in "Jordan" (II) and "Love" (I) and (II). Compare "Humilitie": "On Justice was bestow'd the Foxes brain."
3. *I passe not* means "I care not."
4. *Fine and wittie*: this jangling rhyme and redundancy displays the level to which he fears his art has sunk.
5. *Of stews and brothels*: here we have the same excessively self-punitive voice we saw in "The Church-porch"—"Beware of lust"—and have seen frequently since.
6. *Tic'd* is "enticed."
7. *Arras* is elegant tapestry, different from rude "canvas."

central importance of internal experience and attitude: if, as his mind leaves him, the speaker is left with the phrase, "Thou art still my God," that will be enough. This phrase, like "My joy, my life, my crown" in "A True Hymne," may take its place among the "best in art." The speaker can write this way from his heart even when his brain is gone, and this is the writing that matters. Yet right at this point, at the beginning of the second stanza, he turns upon himself and sees that his writing, in the more usual sense of the term, was actually his "best": his "sweet phrases, lovely metaphors," his "lovely enchanting language, sugar-cane, / Hony of roses." He is intoxicated with a sense of the beauty of his words and affirms them; this impulse is checked, partially, by the recognition that true beauty dwells on high, itself supported by the emergence of the familiar condemnatory voice—"if they will love dung"; yet it is insisted on too, in a kind of balance: "Beautie and beauteous words should go together."

The speaker then returns to the first position—too far, no doubt, when he says that "*Thou art still my God,* is all that ye / Perhaps with more embellishment can say," for this reduces his art further than the poem itself would allow and accepts his loss, more than perhaps he should. But he does all this with a qualifying condition—or is it a prediction?—"So all within be livelier then before."

In "Discipline" the speaker finds himself able, from beginning to end, to ask his Lord to "Throw away thy rod, / Throw away thy wrath"; able to ask him, that is, to be not the God of power and punishment, but the God of love. That he can make this request in this way, that he can maintain this state of prayer, is itself a performance of the confidence and faith with which this book of poems is concluding. This is an achievement of simplicity and directness. But the love of which he speaks is not an easy one: "Love will do the deed: / For with love / Stonie hearts will bleed." Love, that is, will work the afflictions necessary to health and life.

"Who can scape his bow?" the speaker asks. Here, as in "Artillerie," love is imagined in military terms. The bow also evokes the memory of the classical Eros, a figure not, as now, of harmless sentimentality, but full of danger. "That which wrought on thee, / Brought thee low, / Needs must work on me." It is love that brought "thee" to the cross, as a kind of sacrifice; this will "work" on the speaker, both through his own sympathy and in a more threatening sense as well, for he will have his own crosses and afflictions to bear. These are seen here not as contestable, or even as problematic, but as necessary and good things.[12] The poem closes with a plea and an argument: "Thou art God: / Throw away thy wrath." Others may need wrath, but you do not, in part because the effects of your love are, from one point of view, indistinguishable from those of wrath.

There follow now two poems about the Eucharist: "The Invitation" and "The Banquet," the first of which is a call to the feast, the second an account of it. The speaker in "The Invitation" calls to every class of person he can think of, in order of ascending difficulty: "All, whose taste / Is your waste," or "whom wine / Doth define," or "whom pain / Doth arraigne," or "whom joy / Doth destroy," or "whose love / Is your dove," saying that what the sacrament offers is the true version of what the person seeks, or, in the case of pain, that it relieves it. He represents the sacrament as a source of transformation, but not just of wine into blood or blood into wine, but of the self that participates in it: the wine or taste or love you pursue is converted into something else, infinitely better, and with that you are converted too. Even the one "whose love is your dove" needs this. At the end, having "invited all," the speaker calls still upon his Lord:

> Lord I have invited all,
> > And I shall
> Still invite, still call to thee:
> For it seems but just and right
> > In my sight,
> Where is All, there All should be.

This closing phrase, for all its confidence, undermines itself a bit in two ways: both because the speaker here somewhat self-importantly inserts his own judgment and because we now for the first time realize that God is in fact not yet present at the feast, and may never be.

"The Banquet" celebrates the feast itself: "Is some starre (fled from the sphere) / Melted there, / As we sugar melt in wine?" Like "Pomanders and wood," which are good just as you find them, "Yet being bruis'd are better sented," so here God "as broken, is presented." The

---

12. Compare the "bow" of "Affliction" (V), which is not only an instrument of arms but the rainbow of the covenant; and notice that "working" recalls the pomander of "The Odour," which pardon would warm when worked.

feast is a miracle of transformation: "Wine becomes a wing at last."
At the very end the note shifts, as the speaker turns to himself and his
writing:

> Let the wonder of his pitie
> Be my dittie,
> And take up my lines and life:
> Hearken under pain of death,
> Hands and breath;
> Strive in this, and love the strife.

He recognizes here that his account has left out pain, death, strife; but
he finds that he can include them, and do so in a way that accepts these
things and the life to be lived on such conditions. This very fact may
be the best demonstration of the miracle he is describing.

The idea is that the feast is not simply a matter of receiving something
good, but that he must "strive" to make it what it can be for him.
This striving is at least in part a function of his imagination: it is he,
in the poem, who makes the Eucharist what it is; without his act of
imagination, it would be, so far as he was concerned, merely bread and
wine after all. The speaker does not quite say this, indeed it could not
perhaps be said, but this is I think the meaning of his performance in
this poem. "The Posie," which follows next, is perhaps a reaction to
this implicit and dangerous grandiosity, for its task is to reassert Herbert's
personal motto: he and all his works are "lesse then the least / Of all
God's mercies." The motto is apparently modest in the extreme, but
against this is the standard by which he measures himself, which is
nothing less than "God's mercies."

In "A Parodie" the speaker starts to lament the loss of his "soul's
joy," then, breaking the sentence, denies that this can happen:

> Souls joy, when thou art gone,
> And I alone,
> Which cannot be,
> Because thou dost abide with me,
> And I depend on thee.

As in "Gratefulnesse," the speaker starts off on a gesture, becomes
conscious of what he is doing and reflects on it, here rejecting it. But
the rejection cannot last, for in fact sometimes his "Lord" does depart:

"No stormie night / Can so afflict or so affright, / As thy eclipsed light." When this happens, Sin emerges and "raves" at the speaker, saying that God is indeed "lost" to him; what kind of life that leads to for the speaker, "Thou and alone thou know'st." The conclusion presents his deprivation with great vividness:

> O what a deadly cold
> Doth me infold!
> I half beleeve,
> That Sinne sayes true: but while I grieve,
> Thou com'st and dost relieve.

But the person addressed as "thou" has in fact not come. This claim is then an act of hope or faith, or at best of memory; except for one thing, which is that in the poem itself the speaker expresses his certainty—based no doubt on Christ's suffering as represented in "The Sacrifice"—that his Lord himself also knows the experience of total deprivation.

"The Elixir" asks for a simple teaching, that the speaker may learn "In all things thee to see, / And what I do in any thing, / To do it as for thee." In this form the prayer is a model of simplicity and honesty, but in the course of the poem it is transformed into desire for a magical solution to life's problems of a kind that is by now familiar: "This is the famous stone / That turneth all to gold." This poem, like some others in this series, demonstrates not a simple progress toward harmony but Herbert's usual uncertainties, qualifications, and slidings away from states of happiness or understanding momentarily achieved.[13]

---

13. "A Wreath," which follows next, is a performance poem in which the lines themselves are woven into each other like a wreath, the end of one being taken up at the beginning of the next:

A Wreath

> A wreathed garland of deserved praise,
> Of praise deserved, unto thee I give,
> I give to thee, who knowest all my wayes,
> My crooked winding wayes, wherein I live,
> Wherein I die, not live: for life is straight,
> Straight as a line, and ever tends to thee,
> To thee, who art more farre above deceit,
> Then deceit seems above simplicitie.

Then comes the final quintet, of which the first is "Death." This poem redefines its subject, which is no longer to be thought of as "an uncouth hideous thing" but, after God's promises, "we do now behold thee gay and glad, / As at dooms-day; / When souls shall wear their new aray, / And all thy bones with beautie shall be clad." Like "The Bag," this poem exhibits Herbert's capacity to use grotesque images without offense or even surprise: "But since our Saviours death did put some bloud / Into thy face," the speaker says, as though Death had prevailed over Jesus, instead of being conquered by him, with perhaps a hint that his restored health is the result of his actually consuming Christ's blood—a disturbing literalization of the Eucharist. "Thou art grown fair and full of grace"—like a healthy young person—"Much in request, much sought for as a good." The resolution is qualified, especially by the word "half" and by the negative implications of the last line:

> Therefore we can go die as sleep, and trust
> Half that we have
> Unto an honest faithfull grave;
> Making our pillows either down, or dust.

"Dooms-day" begins as a marvelous song of awakening and hope:

> C ome away,
> Make no delay.
> Summon all the dust to rise,
> Till it stirre, and rubbe the eyes;
> While this member jogs the other,
> Each one whispring, *Live you brother?*

> Give me simplicitie, that I may live,
> So live and like, that I may know, thy wayes,
> Know them and practise them: then shall I give
> For this poore wreath, give thee a crown of praise.

This is more complex than first appears, for there is a tension in it between its circular movement, concluding as it began, and the progressive movement of its sentiments. And as the poem proceeds the connecting links between the lines, which make it a wreath, get progressively looser, as if the wreath is undoing itself. To the extent that the circularity works, moreover, it can be seen as threatening, enacting a pattern from which there is no escape.

Each successive stanza is its own rewriting into complexity: through a sense of pain in human life; through the fear that the grave may hold on to us after all ("plead possession"); through the inevitability and irrevocability of physical corruption; to a prayer made on these conditions:

> Come away,
> Help our decay.
> Man is out of order hurl'd,
> Parcel'd out to all the world.
> Lord, thy broken consort raise,
> And the musick shall be praise.

The confidence of the opening stanza is gradually eroded, but then restored through a transformation: no longer is the idea that bones will be raised to the kind of life they once had, but that we shall be enabled to make music. The consort is "broken," just as the altar was in "The Altar," but now it is the Lord who will "raise" it, not the speaker, and what will result is not an architectural creation in stone but music. All this recalls the movement of "Employment" (I), which ends: "Lord place me in thy consort; give one strain / To my poore reed."

"Judgement" anticipates the final moment of God's decision, at which the speaker will not invoke his "merit" but "thrust a Testament into thy hand: / Let that be scann'd. / There thou shalt finde my faults are thine." In what sense are his faults "thine"? This phrase recalls both "Marie Magdalene" and "Clasping of Hands," for here as there the distinction between me and thee, mine and thine, is obliterated by the reciprocal action of the loving other. The faults are "thine" not in the sense that God is a sinner too, but that God has taken them upon himself; yet this assertion is to my ear to simply doctrinal, too una-chieved, to count for much in a verse as full of experience as Herbert's normally is. This speaker is in danger of making it sound too easy.

This poem is followed by "Heaven," reproduced at page 60 above, in which each line is followed by an echo, picking up the last syllable and giving it a new meaning.

> O who will show me those delights on high?
> *Echo.*   I.

The echoing answer in this poem transforms its questions into affirmations; indeed it finds the affirmations in the questions themselves. This is a wonderful kind of conversation, in which the responder is saying you already know the answer to your question, for the answer is embedded in it. Not only you know, you show that the language knows: "wholly" is "holy"; "delight" is "light." The evidence of truth lies in our very forms of speech. Grace is enacted in the song.

Or is it? In discussing this poem in the opening chapter I said that one could read it another way, as false reassurance: all that is really happening, someone might say, is that the ends of the speaker's own words are coming back to him. It is he who sees the echo as affirming a source of meaning in the world; we, by contrast, can see it as the false hope it really is. My own reading, for what it is worth, is that the poem is indeed an affirmation of meaning external to the self, though shadowed by the opposite possibility, by the doubt that always pursues belief; but at the moment I am less interested in justifying that judgment than in saying something about the problem of judgment itself.

This poem, like many of Herbert's, creates an uncertainty and presents it to the reader; in deciding how to read it—whether as grace, false hope, or irresolution—we must make judgments about its meaning. Throughout my reading of Herbert's poetry I have of course been doing this, perhaps most evidently and controversially where I have suggested that a particular speaker exhibits a distortion or confusion that he does not recognize, but we do. How, one may ask, are we to make the judgments required for such a reading? How are we to decide what is a confusion, what a clarification, what is health, what disease?

Here we are at the center of Herbert's verse. It is, I think, our own experience of this poetry, of this mind—our experience of reading, responding, judging, and then doing these things again and again—that enables us to make such judgments. As we read, we gradually come to learn the language in which the poems are composed, the language they half create; inhabiting that language, we use it to make sense of what we read before, finding that we can now explain much of what was once opaque. Our tentative sense that we know better than the speaker does is confirmed when it helps us read the poems that follow more fully and fruitfully, disconfirmed when it does not. Through interaction with the texts and voices Herbert creates, and the person he is in his verse, we undergo slow transformations of our own. Our confidence that some of the movements of this poetry are toward clarity, truth, authenticity, and health, others toward the opposite of these things is thus to a large degree created by our experience of it. It is who we have gradually become in reading this verse that we can best call upon as our guide to understanding it; and it is in this transformation of our own lives that its deepest meaning lies.

At the end of Herbert's book and of this one, we come to "Love" (III), perhaps Herbert's greatest poem. Its achievement is not the work of eighteen miraculous lines, however, but of the whole book of which it is a part. It is because "Love" (III) speaks at last for us, saying what we have long known to be true—especially about Herbert's loveability, for we have ourselves loved him; and hence about the possibility for love in the world—that this poem has the incredible power that it does.

Love (III)

L ove bade me welcome: yet my soul drew back,
        Guiltie of dust and sinne.
But quick-ey'd Love, observing me grow slack
        From my first entrance in,
Drew nearer to me, sweetly questioning,
        If I lack'd any thing.

A guest, I answer'd, worthy to be here:
        Love said, You shall be he.
I the unkinde, ungratefull? Ah my deare,
        I cannot look on thee.
Love took my hand, and smiling did reply,
        Who made the eyes but I?

Truth Lord, but I have marr'd them: let my shame
        Go where it doth deserve.
And know you not, sayes Love, who bore the blame?
        My deare, then I will serve.
You must sit down, sayes Love, and taste my meat:
        So I did sit and eat.

I leave "Love" (III) without comment, not because it does not warrant any but because it warrants so much. This was the poem that Simone Weil found as perpetually transforming of her life as the Lord's Prayer, and like that prayer, she used to repeat it daily. One recent critic devoted two chapters of a book to its explication. For us, let it stand as marking the point where I stop telling the reader what a poem means, leaving

The Church.

Love

Love bad me wellcome yet my soule drew back
　　　Guilty of dust and sinn.
But quick-ey'd Love, observing me grow slack
　　　From my first entrance in,
Drew neerer to me, sweetly questioning
　　　If I lack'd any thing.

A guest, I answerd, worthy to be heere:
　　　Love said, yⁿ shall bee hee.
I the unkind, ungratefull? Ah, my deare
　　　I cannot look on Thee.
Love took my hand, & smiling did reply,
　　　Who made yᵉ eyes but I?

Truth Lord, but I haue mard them: let my shame
　　　Go where it doth deserue.
And know yⁿ not, says Loue, who bore yᵉ blame?
　　　My deare, then I will serue.
You must sitt downe, says Loue, & tast my meat
　　　So I did sitt and eat.

Finis

The Williams manuscript version of "Love" (III)

Loue.

Loue bad mee welcome. yet my soule drew backe
        Guilty of dust & sin.
But quick-ey'd Loue obseruing mee grow slack
        From my first entrance in,
Drew neerer to mee sweetly questioning,
        If J lack'd any thing.

A guest, J answer'd, worthy to be heere:
        Loue said, you shalbe he.
J y vnkind, vngratefull? A: my Deere
        J cannot looke on thee.
Loue tooke my hand, & smiling did reply,
        Who made the eyes but J?

Truth Lord, but J haue marr'd them: Let my shame
        Goe, where it doth deserue.
And know you not sayes Loue, who bore y blame?
        My Deere, then J will serue.
You must sitt downe sayes Loue, & tast my meat
        So J did sitt & eat. —

Finis.

The Bodleian manuscript version of "Love" (III)

it wholly to him or her. In some sense all of *The Temple* leads up to this, and all of this book does too.

In closing I want to raise with the reader one question. I have spoken from the beginning of reading Herbert's poetry as "learning his language," and this is in a sense what both you and I have done, in our different ways. The question is this: What does it mean to have done this?

A poet like Herbert does not simply offer us a set of new perceptions or feelings or experiences; his poetry stimulates in us a kind of life hitherto unknown. What does it mean to turn from that life to our ordinary experience, to the light of common day? In thinking of this I am again drawn to the image of travel, as I was in the Preface, imagining now the experience of the anthropologist. Suppose you went to visit and live with a tropical people who sang songs of great beauty, around which they organized their day—dawn songs, noon songs, and night songs. When you lived with them, you too would naturally use their songs to shape your day; when you flew back home you would leave behind not only the people, but their songs and the kind of life they made possible for you, and this would be a loss you would have to address. In reading Herbert, or any writer of similar originality and power, there is likewise this simultaneous promise and danger: that you will change as you read, and that what are now experienced as gains will soon be felt as losses.

In this reading we have been led outside of ourselves and our world to another position, broken out of what seems natural or familiar, and acculturated elsewhere. We cannot simply move from this language and mind back to what was our own—a part of the self and imagination remains on the island, singing its songs—and we cannot translate its terms into ours either. To create this very difficulty for ourselves is ultimately I think the reason for reading literature of this kind. In reading Herbert's poems we are given a brokeness of language and self that in some way parallels his, which it is our task and opportunity to face.

Afterword

When this book was nearly finished, I returned to England in order to examine the manuscripts, to visit Herbert's church at Bemerton, and to return to Leighton Bromswold. While I was there I happened to go to Westminster Abbey, and the school next door, which was Herbert's, and to visit Trinity College in Cambridge, where he was first a student, then a fellow, before becoming University Orator. I thus touched on most of the places he lived, from a very early age on.

I was most struck by the manuscript in Dr. Williams's Library, called *W,* which Herbert compiled in the mid-1620s, perhaps with an eye to publication. This is a small leather volume, bound with blank pages. Into it Herbert's poems were transcribed, in what is called the "secretary hand" of the time, which to my eyes at first looked crabbed, but in time beautiful. Whether this was written by an amanuensis, or by Herbert himself, we cannot be sure, though the Latin poems, and the corrections in the English ones, are apparently written by him in a different hand, with a different pen, as are the page numbers. The ink in which the poems are written is jet black and clear against the fine paper, fresh and immediate, almost as though written yesterday.

This manuscript is different from a printed book, partly because it is written by hand, partly because it is unique. Here are Herbert's poems, in a single volume, written with a pen, vulnerable to time and accident. He could have lost this book, or thrown it away; but he kept it and later added to it leaving a now-lost manuscript with ambivalent directions as to publication. Reading this volume of his verse carries one back in imagination, behind the publication, to the writing of the poems themselves, which were composed after all as part of human life, not produced for consumption in twentieth-century classes on English poetry. The voices in which they are composed, including the sermon voice, are his own. This is the real thing.

To see it this way helped me understand Herbert's audience, which was not after all the modern critic or student, but the person he hoped

Children's benches at Leighton Bromswold

these poems would help: the "dejected poor Soul" whom they might "advantage," or the "kinde man" who might "thrust his heart / Into these lines," as Herbert says in "Obedience." I have myself tried to write my own book from the part of myself to which these poems seem to me to be written, and to the analogous part of my own reader.

The church at Bemerton is small, as I knew it would be, and it has been much restored—though the door is still the one Herbert must have used, daily, when he crossed the lane from his rectory, a handsome house with a view of the Salisbury water meadows. A couple of miles away is his other church, Fuggleston, on the edge of the grounds of Wilton House. If that is where his relatives, the Earls of Pembroke, worshipped, Fuggleston would have been a more important part of his parish than Bemerton. Wilton House is grand, indeed palatial, and one can imagine Herbert's dependent condition: in one sense belonging to Wilton House, in another far below it.

The church at Leighton Bromswold, not quite finished when Herbert died, is a beautiful and somber building. The pews are all of oak, almost all original, and so designed—with a ridge in the back—as to enforce a straight-backed and uncomfortable posture. In the back of the church are rows of benches for the children, who sat between the men on one side and the women on the other. The two pulpits, made famous by Walton, are indeed identical, and beautiful, likewise of oak. The whole has a distinctly Puritan feeling: it would not be out of place in a seventeenth-century church in Massachusetts. The choir is flooded with light through clear glass windows. I have not been able to discover whether the restored church had colored windows, later destroyed in the Civil Wars, or whether they were always clear. (Some fragments of stained glass in the south transept may be relics of medieval windows.) In the choir, the benches face each other as usual, but they were not apparently for choristers, but for communicants, who would partake of the Lord's Supper at a table in the middle of the sanctuary.

The church is locked, and not much visited. One has a sense of timelessness, as though this church really is very much as it was when finished in the 1640s.[1]

To hold in one's hand the manuscript book that Herbert held, to open the door at Bemerton he opened, even to see the arches and cloisters at Westminster and the great court at Trinity that he saw often, gives one an odd sense of physical proximity and spiritual distance. It is true that the context of his life can indeed be made clearer by seeing the churches, by walking the path from Bemerton to Fuggleston along the River Nadder, but one never crosses the line between Herbert, living then, and oneself, living now.

Suppose somebody gave you a penknife used by George Washington: it would presumably puzzle and bemuse you to think that what is now held in your hands was once held in his. But the knife does not tell you anything, nor does it establish connections; it means something only because of what you already know about George Washington, of whom it is a relic. And relics decay: the paper ages, the leather cracks, the stones of the church turn to dust, as Herbert's own body has done,

---

1. The tower came slightly later than the rest, paid for by the Duke of Lennox. It is a very early example of a classical style that was to become enormously popular, and it has been suggested that its architect may have been Inigo Jones. See Arnold Taylor, "The Seventeenth-Century Church Towers of Battersea (1639), Staines (1631), Crondall (1659) and Leighton Bromswold (c. 1640)," *Architectural History* 27, (1984):281, 290.

lost beneath the parquet floor of the church at Bemerton. Even the pews and pulpits at Leighton Bromswold, while in one sense deeply eloquent, are in another silent; and they, too, slowly decay.

But not everything is subject to the process of decay, and not everything is silent or unspeaking. The poems themselves, the voices in which they are written, speak to us freshly and immediately. In a sense they cannot age, for they continue to exist, and to be accessible, in a realm outside of time, where living mind speaks to living mind. Of course a set of poems means differently to different readers in different cultures, but so long as one can learn the language in which they are composed, whether Homer's Greek or Herbert's English, they retain their immediacy and presence. And in reading them one makes contact not just with an object or artifact, but with a speaking person.

Why do I read them with such care and attention, why devote years of my life trying to understand them? Partly to learn the language of this different person, acquainting me with other ways of imagining the world than my own; for all life is imagined, including yours and mine. The impulse is like that of travel, to learn other ways of being human. We live somewhere else for a time, and return to our own world as different people.

Herbert makes this possible, and rewarding, by realizing so completely the language with which he leads the center of his life. This language is not just any language, but that of Christian theology, as powerful a source of meaning as any in human history. His way of writing is not simply to replicate it, but to test it, to transform it, to create it anew; in so doing he shows how this language can itself work not as a system of dogma and doctrine, not as a set of declared truths propounded from on high, in a super version of his sermon voice, but as a ground of life. He breaks this language down, as he breaks down his own mind, and in doing this redefines theology itself, not as doctrine but as an activity of the heart and imagination—an activity in which, through his poetry, he has also engaged us as his readers.

I am reminded of a picture I saw on the same trip, by Corot, of a marsh on a gray day. In one sense it is simplicity itself, just a marsh bordered with trees under a gray sky. But in another sense it is most striking: the light breaking off the waters, the weight of the air, the marshes and colors are full of original life. The picture recalled to me what I have often seen, in Michigan and on Cape Cod, in such a way that I can see it differently now. In this sense it recreates the marshes themselves. The painting is an act of creation that reenacts the continuous creation we see in nature itself, and thus connects human life and the creative processes of the universe. So too George Herbert, in creating voices and images, making a familiar language read and ring in new ways, offers his reader an experience of creation, in language, that mirrors or reenacts the larger creation of which we are all a part. And this one, even more than the painting or the church, lives freshly in a dimension that is not bound by space or time, where minds that do not coexist nonetheless can meet. This confirms both the existence of that dimension and our own participation in it: "beyond the starres heard."

Acknowledgments

Many people have been good enough to read all or part of this manuscript and given me their comments, which have been of enormous help. I am especially grateful to A. L. Becker, Thomas Eisele, Russell Fraser, John Knott, William Ian Miller, Michael Schoenfeldt, Kent Syverud, and Mary White. Adriana Diakiw and Alice Fulton each gave the manuscript attention of an extraordinary kind, affecting both my readings of particular poems and my sense of the book as a whole. Thanks can only acknowledge, not repay, such generosity. All errors of fact and judgment are of course entirely my own.

In addition, I wish to thank Oxford University Press, by whose kind permission I use the Hutchinson edition of Herbert's poems as the basis for my own texts; the Bodleian Library, in Oxford, for permission to examine MS. Tanner 307 (commonly known as B) and to reproduce two poems from it; Dr. Williams's Library, Gordon Square, London, for permission to examine the manuscript in their possession (commonly known as W) and to reproduce two poems from it; the Houghton Library of Harvard University for permission to reproduce the portrait of Herbert by Robert White; the Huntingdon office of the Cambridgeshire County Record Office, especially its deputy archivist, Philip Saunders, and the community at Little Gidding, especially Pat Saunders, for assistance in learning about the history of the church at Leighton Bromswold; the John Simon Guggenheim Memorial Foundation and the University of Michigan Law School for essential financial support; and Marcia Beach for her painstaking and intelligent assistance in preparing the manuscript for publication.

I began this book at Clare Hall, Cambridge, several years ago and put some finishing touches on it there on a visit early in the winter of 1993. I am more grateful than I can say to those who maintain that remarkable and civilized community of scholars for creating a perfect environment for this kind of work.

Further Notes

Method

While I hope that this book can simply be read on the terms on which it presents itself, some readers may be interested in the choices I have made in writing it as I have done.

To start with the obvious, this book is in aim and structure rather different from most. It is partly an introduction to the poetry of George Herbert; partly a commentary upon many of the poems, and in this sense a kind of companion to the verse; partly an extended critical essay, setting forth my sense of the way this poetry works; and partly a set of reflections on certain themes and issues that arise in the poetry, especially those having to do with the nature of Herbert's theological language and his own relation to it. In all of this I work out of the idea that the reader as well as the text is present in every reading, and that all of our readings will therefore reflect the histories of our own minds. While my main interest is in the poetry of Herbert, the book is of necessity an argument for its own procedures as well, and an argument that can be generalized. I have tried to write the kind of book I myself would like to read, about Herbert and other writers too.

This is not the sort of scholarly monograph that approaches a poet's work mainly by way of other critics and scholars. I mean this as a claim that Herbert's poetry, and other work of similar quality, can be read by an ordinary interested reader, bringing to the process whatever he or she happens to be at the moment. While I have by now read a good deal of Herbert criticism and scholarship, I rather deliberately avoided doing this at the beginning of my own work with the poems. I wanted to engage as directly and whole-mindedly as I could with Herbert's poetry from the point of view defined by my own education and experience at the time. Indeed, I originally did this reading without any clear idea that it would lead to a book, for its own sake; and the book I have written is meant to validate this way of approaching literature.

I mean this book to reflect the view, then, that literary texts can be read not as objects of analysis, but as expressions of human minds, as if they had something to say to us. My sense of reading Herbert is that I am listening to the voice of another person, from another world, with the aim of learning something of value in my own life. Of course such an approach may be dismissed by some as naive or unscholarly, but I mean it as a serious argument for the value of this way of reading, and this way of writing too.

This may help explain why my book is more personal and autobiographical than is usual. In it I try to bring to the foreground what is significant in my own life and education that makes me see Herbert, and listen to him, in the particular ways I do. But I mean this as an argument too, and not just about Herbert: all of our readings are from particular points of view and not from our theoretical or political commitments only, but, if our readings are real ones, from points of view defined by the histories of our minds much more fully imagined. My book is thus meant to be an argument by performance for a more direct and personal engagement not only with the poetry of Herbert, but with literary texts more generally.

Of course I do not think that mine is the only way to read these poems. It flows from what I have said that the reader should expect his or her engagement to be somewhat different from anyone else's. My object here is not to control that engagement, or to direct it, but to facilitate it. My hope is that this book presents one person's experience of this poetry in a way that is helpful to others but does not claim that it is the only possibility. The ideal reader of this book will at the end focus so hard upon her own continued reading of Herbert that she forgets all about what I have done.

I have repeatedly spoken of reading Herbert's poetry as a process of learning his language. This implies, as I have suggested, that the activity is not linear, working by discrete increments, but far more complex, involving shifts in the whole mind and imagination; that it is incomplete and imperfect; and that the reader is always present, transforming what he learns.

Thinking of this work as learning a language has another dimension, for it is not only in reading the work of a poet that we can think of ourselves as learning a language. The center of our social life can in fact be seen as the process by which we learn and respond to each other's languages, across national and religious boundaries and within our own society, institutions, and families as well. The art of establishing and managing relations with others is largely a matter of learning first to understand the language of another, and then to create a space in which that language can be placed against one's own. This is what the world is like to you; this is what it is like to me; between them there are of necessity gaps and irresolvable differences; these define the central issues we need to address, each of us recognizing that his or her language is not a superlanguage, entitled to override the other, but one way of meaning among many. This is true as man talks with woman, parent with child, Christian with Muslim, white with black, you with me, and so throughout our world. Learning the language of another is thus at once an intellectual, ethical, and political activity. It is perhaps the most important kind of understanding of others: learning what things are like from another's position—both in another culture (or point in culture) and as another mind and person—and how, by what question and claim and gesture, the writer has found it possible to use the language that defines his or her world.

The kind of education this experience offers is the modification of one's own mind, as initially strange practices become familiar and our sense of what is natural begins to change. Our response will lie largely in the way we use the language we have learned, in the kind of relation we establish with it, both as reader and as writer; in the way we ourselves learn to talk. Poetry, at least of Herbert's kind, is a heightened and clarified form of speech itself; it can show us something of what is involved in the process of learning the language of another and may teach us, in the process, something about the problematic character of our own language too, and the hearts and minds that use it.

Finally, I would like to say that I am uncomfortably conscious that the demands of space, and of my own method, have required me to omit many poems it would have been good to discuss. In particular, I wish I could have included some discussion of Herbert's translation of Psalm 23, written in such a way as to erode the trust which is the most prominent feature of the original; of "Providence," including a comparison with the Psalm from which it is drawn; of his most opaque poems, like "Hope," and his least strong, like "Lent," "The British Church," and "Sunday"; of certain wonderful poems, such as "Employment" (II), "Vanitie" (I), "The Pearl," "Christmas," "Marie Magdalene," "The Size," "The Search," and "Sighs and Grones." And throughout, I wish it had been possible for me to focus attention more sharply on Herbert's incredible facility with form: his remarkable stanzaic variations, perfect ear, and capacity to write English in natural sentences that not only adhere to the requirements of form, but transform them. The choices made in composing a book always involve losses, and I want to acknowledge that these are some of mine.

Text

My presentation of Herbert's poems for the most part follows F. E. Hutchinson, ed., *The Works of George Herbert* (Oxford: Clarendon Press, 1941), reproduced here with kind permission of Oxford University Press. Most editions subsequent to Hutchinson's simply reprint the first edition of 1633, with small emendations. Hutchinson, by contrast, gives priority to the manuscript *B*, now in the Bodleian, and some as well to the earlier manuscript *W*, in Dr. Williams's Library, Gordon Square, London. While not in Herbert's hand, *B* is the copy submitted to the university for licensing, and bears the signatures of the men who approved it, while *W* was apparently revised by him. In his part of the introduction to the facsimile text of the manuscript, *The Bodleian Manuscript of George Herbert's Poems: A Facsimile of Tanner 307*, Amy Charles and Mario Di Cesare eds. (Delmar, N.Y.: Scholars' Facsimiles and Reprints, 1984), Mario Di Cesare makes persuasive arguments for the relative importance of *B* compared with the first edition. My own view is slightly different from his. I think *W* is the more carefully prepared of the two MSS, and it has Herbert's own corrections, which I think are entitled to great weight, at least where the poems are not heavily rewritten later.[1] *B*, though much larger and more costly, and though written in a more ornate hand, shows many of the signs of rush and carelessness—at least on the part of some of the scribes, for it was evidently transcribed by several people. There is no doubt

---

1. The poems with several stanzas often have a rough mark, a kind of slash, running from one stanza down to the next, which also seems to have been done in Herbert's hand, as do the flourishes at the end of the poems. It looks to me as if this book, at first prepared with care for private use, was later corrected as a fair copy for a contemplated publication, which for some reason never took place.

that it was the copy submitted to the university for licensing, for the signatures of the licensors appear on it. It may have been the copy used by the printer in preparation of *B;* but, if so, the printer imposed his own standards of punctuation with great freedom.

I have generally followed Hutchinson's edition, but with a few changes, the most important of which are (1) in the lineation of "The Collar" I follow *B* in its entirety, for reasons set forth by Di Cesare in his introduction; (2) in "Easter-wings" I follow the design in both *W* and *B,* rather than the 1633 edition.

Bibliography

This introduction to the poetry of George Herbert has, like any work of criticism, proceeded from a particular point of view. Others working on the same poems will naturally see different things in them and ask different questions of them. As a way of inviting the reader to further reading, I shall here briefly describe the works on George Herbert that I have found most valuable, indicating differences of emphasis and interest.

F. E. Hutchinson, *The Works of George Herbert* (Oxford: Clarendon Press, 1941) is the standard edition of his poetry and prose, in English and Latin. It has a useful biographical introduction and contains extensive notes on the poems, which are often highly illuminating. A good shorter edition is *The English Poems of George Herbert,* edited by C. A. Patrides (London: J. M. Dent, Everyman ed., 1974). Unlike Hutchinson's edition, which makes editorial emendations, this one reprints, with only the smallest modifications, the text of the first edition of 1633. It has brief but helpful notes and an extensive bibliography. Also valuable are *George Herbert: The Complete English Poems,* edited by John Tobin (London: Penguin Books, 1991) and *George Herbert and Henry Vaughan,* edited by Louis L. Martz (Oxford: Oxford University Press, 1986).

An essential aid to the reading of Herbert is Mario A. Di Cesare and Rigo Mignani: *A Concordance to the Complete Writings of George Herbert* (Ithaca, N.Y.: Cornell University Press, 1977). The life of Herbert is best told in Amy M. Charles, *A Life of George Herbert* (Ithaca, N.Y.: Cornell University Press, 1977) and in the second chapter of Joseph H. Summers, *George Herbert: His Religion and Art* (Cambridge, Mass.: Harvard University Press, 1954). The texts are best discussed in *The Williams Manuscript of George Herbert's Poems: A Facsimile Reproduction,* with an introduction by Amy M. Charles (Delmar, N.Y.: Scholars' Facsimiles and Reprints, 1977) and *The Bodleian Manuscript of George Herbert's Poems: A Facsimile of Tanner 307,* with an introduction by Amy M. Charles and Mario A. Di Cesare (Delmar, N.Y.: Scholars' Facsimiles and Reprints, 1984).

One might begin the history of modern criticism of George Herbert with Rosemund Tuve, *A Reading of George Herbert* (Chicago: University of Chicago Press, 1952). This is a beautifully written and intelligent book, the aim of which is to locate Herbert firmly in his intellectual and cultural tradition. Especially important is her discovery, described in a long first chapter, that "The Sacrifice" is not original in form but derives from an early liturgical form, the medieval complaint of Christ to his people. In the rest of the book she explains the background of other images or symbols, showing how these acquire meaning from their prior uses. Her book is thus what might be called an iconography of Herbert's poetry. In general terms her aim is similar to that of the present book, for it too could be defined as learning the language of George Herbert, but the dimension of language that interests her is different: less a matter of voice and gesture, more a matter of symbol and image. She is particularly valuable on the nature of belief (105), although her sense of that differs from mine. Poems that her approach helps clarify include "The Bunch of Grapes," "The Agonie," "Sion," "Sunday," "Justice" (II), "Whitsunday," and the "Jordan" poems.

Joseph H. Summers, *George Herbert: His Religion and Art* (Cambridge, Mass.: Harvard University Press, 1954) is meant as a one-volume statement of what needs to be known about Herbert's life, the texts, the religious background, and so on. Summers is especially good on later uses of Herbert, particularly by Emerson—who quoted five stanzas of "Man" in the final chapter of *Nature*—Thoreau, and Dickinson. As he tells the life story, a great deal is made of Herbert's want of meaningful employment in the late 1620s, which Summers connects to the two poems entitled "Employment" as well as others on that theme. He elaborates a vision of the poems as hieroglyphs, that is as artifacts with meanings at several layers and of several kinds, drawing on the typological interpretation of the Bible as a model (see 127 and 140 for brief summaries). Anticipating a position later taken by Stanley Fish, he sees a deep connection between what the poems achieve and the kind of catechizing that Herbert describes in *A Priest to the Temple*. He has a fine analysis of "Church-monuments"; he neatly explains the problematic use of the word "handkerchief" in "The Dawning"; he has good readings of "The Pearl," "Mortification," and "An Offering." He traces some of Herbert's formal inventiveness to the translation of the Psalms by Sir Philip Sidney (finished by Herbert's own relative, the Countess of Pembroke). He has an extended treatment of allegory, which is close to what I mean by myth-making. My only difficulty with this book is that reading of the poems is occasionally marred by a habit of quoting passages as though they simply represented what Herbert believed, without much regard for the sort of shifts of voice and feeling to which my own book has been directed.

Louis L. Martz, *The Poetry of Meditation: A Study in English Religious Literature of the Seventeenth Century* (New Haven, Conn.: Yale University Press, 1954, rev. ed. 1962) contains two interesting chapters on Herbert. The first connects Herbert's poetry with the practice of formal devotions, particularly as defined by St. Francis De Sales. He is especially good on the "Jordan" poems and on Herbert's use of the Psalms, both in the Coverdale (prayer-book) version, and in the translation by Sir Philip Sidney and the Countess of Pembroke. In the second chapter, dealing with the structure of *The Temple*, he suggests that "The Church Militant" is not simply, as it may seem, "a rather desperate effort to salvage, if only by way of appendix, a very early poem," but actually has a role, for it represents the active life to which contemplation and devotion ultimately may lead. Then, and more helpfully, he traces out in brief terms certain sets of thematic and sequential connections among the poems in interesting ways. He thinks that after "The Flower" Herbert's griefs really do melt away, in the movement towards "Love" (III). His readings of "The Search," "The Flower," and "The Forerunners" are all of interest.

Another significant book is Arnold Stein, *George Herbert's Lyrics* (Baltimore: The Johns Hopkins Press, 1968). The first chapter deals with Herbert's interest in plain speech, helpfully locating this in an extended tradition. The most valuable chapter is the second, "The Movement of Words," dealing with Herbert's prosody or "metrical rhetoric." Stein here analyzes the metrical and rhythmic structure of Herbert's poetry with great particularity, showing how Herbert uses stress, juncture ("the pause and transition between syllables"), and phrasing to give movement and life to his verse. The central devices Stein identifies are the increasing intensity of stress in the life of a poem, the loosening and contracting of rhythmical movement, and the augmentation and diminution of phrases.

Chapter three deals with poems of complaint, praise, and love, showing how Herbert in each case engages in a practice and at the same time brings to the surface its inherent difficulties, which characteristically lead to a transformation of the form. Thus every complaint becomes a declaration of praise and love; attempts to escape from love, or to compel it, move in the direction of contemplation. The last chapter, "Questions of Style and Form," offers detailed and persuasive readings of "Mortification," "Life," "Virtue," "Love" (III), and "The Flower." To my ear he does not pay enough attention to the ways in which the various speakers of the poems are differentiated from each other, and from Herbert, but the readings are generally careful and persuasive. In a characteristically elegant phrase he says that Herbert "is the master of an essential artistic illusion by which the flow of invention may seem to discover its own form, as if spontaneously" (154).

In his book *Self-Consuming Artifacts: The Experience of Seventeenth-Century Literature* (Berkeley and Los Angeles: University of California Press, 1972) Stanley Fish has a long and brilliant essay entitled "The Dialectic of Self in Herbert's Poetry," in which he argues that the structure of Herbert's poetry is, often at least, to carry the reader to a point at which poetry itself is seen to have no function, the poet and the reader to have no role: everything is done by God. The value of the artifact is not in the thing itself, but where it leads the reader; when it is done, it has consumed itself. This position is persuasively argued, sometimes perhaps overargued; it has certainly influenced my own reading of Herbert. For Fish this position is part of a set of larger theoretical issues, about the location of meaning in literary experience.

He is especially good on "Sepulchre," in which, as he shows, the terms "heart" and "stone" undergo a reversal; on "Even-song," which begins by drawing distinctions and categories, but ends by denying them; on "The Holdfast," which drives poet and reader alike into acknowledging that they can do nothing (though I think he misses the sermon-voice aspects of the closing couplet); on "The Pearl," which he sees as about intellectual pride; and on "The Altar." One of his points is put neatly this way: "To read many of Herbert's poems is to experience the dissolution of the lines of demarcation we are accustomed to think of as real" (164). In this context, he reads, with a sure touch, "Church-monuments" as enacting the dissolution it describes. The strongest version of his position is that the poems are ultimately revealed to have as their true author no one else than God; this is what makes them morally permissible, and the only thing that could do so.

Fish also has a short book on Herbert, *The Living Temple: George Herbert and Catechizing* (Berkeley and Los Angeles: University of California Press, 1978), which is built, like his essay, on a unifying idea, but a slightly different one. Here he draws on the model of catechizing, as it is described by Herbert in *A Priest to the Temple*: as a dialectical activity meant to lead the catechist to independence of mind and responsibility. This, says Fish, is what Herbert tries to achieve in his poetry as well. He then makes his own artifact "self-consume," when he insists to his reader at the end that this model of poetry has its origin in his own reading, not in the poems themselves. Of course others will bring other schemas to the reading, among which— and this is the crucial point—no external judgments of value can be made. This is a highly intelligent work, well worth attention, though I think his interest in literary theory sometimes diverts him from the poetry itself.

Helen Vendler, *The Poetry of George Herbert* (Cambridge, Mass.: Harvard University Press, 1975) is an important book, worthy of the attention of anybody interested in Herbert. The first chapter consists of a reading of "Vertue" (which is especially interesting in its discussion of "my music"). The second chapter is to my mind the best. Entitled "Alternatives: The Reinvented Poem," it is about what I have called Herbert's method of writing by perpetual rewriting. She has a good reading of "Prayer" (I) as a movement from commonplace to anger to reconciliation, and good readings as well of "The Temper," "Affliction" (I), "The Flower," and "The Rose."

Later chapters deal with emblems and allegories; with Herbert's imitators and adapters, who define his achievements by their own failures; with liturgical poems, which she thinks are generally less good than the others; with ethical and speculative poems; and with formal patterns, where she has fine analyses of "The Call," "Antiphon," "Grace," and "Heaven." She is more interested than I am in judging the quality of particular poems, and her judgments would often differ from mine. For example she thinks rather little of "To all Angels and Saints," "Sion," and "The Offering," all of which I admire.

Barbara Leah Harman, *Costly Monuments: Representations of the Self in George Herbert's Poetry* (Cambridge, Mass.: Harvard University Press, 1982) is especially valuable for its summary of the critical controversy between Fish, who tends to see the poems dissolving, and Vendler, who focuses on Herbert's reinventions and reconstructions (see 79–80, 172–73). The center of the book is an account of collapsing and dissolving poems, with valuable readings of "The Collar," "Miserie," "Redemption," "Mortification," "The Pilgrimage," "The Temper," "Artillerie," and "The Flower."

Chana Bloch, *Spelling the Word: George Herbert and the Bible* (Berkeley and Los Angeles: University of California Press, 1985) is a book of great value. In it the author patiently and carefully describes the biblical background to Herbert's verse, focusing on particular words, images, and forms. Like Tuve, she is interested in a richer understanding of the traditions and materials with which Herbert worked; like Vendler, she focuses upon the new uses to which he puts these materials. Particular words enriched by her reading include "dust," "rest," "thorns," and a good many others. She draws an analogy between the way in which the scriptures were often read in Herbert's time, typologically and by collation, and the way his own verse asks to be read. She is particularly good on "A True Hymne," "The Altar," "The Sacrifice," "The Call," "Prayer" (I), "The Forerunners," "Antiphon" (I), and "Love" (III). Her analysis of the resonances of the title of the whole book of verse, *The Temple*, is splendid.

She is interested in explaining Herbert's love of proverbial expressions, which she does gamely, but to me not wholly persuasively. Perhaps best of all, she compares Herbert's whole book with the book of Psalms, in purpose and organization, in a way that is highly persuasive. Like the other critics mentioned, she tends to organize the poems by type rather than, as I do, by sequence.

Love Known: Theology and Experience in George Herbert's Poetry (Chicago: University of Chicago Press, 1983), by Richard Strier, argues "for the centrality of a single doctrine to George Herbert's poetry and theology: the doctrine of justification by faith" (xi). It persuasively resists an earlier view, having its origins in Walton, that defined Herbert as a sweet Anglican, and instead locates him squarely in the mainstream of Reformation thought, especially with reference to the view that man can do nothing to help himself, but depends entirely upon God for salvation. Strier also resists Vendler's claim that the poetry can be read for its human value without much regard to its theology. In particular, Strier sees Herbert writing against the rationalism and self-sufficiency of "covenant theology," which imagines man and God striking a sacred bargain (a topic I discuss under the rubric of promises). Poems in which he sees Herbert at work in this way include "The Pearl," "Obedience," and "Artillerie." He is rightly insistent (especially at 145) that theology is not merely a matter of propositional belief, but of experience and feeling; some of his readings, however, end in a more solid theological and doctrinal affirmation than I would give them. He is especially good on "The Sepulchre," "Sinnes Round," "The Glance," "Deniall," "A True Hymne," and "Fore-runners." Strier is interested in the meaning of sequence, and discusses the relations among the poems that open the book.

Debora Kuller Shuger, *Habits of Thought in the English Renaissance: Religion, Politics, and the Dominant Culture* (Berkeley and Los Angeles: University of California Press, 1990) contains a fine essay on the structure of *The Temple*. It sees the three parts as differentiated by the sense of human personality they assume. "The Church-porch" assumes a human actor that is autonomous, in control of himself, and rational; it addresses him by telling him how to perform his social and ethical roles in an appropriate fashion. "The Church" assumes a private, passive, spiritual, and anguished self, the experience of which it expresses. "The Church Militant," consisting of a long history of the church, assumes that human beings are simply minor actors in a larger, providential drama.

In *Prayer and Power: George Herbert and Renaissance Courtship* (Chicago: University of Chicago Press, 1991) Michael Schoenfeldt takes the valuable and original step of reading Herbert's poetry against the background of the language and practices of court behavior. These are relevant not only because of their role in the general culture, but because Herbert himself had been trained in them. Particularly as University Orator he was engaged in public life, from time to time actually addressing the king himself, and part of the skill of the courtier and orator alike is to advance one's own position through rituals of submission. In this context Schoenfeldt has fine readings of "The Thanksgiving" and "The Reprisall," which explore the inherent self-aggrandizement of the "submissive" courtier. Schoenfeldt's readings pick up resonances that one might otherwise miss, for example the element of negotiation in "Praise" (I) and "Submission." In similar fashion, he traces out the element of hostility necessarily present in relations of such inequality, studying for example the ways in which God is imagined as a torturer, "stretching and racking" the speaker, as in "The Temper" (I) and "Justice" (II). On the other side is the aggressive force of prayer, the "engine against th' Almightie," and Schoenfeldt persuasively analyzes its social and rhetorical structure, especially in connection with "Gratefulnesse." The last two chapters, richly suggestive, are both about "Love" (III), the first connecting it to the language and practice of invitation by a superior, the second to the language of sexuality that runs through Herbert's poetry. As with Tuve and Bloch, Schoenfeldt's aim is less to provide novel readings of the particular poems than to enrich our understanding of them by connecting them to their cultural context, and in this he succeeds admirably. He is especially good on "The Bag," "The Flower," and the "Jordan" poems, in addition to those mentioned above.

Index

References to reprinted poems are in boldface type.